WITH PASSION
AND COMPASSION

WITH PASSION AND COMPASSION

Third World Women Doing Theology

Reflections from the Women's Commission
of the Ecumenical Association
of Third World Theologians

Edited by
Virginia Fabella, M.M.
and
Mercy Amba Oduyoye

ORBIS BOOKS

Maryknoll, New York 10545

Third Printing, September 1989

653448

The Catholic Foreign Mission Society of America (Maryknoll) recruits and trains people for overseas missionary service. Through Orbis Books Maryknoll aims to foster the international dialogue that is essential to mission. The books published, however, reflect the opinions of their authors and are not meant to represent the official position of the society.

Manuscript editor: Lisa McGaw

ORBIS/ISBN 0-88344-623-6

Contents

v

PART THREE
LATIN AMERICA

Foreword

With growing force, Third World women are shaking up traditional pieties and preconceptions in every sphere of religious life. The field of theology is no exception. Up until now, students of Christianity, whether engaged in private, group, or classroom study, in church or seminary, have had almost nothing to say about the oppressive patriarchal patterns of subordination and super-ordination from a global perspective. Today, Third World women are demanding that theological scholarship must undergo a rigorous reassessment of its own role in perpetuating and reinforcing racist attitudes and sexist practices.

In this book, *With Passion and Compassion,* Third World women theologians connect the entire spectrum of their worldview to the histories of their countries; histories grounded in patriarchy, colonialism, and missionary paternalism; histories so full of misogynist contempt and militaristic culture that African, Asian, and Latin American women have been denied their full humanity. In other words, the *weltanschauung* described in this book primarily arises from the inevitable trials and tribulations that come with being a woman of color and poor in a world that despises both.

The thinking in these pages is indebted to Third World women who envision a new Church *from* the Bible, in opposition to the ecclesiastical patriarchs who embrace the historic continuity of religious traditions and want to conduct the church *by* the Bible. They are women who are willing to live under the manifest will of God who has ordered the life of the Christian church into an inclusive community of equals.

The Third World women theologians included herein are long-suffering custodians of truth. As outstanding pioneers in the struggle for a globally inclusive church, they are protesting against an uncompleted Christianity. They believe that there can be a new creation of the commonwealth of God on earth. Their aim is to return to the inclusive principles and practices of the apostolic church insofar as these accord with the revealed teachings of Christ. These churchwomen are speaking out against those who care more for their clerical oaths and social roles than for the Word of God. Under the pressure of day-to-day female persecution, women theologians from Africa, Asia, and Latin America are persuaded that Christian women must not tolerate sacred and secular arrangements that result in the horrors of injustice, cruelty, and wide-spread violence against women.

Common to Third World women theologians is the firm conviction that Christians are morally bound to cooperate with the forces of good and equally bound to refuse cooperation with the evils of patriarchy. The Church must be composed of committed disciples, struggling against alienation and the violence of the powerful for a more just and human world. United in a bond of love to God and to each other, followers of Christ are called to resist oppression, to oppose authorities and laws that rob humans of their birthright of freedom and dignity, and to be noncompromising in their attack against unjust social structures. The price of enduring individualized social injustice is global social destruction.

The present text emphasizes that authentic Christianity can never be divorced from practical life. A God-pleasing faith must take into account the political economy and social realities in order for believers to recognize evil and bring about change. Christians have the responsibility to make the church community live according to the Gospel truth.

The theological premises and assumptions which are inherited from the indigenous communities' religious traditions emphasize the continual struggle and interplay of passion and compassion as the highest good. What the writers of this book make clear is that passionate compassion is the essential quality of justice. It is akin to steadfast fortitude in the face of formidable oppression, and serves as the most conspicuous feature in the construction of Third World women's theologies. Their thesis is that African, Asian, and Latin American women embrace this moral quality of life not as an ideal to be fulfilled but as a balance of complexities to be achieved, in order that suffering will not overwhelm and liberation is possible.

KATIE G. CANNON

Introduction

THE AUTHORS

Those who have brought to birth this volume of essays are women from the Third World. That is what we call ourselves. The current move to introduce the term "two-thirds world" attempts to acknowledge that in geographical space, and certainly in population, those who occupy the underside of the purchasing and ruling powers in the human community constitute *more* than a third. As part of the Ecumenical Association of Third World Theologians (EATWOT), we maintain our stance and our name, for EATWOT's Third World seeks to present a different reality, a reality not dependent on numbers or location.

Originally a choice to stay unaligned either with the capitalist West or the socialist East, the term "Third World" has accrued to itself deep theological meaning as persons from those geographical areas marked by poverty and oppression began to theologize and to discover the underside of the industrialized and affluent North. "Third World" has a meaning not based on numerical strength but on quality of life. Its concern is with seeking the environment in which all human beings can live a life compatible with their status as beings in relation to God. It has virtually shed its original parameter of a divide created by politico-economic powerplays among supernations. "Third World" for EATWOT is a supra-geographic term, for even following the "money equator" that twists and turns to include Japan and Australia, there is a Third World on both sides of it—people whose humanity is being denied.

We, the women who came together in Oaxtepec, Mexico, in December of 1986 to reflect on what it means to do theology from Third World women's perspective, share this description. For most of us, doing theology in the colonizer's language is itself a sign of Third World–ness. Words carry weight, but we refuse to let semantic debate divert us from the course of our liberation. That some of the papers in this collection of essays had to go through two or more translations to arrive at the English language demonstrates our Third World diversity as well as the demand imposed on us if we wish to communicate with world powers who feel no need to learn Third World languages and cultures.

The papers presented in this volume have come from a process which began in New Delhi, India, at the first assembly of the Ecumenical Association of Third World Theologians, in 1981. The Association had assumed that by naming the structures that divide human beings, making some more powerful than others, and by taking a liberative stance, all was taken care of. We, the women of the Association, were just as concerned to name the demons and to have them exorcised. Sexism was one such demon, and it existed within the Association itself. Our voices were not being heard, although we were visible enough. It became clear to us that only the oppressed can truly name their oppression. We demanded to be heard. The result was the creation within EATWOT of a Women's Commission, and not a Commission on Women as some of the male members would have it. Rather than see ourselves solely as victims of male domination, we formed a sisterhood of resistance to all forms of oppression, seeking creative partnership with men of the Association.

THE SOURCES

Oaxtepec presented us the opportunity for an overview of what the Women's Commission had done during the brief years of its existence. It provided us the occasion to share what it means to do theology from the perspective of Third World women.

The preparatory work that led to the Intercontinental Women's Conference held in Oaxtepec, Mexico, on December 1-6, 1986, began with national meetings on the three continents of Africa, Asia, and Latin America. The national groups met with the purpose of sharing their local experiences and reflections, seeking synthesis and particularities. These national consultations were expanded into sub-continental and continental meetings, with each phase building on what had gone before, on the grounds that no experience was too marginal to be included in the global. In Mexico, representatives from the three continents who had taken part in the process met to share, evaluate, consult, and project. The papers in this volume have all been presented in some form during one of the three phases of the process. They bear the imprint of a collective task as well as the marks of personal passion and compassion in a world which appears more dominated by suffering than by joy.

A study guide suggested by the Commission directed the attention of the participants in the process to five main areas: Bible, christology, ecclesiology, spirituality, and the methodology of women's theology. It also commended the use of the EATWOT general process of including contextual analysis in all its theologizing efforts. For the Commission, contextual analysis means going beyond telling our stories of resistance to, and participation in the struggle against, the forces of death and dehumanization. It involves taking a critical look at our reality and the web of oppressions of which sexism forms a part.

It was not an easy task to select the papers for this volume that would represent the range of theological themes and at the same time demonstrate the multi-faceted character of the Commission's work. We have consciously selected papers that reflect the ecumenical nature of our quest. Especially where studies on the Christ event and the Church are concerned, we have tried to include essays of both Catholic and Protestant origins, to show not only their differences and similarities but also how at times they are complementary. We are painfully aware of the absence of Orthodox input.

We have also attempted to include as wide a range of geographic areas as possible. The absence of contributions from the EATWOT minorities from the U.S.A. is part of the design put forward by the Commission. The context of women from the minority groups in the U.S.A. is considerably distinct and as such needs a separate intra-EATWOT dialogue.

It is to be observed, moreover, that the method of contextualizing our theological reflections and perceiving our context from a theological standpoint leads to unavoidable repetitions. We have risked those repetitions to emphasize the importance of context in Third World women's theology. Essays that omit a delineation of their Third World context presupposed a preceeding input when originally presented.

The essays that were finally selected constitute but a fraction of the total produced in the course of the Commission's work. However, the salient thoughts and reflections of the papers from each continent have been woven into the final statement of each continental consultation. We have included all these final statements in this volume. What could not be included, to our regret, are all the discussions among the women that facilitated the writing, revising, and editing of all the papers, which manifest the collective nature of our theological endeavor.

To introduce the contents of this collection, we have chosen to present highlights from some of the essays instead of summarizing each one. Though the sections of the book are divided according to continental contributions, in order to facilitate cross-referencing, we will present the highlights in thematic fashion.

METHODOLOGY

A key requisite of our methodology is that our reflections are done by Third World women ourselves. Our theology must speak of our struggles and the faith that empowers us. Our theology goes beyond the personal to encompass the community, and beyond gender to embrace humanity in its integrity. Our theology takes cognizance of academic studies but insists on the wider spectrum of women's experience and reality for its inspirations and insights. Being contextual in the Third World has meant that women's theology has embraced the religio-cultural besides the socio-economic and has engaged it in a living dialogue. For most of the women, especially those from Asia and Africa, it is a dialogue of life which forms part of our daily experience. Theologizing in the light of our Christian faith, we have learned to appreciate the insights and spirituality of other faiths and seek avenues for interfaith dialogue, not just to enrich Christian theology but as a community responsibility owed to all people of faith.

The context of poverty, multiple oppression, and tokenism shows up as a common experience of all the three continents. The Third World is a cross-ridden universe of economic, political, and religio-cultural oppressions within which women are doubly or triply burdened. Liberation thus takes on an existential meaning, but its goal, as capsulized in Virginia Fabella's paper on methodology, is the "liberation of all men and women from whatever binds them, both internally and externally." Thus freedom from selfishness and acquisitiveness is just as vital as liberation from all exploitative and unjust practices and structures, whether political, economic, or social, whether based on gender, race, or creed. Liberation leads to wholeness.

SPIRITUALITY

Women's theology comes as words that are lived. All the essays are fruits of a spirituality and hence come out of, and go beyond, scholarly pursuits and interests. The term "spirituality" thus needs more explication to illustrate how it is evidenced in women's lives.

Luz Beatriz Arellano speaks of spirituality that arises from the faith experience of Nicaraguan women engaged in the process of building a new society. Spirituality for Nicaraguan women means discovering God as a God of life in their experience as not only bearers and sustainers of life but also as promoters and defenders of life and peace in the midst of aggression and threats of death. Spirituality is a close following of Jesus who exemplified the freedom to give up one's life that others may have it to the full (John 10:10). In this sense it is an ecumenical spirituality "shared not only with Christians who belong to the various churches, but also between Christians and non-Christians." The values and aspirations found in the people's struggle for liberation are at once Christian and human.

Mary John Mananzan and Sun Ai Park discuss spirituality from their Asian perspective. In the light of Asia's multiplicity of religious traditions, they also refer to ecumenical spirituality, setting it forth as an important feature stimulating the search for the "unity of humankind in humility and reverence towards all life and belief systems." The view of salvation here is communal, historical, and cosmic. "Ecumenical spirituality activates and expands our visions and living." How this spirituality is utilized in the church becomes the burden of another set of papers.

WOMEN AND THE CHURCH

In all the essays there was clear expression that not enough is being made of women's spirituality in both the Catholic and Protestant churches on the three continents. Though there were vast areas of similarities, there were also evident differences.

The Africa papers point to the heavy hand of colonialism, the paternalism of the missionary period, and the legacy of Western Christianity as the factors that influence women's participation in the church. To these they add the further impetus to patriarchal attitudes that both Islam and African traditional religion lend to the church. These constitute a triple jeopardy, and yet from African traditional religion women have derived and continue to derive precedents for more effective response to Christianity. It is from their own religious tradition that the role of women cultic-functionaries has been asserted. That women continue to be "owners" of traditional shrines has empowered African women stirred by the Holy Spirit to begin movements of prophecy, prayer, and counselling that have become churches.

The overall picture painted by Christine Tse shows how cultural stereotypes are reflected in the Asian church. The church employs the myth of divine origin of male superiority to buttress men's dominion over women, and that of "order" to justify hierarchy on a theological basis. Asian Christianity, being a minority religion, has acculturated into the ethos of the dominant male-oriented religions and philosophies like Islam and Confucianism. In spite of all this, women demonstrate that we can be effective partners when inclusiveness becomes the principle by which the church lives. For this to happen, church women have to work together not only towards demythologization but also the dismantling of the church's patriarchal structures.

Maria Pilar Aquino from Latin America directs attention to the conflicts of opposing interests in the church. At its center the church reproduces the relationships of class and gender oppression as experienced in society, while professing an option for the poor which in fact should also mean an option for women's humanity. On the periphery is the world of Christians whose dreams, defeats, successes, and interests are fuelled by the message of the gospel of liberation. These are the basic ecclesial communities (BECs) which have come into being in the past twenty years and have begun a process of renewal of the Church in Latin America. Women in these BECs have become aware of their dual oppression as poor and as women, and have begun to view themselves as creators of a new alternative, challenging the male structures of the Church.

As one reads of women's lives in the Church, the evidence begins to emerge that "women become dangerous" when we question "the powerful and masculine models of the internal structures of the church," and as such our presence has been construed as a source of tension. The mark of faith and hope and love is that through all this, women together strive to find new paths to become effective partners in the church, impelled by the love of Christ demonstrated not only in the cross but also in the affirmation of women's bodies and our full humanity. Women's relationship to the Church is founded on their christology.

THE CHRIST OF THIRD WORLD WOMEN

The combined papers of Elizabeth Amoah and Mercy Oduyoye illustrate the words of grassroots women's spirituality—what African women see in Jesus. Women's bonding with Jesus is that of persons who, while marginalized by society, continue to call attention to the periphery and to act as if that were the center. African women demonstrate an affinity with Jesus as a person who is sensitive to the misery and oppression of the weak and seeks their empowerment for liberation.

Both Louise Tappa and Thérèse Souga center their African contribution on Jesus' encouragement of women's self-affirmation. Louise asserts that if

"Christology is to work out the full meaning of the reality of the Christ event for humankind" then the procedure for articulating it should be that "of contemplating and thinking of Christ in relation to our situation and our praxis." Thérèse follows this method and maintains that "Jesus bears in his person the conditions of the weak and hence those of women." However, African women warn that it is vicarious suffering, freely undertaken, which is salvific, and not involuntary victimization. The passion of Christ was a voluntary result of his spirituality.

In the synthesis of two christological studies found in the Asian section, we also find a christology that relates to the passion of Christ as the suffering of Jesus is related to the active suffering of women. It is active, not merely passive, suffering for the sake of God's reign that has salvific value.

THE BIBLE IN WOMEN'S THEOLOGY

Rereading the Bible is a basic procedure of theological reflection for women. The Commission study guide included Bible as one theme. Two biblical expositions are included in this collection. Teresa Okure's article provides an example of how a systematic study of the figure of Eve can provide liberating insights for women's self-perception. Elsa Tamez contributes further methodological strands for the rereading of the Bible from her Latin American experience and perspective. The fact, however, is that Bible studies have permeated all the other theological themes, as seen in Ana Maria Tepedino's reflections on women in theology.

Ana Maria forms her biblical image of Martha not solely from the oft-interpreted Lukan passage but from the gospel of John. In John 11:17-44, Martha is shown as a disciple, a woman of faith, full of life, initiative, and determination, and abounding in hope. Further, Martha is a theologian who presents to the members of the Johannine community a theological synthesis of messianic faith that they may know that Jesus is the Christ and that, by believing, they may have life in his name. Her confession is not in reaction to a miracle, but a response to Jesus' revelation and challenge, both as friend and master.

OUR FINAL WORD

This volume was made possible through the efforts of groups and individuals whom we would like to acknowledge before concluding our Introduction. First and foremost are all the teams of women who facilitated the Commission's work and contributed to this collective endeavor. The national, continental, and intercontinental meetings all benefited from the collaboration and active involvement of women, many of whom belonged not to EATWOT as an association but to the Commission's network of women engaged in doing theology.

Our gratitude also goes to all those who have given us both advice and assistance in preparing this volume. In particular we would like to mention the Orbis editors and copyeditor.

Finally, to our partners in the liberation struggle who provided us with funds to carry out our work, and who have encouraged us and exhibited sustained interest in EATWOT and the Women's Commission, we say, Thank you.

VIRGINIA FABELLA AND
MERCY AMBA ODUYOYE

Part One

AFRICA

1

Church Women of Africa: A Theological Community

Rosemary Edet (Nigeria) and Bette Ekeya (Kenya)

INTRODUCTION

The situation of women and the nature of Christianity in Africa are both shaped by the histories and cultures that are molding contemporary Africa. Our contribution is primarily a descriptive one, sharing the context in which women try to live theologically in Africa. We begin with an overview of Africa's realities as shared by Rosemary Nthamburi of Kenya and Lloyda Fanusie of Sierra Leone, and from our own studies, then we consider women's lives in Africa, with an emphasis on how the changing culture affects and is affected by women. Lastly, we place women in the context of the church and reflect on the shape and content of African women's contributions to Christian theology in Africa.

We are, of course, situating women's lives in the realities lived by all of Africa's peoples—women and men—and within which the church operates. The Christian church has suffered and is suffering from a growing cultural alienation because evangelization has not been that of cultural exchange but of cultural domination or assimilation. There has been an imposed model of development accompanied by an ideological, cultural imposition, which has led to lifestyles that are both inconsistent and alienating for Africa's peoples. The result is a loss of cultural and material identity. Periodic attempts are made by governments to inculcate nationalism into citizens.[1] Unfortunately, recita-

---

Translated by Phillip Berryman.

tion of the national pledge or refraining from wearing miniskirts does not turn one into a nationalist, for being a nationalist is an attitude and a commitment to the community that needs stronger roots than an enforced discipline. Nationhood may be imposed by colonial exigencies, but nationalism cannot be an imposed concept; it is a commitment.

As in colonization, so it is with "Christianization"; a cultural and religious alienation or lopsidedness has been introduced into Africa. One such experience is that brought about by evangelization in a male-dominated church, both structurally and ministerially. This is not denying the elements of male domination in most African cultures. However, culturally there is no discrimination on the spiritual or religious level. Ironically, Christianity, which teaches that "in Christ there is no male nor female, Jew nor Greek," turns around and sees to it that women are grouped with children in churches. Women are regarded as unfinished handiwork of God and as such are like children. The likeness of God in women is totally neglected, and the neglect is justified by the biblical creation story.

According to Genesis 1:27, the bisexual, androgynous human race as the image and likeness of the creator God is the primary source of our understanding of this God. Both Genesis 1 and 2 indicate that when God shares God's being ad extra with that which is not God, the result is bisexual humanity. Thus the one God of the Judeo-Christian tradition nevertheless exists so richly and fully that God's created image can only be pluriform, even sexually. In both chapters 1 and 2 of Genesis there is unity and diversity in the human image and likeness of God, but neither domination nor subordination.

The literary form of Genesis 2 has been the occasion of many misinterpretations that have destroyed the partnership of man and woman as the image and likeness of God. If the church is the body of Christ or the people of God, then all the members of the body work toward the betterment of the whole body. All are necessary and the dysfunction of one organ incapacitates the whole body. The present malaise in the church might be due to the fact that it has refused to allow women to function normally in the church but has reduced them to all-purpose workers, for example, fund-raisers and rally organizers. As such the feminine image of God is overshadowed and is not utilized by the church or by humanity in most cases. This is the situation that prompts the special attention we wish to call to women's lives in the midst of Africa's realities.

AFRICA'S REALITIES

In an essay on the possibility of a new image for the African woman, Rosemary Nthamburi opens with the following statement:

The African states have been through the traditional society, colonialism, and have now entered into a state of independence. As they experience these historical events and changes, African women labour under disabilities in employment, law, and sad to say, in Church.[2]

We know of course that contemporary Africa is at once traditional, colonial, and neocolonial. The countries are independent—almost all of them—but it is a fact that little is done independently of global politico-economics managed mostly by the nations of the Western hemisphere. Women share the bitter fruits of the exploitation of Africa by outsiders, but women's disabilities also have authentic roots in Africa's indigenous structures.

Africa's traditional society was by and large not as fair to women as we would like to think. Sometimes women were regarded as secondhand citizens; often they were used and handled like the personal property of men, exploited, oppressed, and degraded.[3] Under colonial rule women fared no better, for all the disabilities of Western Christian culture were added to the already burdensome African situation. So it is no wonder that even when it has meant taking up arms, African women have fought as South African women fight today, to resist Western and racist exploitation of Africa. In spite of this involvement, the social status of women has not changed much; neither have stringent cultural provisions seen much modification in the direction of liberating women from dehumanization.

When analyzing women's contemporary experience, we cannot ignore the fact that in the realm of religion Africa has Christians, Muslims, and traditionalists moving side by side,[4] influencing and validating one another's concepts—mostly in ways that are unfavorable to women. The expansionist move of the religions of the world and the spread of populations means that religious groups like the Bahai, Hindu, and Buddhists are present and active in Africa[5] just as they are in other parts of the world.

In this religious pluralism, African women and men practice one or the other of these religions, but no one escapes the African traditional religion of one's own people. It is woven so tightly into the culture that none can claim to have moved completely out of the spirituality of Africa's own religion as distinguished from the "new religions" that have arrived in Africa, be that religion Christianity or Islam.

Concerns for peace and justice, for equality and liberation for all human beings characterize the endeavors of all persons and groups who see the church as a positive factor in Africa. Europeans had imposed systems that Africans knew little about to replace African systems about which in turn the Europeans knew little. Missionaries and colonizers were responsible for worse evils, such as racism, exploitation, domination, and a class system—all of which they introduced. They grabbed and sold land.[6] Africans now demand justice and equity vis-à-vis the West.

To what extent is this quest for the humanization of interaction in the realm of North-South relations extended to justice and equity between women and men in Africa? From our studies we have come to some insights on the factors that influence women's lives in contemporary Africa. One thing that struck us is the strong hold Africa's traditional culture has on women. It is to this that we turn.

WOMEN'S LIVES

In the changing culture of Africa one finds the intermingling of many styles of life: ". . . the literate and elite groups interacting with an illiterate and unsophisticated majority. The Haves and the Have-nots continue to enjoy their lives according to their means. Women are found among the Haves and the Have-nots, in government jobs and in private enterprises, among the able-bodied, the disabled, and the needy."[7] Women are not protected from the vicissitudes of life in Africa. In all this the demands of tradition are applied more to women than to men. Yet African women are expected to bear all this without protest. Least of all is any protest against sexism expected from women.

In most parts of Africa women are still the property of the men who father them or marry them. In some societies it is the uncle who holds sway over a woman's life. It makes little difference. Any talk of women's liberation is met with cynicism, hostility, or ridicule. A woman who has a vision concerning her life that contradicts the traditional role the male-dominated society has laid down for her pays a terrible price for daring to pursue that vision. Neverthe-less, women all over Africa are quietly but surely struggling to be free to realize their fullest potential as persons both within and outside the established social customs and church traditions. Women with a theological vision that sees beyond the traditional patriarchal interpretation of a few passages of the Bible are learning to delve into these interpretations and to expose those negative sexist designations that are added to burden women with an eternal sense of guilt and condemnation. Both men and women need to be freed from this so-called divinely willed, subordinate state of women. To do this, African women are beginning to reclaim what is positive in the traditional culture and to question all that is negative.

Traditionally, women play vital roles in religion and contribute their quota to the community worship life. It is a bit confusing to talk about the progress or regression of women's role in religion, be it traditional or Christian, without some knowledge of what women did in the traditional society. Suffice it to say that in African traditional religion, the salvific ministry associated with acts of healing, driving away evil spirits, promoting fertility, and encouraging success in life's ventures was performed by priestesses and priests alike.[8] These persons who officiate at communal worship do get professional training under the tutelage of a chiefpriestess or priest of the particular deity. They, like those in the Christian ministry, have been called by the deity. They have to obey or face dire consequences. In African traditional religion, therefore, women profes-sionals occur who can be equated to ministers, pastors, and priests in the Christian churches, and they undergo a period of training for their offices.

Traditionally, then, women have liturgical functions just like men, depend-ing on their calling. These women operate in their capacity as professionals: they conduct the services, that is, offer prescribed sacrifices or perform rites as occasions demand. Furthermore, women participate in community worship as cantors, choristers, gift-bearers, and sometimes as cooks and dancers. What is important in each case is *participation* by all the members of the community, since each member of the community is saved as being part of the community. Also, each assembly for rites or sacrifice is an act of solidarity and reinforcement of life and links of relationships. In the traditional act of worship, women display commitment to the community by their services irrespective of the capacity in which they serve. The role of the professionals among them is that of ministering to the needs of the community—pouring libation, healing the sick and afflicted, treating the barren, and generally offering prayers for the community.

With this understanding of the African background, it would not be an exaggeration to say that in contemporary Africa people are hungry for friendship, for celebration, as life gains a meaning when one goes through one rite of passage after another. This search for celebration of life is fueling the proliferation of spiritual movements and occult societies that are emptying the churches.[9] With such an opportunity for ministry, the church in Africa continues to under-utilize the gift of womanhood, which it does not fully appreciate. Is the church suffering from its lopsided structure and outmoded ecclesiology and Christology? The church in Africa seems to be going through an identity crisis.

Both community and identity are problems in today's society and today's church in Africa, because a person's identity is tied up with one's roles and with the need to fulfill the ongoing expectations of others. There are a few roles where the expectations are not changing, especially those of wife and mother. Traditionally a woman's identity was that of wife and mother. She was known as the mother of such-and-such a child and her own name disappeared into obscurity. Priestesses were known by the name of the deity they served. This way of identifying persons fitted into the Christian designation of wives as Mrs. So-and-so (the names being those of the husbands). Children today tend not to know their mother's name, but all can give their father's name at a very tender age. This situation makes it harder now for women to be confident about the meaning of their role in church life, for identity is molded by role and regulated by the relationships we have. Is the mother related to the child only as the wife of its father? Are women to be identified and related to only as being female?

Christianity has come as a mixed blessing for the African woman. It promised an elevated personal dignity and equality with the menfolk yet never quite brought about the fullest enjoyment of this promise. Nevertheless, being "naturally" or "incurably" religious, the African woman has accepted Christianity as her new religion. She has thrown herself into it with a zeal that surpasses that of men. Deep down she remains African but permits the new faith to enrich her traditional person without experiencing any spiritual conflict; religion, belief in God, is the integrating factor of her life. Her life is religious. As a Christian she witnesses to the depth of her commitment to her family and to the Christian community. In times of crisis she would most likely resort to her traditional rituals; she most certainly would not leave anything undone if it were likely to affect her children adversely. Western theologians have labeled this "syncretism." We believe that the best judge of what this phenomenon in religion really connotes is the African woman, and she is yet to be consulted by theologians. To the priestly hierarchies her role in the church is to be supportive, not consultative.

WOMEN IN THE CHURCH

Perhaps the major task in building the church in Africa is the fundamental rethinking of the basic approaches to the theology of the church, because the one consistent and persistent scandal that obscures the full symbolic presence of the church as the sacrament of communion between God and humanity is male predominance. The vision of the church as androgynous can contribute significantly to the crisis posed by the need to renew the church in contemporary African society.

Only a practically androgynous church truly reflects the ontology of Judeo-Christian creation theology (Gen. 1:27; 2:23) and of Christian redemption theology (Gal. 3:28; 2 Cor. 5:16). If God's very being is the communion in the one divine nature of the three divine persons, and if bisexual humanity is the image and likeness of this God, then certainly the church of Jesus Christ, in whom there is perfect communion of the divine and the human, must be an exemplar of androgynous communion.

Ironically, the church is customarily referred to as female while the whole structure and hierarchy are predominantly male. No wonder the symbolism of birthing and the female womb-essence means very little in the church. As a sacrament, both sign and cause of God's saving communion with creation, the church must reflect in its own being both the being of God and of God's created world. Since both God and Christ must be thought of as neither male nor female, so must the church if in truth it is the body of Christ.

If we in Africa base our theology of the church on the Bible, then we shall not fall into the one-sided ecclesiology that we have inherited from the missionaries. We are not saying that only the Bible is the source of theologizing. We are saying that revelation has to be interpreted and applied to our contemporary situations and experiences. Culturally, women's experiences are different from men's experiences on the societal level. Hence feminine interpretation is indispensable as a balance to the masculine. The church in Africa must reflect the feminine face of God as traditional religion tries to do through the institution of the priesthood as a function for both women and men. The African Independent Churches are attempting to do the same. By doing this, a balanced ecclesiology will emerge to make real humanity's likeness to God.

Furthermore, women have always held positions in African traditional religion. Let the church not deny us these opportunities in its structures, because they bring about the desired balance for which humanity is searching.

Call it complementarity if you please. Humanity will keep its image and likeness of God if both male and female work as a body. To achieve this we propose that Mariology be revitalized with emphasis on Mary as a human Christian believer whose faith was lived out in her status as woman. Second, there should develop a theology of God as Mother to complement and balance that of God as Father, since neither is meant to connote biological realities but to approximate our affirmation that God is the source of life and that God cares for this creature that is only a little lower than the divine ones. God is a God who saves, a God who gives life, the new life in Christ that redemption is all about. This theological emphasis is one that women in the church will help to articulate.

At present there are very few women ministering in the church as theologians, but women are to be found in other areas of the church's ministry as participants in the common priesthood of Christians. Women are in the ministries of healing and teaching, counseling and organizing for community tasks. Women exercise the ministry of teaching and of prayer. Women religious, deaconesses, and a few ordained into the liturgical ministries participate as much as they are allowed to do by the various male hierarchies that control the exercise of charisms in the church. Some women have skirted this male domination of Christianity by founding Christian communities within which they can be obedient to God rather than to men.

In the church's mission, goals are set for the community by members who are committed to these goals. These goals in turn touch the real needs of the church. Participation in the setting of goals and in a clear communication of the goals to committed members highlights the importance of the lateral ministry in the local church. Programs are the means of achieving these goals, and it stands to reason that women, who for the most part are expected to participate, become involved in other aspects of the process. As this occurs, the church will be seen to be reaffirming the transcendent vocation of womanhood, which has been systematically obscured, thwarted, or corrupted, even in our own time, on the continent of Africa. In society as well as in the church, women are the persons who join force with grace, with Mary as their model, as the one who through God's incarnation in Christ has made the world aware of the grandeur of both spiritual and physical motherhood. Women's selflessness in service is a quality necessary for genuine Christian life and growth.

WOMEN'S THEOLOGY

When African women do theology, they cannot help but reflect critically on all the experiences that we have shared here with you—and more besides. Arising out of our cultural roles, we are an asset to Africa because we work in the fields, at home, and now in the modern sectors of the economy. Yet this has not earned us independent identities or decision-making rights in the communities that we share with men. We continue to labor under the definition of womanhood that is rooted firmly in the functions of child-bearing and home-making. Since this attitude has remained unchanged it handicaps our participation in church and in society. As Rosemary Nthamburi has observed, the contemporary woman in the theological field has to work to "uncover all oppressive social structures which discriminate against women so that women can take their proper role alongside men in the society, and in the declaring of total liberation from all forms of oppression. It should be an act of humanization."[10]

In describing the roles that women play in the churches in Africa, one is struck by how traditionally feminine they are. We do not dispute the validity and necessity of these ministries, but we are distressed by the obvious lack of decisive action against societal exploitation and injustice. For women, Jesus is attractive because he is a fighter for justice, a healer, and a teacher. We retell the story of Jesus because it speaks directly to those areas of our lives where the reality of God is active and compelling. We find God in social justice and in the services of the church that respond to this need in society.

In Africa the concern with building up the church has become all-consuming and has limited woman's yearning for a fresh look and for decisive, liberating action, action that can provide her with the opportunity to function as an agent of God's liberating movement through the church of Christ. As Lloyda Fanusie puts it: "the active involvement of women in the church can only be a reality when women are seen as real people, created in God's image."[11]

We are convinced that the church can be more relevant and more effective in Africa and that, given the chance to act as full humans, women can equal men in their service to the church, as they are doing in other walks of life where the barriers to women's intensive participation are crumbling. One area in the church's life that needs to see a new phase is its theological emphases. This, we believe, is an area in which women should be fully involved.

For the purpose of this discussion we are describing theology in terms of finding ways in which knowledge of God and God's will for humanity and the universe are understood and responded to. From this broad description we can divide the theological enterprise into nonacademic and academic or, more precisely, grassroots and professional. The two are related, for they overlap and in many ways complement one another.

In grassroots theologizing we find that African women in the traditional African community are quite accomplished theologians in their own right. The domestic role of women in Africa involves a lot of religious ritual. In community worship, women are priestesses. Both are sacred duties in which the traditional woman finds her deepest fulfillment and joy. This deeply spiritual life is sustained by a theology yet to be set down on paper but all too evident in women's prayers.[12] The domestic rituals that revolve around the mother and her children are the traditional woman's deepest theological experiences. Her performance of these rituals is itself a theological statement. It is a statement of faith in the one God manifested in traditional religion as in Christianity. It is a statement of human dependence on constantly staying in touch with God and of the sanctity of covenantal relations. In times of great crisis a woman will resort to special ritual provisions whether she is baptized into Christ or not. Women who are not baptized do so more readily than Christian women. While remaining strong believers in the efficacy of prayers, Christian women seldom resort to the ritual provisions of their churches.

Christian women who are more single-minded in their Christian theologizing are those who occupy more prominent places in their Christian communities, such as prophetesses in the Independent Churches or leaders of basic Christian communities in the Roman Catholic Church. Such women will need to live exemplary Christian lives, which may require that they sever themselves from the traditional practices that the particular cultural community expects of them. It is a very hard stance to take, but if such women are to remain heads of church-sponsored projects, they have to dissociate themselves from all that the Christian community considers to be incompatible with Christianity. By what theological criteria do these women make their decisions? We have to consult them.

Women in such leadership positions desire to know more of the biblical background of their faith and more especially concerning the significance of women in the Bible for the church, and for Christian theology. Women's theology in Africa is being done in Bible studies, where women cease to be the docile and passive recipients of the wisdom/doctrine of the clergy. They are questioning the established order of things. In fact, the awakened awareness of the traditionally unquestioning women has scared some ecclesiastics into phasing out diocesan programs involving women's development and leadership.[13] It has become uncomfortable for the clergy concerned to head a congregation of women who demand to know the wherefore, the what, and the how of their church's teachings and practices.

The rising number of young women with university degrees in religion include a few who are to be found quietly engaged in "revolutionary" activities, such as working with the destitute and the marginalized. They are theologians of the "seed growing secretly." Such quiet proclamation of the word of God is indispensable in an Africa that is fast following the line of materialism and godlessness. On the other hand, there are in Africa those inspired by the dauntless courage and faith of relentless fighters such as Winnie Mandela, women who tackle anti-women legislation and church regulations. She who would seek to call Africa to women's perspectives needs the spirit of justice and equity that moves the anti-apartheid struggle. Such a move can be sustained only by a theology of hope.

THE THEOLOGICAL TASK

Faced with their own particular experiences as women who have recently ventured into what is said to be a man's domain, African women theologians have the task of reclaiming the theological heritage stored in the participation of African women in traditional religion: the grassroots theology of Christian women and the theology that undergirds the spirituality of Christian women in Africa, especially those in the African Independent Churches. Inclusiveness has to be a mark of the enterprise, for there are, as we have pointed out, theologians to be found in all realms of the woman's world. The feminist perspectives to be gained from research demand that all women be reckoned as resource persons for this work. Not all can be or wish to be "writing theologians," but there is not a single African woman's experience of life in church and society that the theologian can afford to ignore. A critique of the status quo and strategies for dismantling sexism and for pointing to women's experience and hopes for Africa is a task for all women. Those who would be called theologians stand as servants to this cause whose goals affect all women and men.

We have tried to present a picture of Africa that is based primarily on experiences in two countries that share a history of forms of British colonialism: Kenya and Nigeria (with supplements from Sierra Leone). Today these countries are in the throes of the neocolonial exploitation of Africa. Experiences of church life present a variation on the old theme of missionary paternalism and the struggles for the birthing of authentic African Christianity. We have presented a realistic picture of African women's lives, a picture that in the church remains very traditional. There is very little encouragement for women to take the church's mission, ministry, and theology as a sphere of women's service. This is the reality within which we embark on our theological task. It is a labor of faith, hope, and solidarity.

NOTES

1. An example of these periodic efforts is the war against "indiscipline" that the military government of Nigeria launched in 1984 since it returned to power after the Second Republic under Shagari was ousted.

2. Rosemary Nthamburi, "On the Possibility of a New Image for an African Woman," a paper submitted to the Continental Consultation on Theology from Third-World Women's Perspective (EATWOT Women's Commission), Port Harcourt, Nigeria, Aug. 19-23, 1986.

3. Ibid.

4. Lloyda Fanusie, "Women and the Church (Protestant)," paper presented at Port Harcourt, Nigeria, August 1986 (EATWOT Women's Commission).

5. Ibid.

6. Nthamburi, "New Image."

7. Fanusie, "Women and the Church."

8. P. Temples, *Bantu Philosophy* (Paris: Presence Africaine, 1969), pp. 142–43; H. Sawyer, "Sacrifice," in *Biblical Revelation and African Belief,* ed. Kwesi Dickson and Paul Ellingsworth (Maryknoll, N.Y.: Orbis Books, 1969), pp. 58–59; K. A. Opoku, *West African Traditional Religion* (Accra: International Press, 1978), pp. 74–81.

9. P. J. Murnion, "The Parish as Source of Community and Identity," *The Parish in Community and Ministry* (New York: Paulist Press, 1978), p. 101. This situation was vividly reported at the Port Harcourt Consultation by Rosemary Edet and in Elizabeth Amoah's paper given at the consultation (see n. 12, below).

10. Nthamburi, "New Image."

11. Lloyda Fanusie, "Women and the Church."

12. Elizabeth Amoah in her paper on "The Vital Aspects of Women's Experience of God," presented at the Port Harcourt Consultation, gave a survey of women's spirituality as it breaks through in the "Spiritual Churches" of Ghana. She concluded: "Definitely there is a thirst for something . . . in our struggles to create the just and peaceful existence that we desire."

13. The reference here is to projects of the Catholic Secretariat in Kenya, where one department deals specifically with Development Education Programmes (DEP). The target group is women. Women leaders of small groups undergo courses in conscientization. These courses are of two kinds: Women in National Development of Women (WINDOW) and Development Education Leadership Training in Action (DELTA). Both WINDOW and DELTA are designed primarily for coordinators of women's groups.

2

Women and Men Building Together the Church in Africa

Dorothy Ramodibe (South Africa)

INTRODUCTION

The theme "Women and Men Building Together the Church in Africa" is problematic for me as an ordinary woman from Soweto, Johannesburg—a woman who has experienced terrible oppression from men in our society and even in the church, where I expected my salvation to come from, the church that one would have expected to be a refuge for the weak, poor, and downtrodden. We need to ask the question: Is it possible for women and men together to build the church in Africa when there is exploitation, oppression, and domination of women by men? Is working together possible when there is no equality between men and women?

To me, this sounds like the same apartheid drums that I hear at home, where people (particularly P. W. Botha) call upon whites and blacks to build together the "nation" of South Africa while apartheid remains intact. No, there can be no cooperation between whites and blacks as long as legalized inequalities exist. It cannot happen until there is equality and justice. No, there can be no cooperation between women and men as long as the oppressive and exploitative structures of the church remain intact. There can be no cooperation as long as men retain their dominant position in the church. The problem here is that the church uses the traditional understanding of the theology, or doctrine, of reconciliation, which consciously or unconsciously assumes that you can reconcile justice with injustice, righteousness with unrighteousness, good with evil. Actually they want to reconcile the devil with God. This traditional theology of reconciliation does not insist on repentance as a prerequisite for reconciliation. Those who understand reconciliation in this way will always call for peace where there is no justice. You will hear them saying, "For the sake of

14

peace let us be reconciled" without their lifting a finger to deal with the injustices. I am going to argue that for reconciliation to be possible we must do away with evil, injustice, and sin.

There is another question that we have to ask: Which church are we building—the historical church of the dominant classes or the church of Jesus Christ? Is it the old, oppressive church or is it the "new," liberating church? Are we invited to participate at the will of the dominant group in this old church, just to be accommodated, to be co-opted into the system, to collaborate in our oppression? Are we asked to soothe the consciences of men by being seen to be working side by side with men when we have no powers at all?

Behind the questions raised here, I sense a common theme: women are being asked to join men in continuing the work long begun by men. I shall argue that it is impossible to correct, develop, or improve the church, within the same old system, to accommodate women. Women want to *change* the church and not simply "improve" it. Women want *liberation* of the church from men. The theme, on the other hand, seems to suggest development rather than liberation.

THE ROLES OF WOMEN AND MEN

Allow me at this point to address the current problems of *(a)* women and men in South Africa, and *(b)* women and men in the church. Only in the light of these two issues can we look ahead to "building together the church in Africa."

Women and Men in South Africa

African tradition and culture present themselves to women as an oppressive system. It has a male-domineering factor. It is a patriarchal system. This oppressive patriarchal system was found in South Africa even before whites came with their Western capitalistic culture. Capitalistic culture has reinforced the oppressive system, out of which it derives more benefits. The patriarchal system has been continued to date by those who see culture as *static* rather than *dynamic*. To me, static culture is oppressive culture, and the patriarchal system legitimizes the domination of women by men.

African theology, we should note, has almost fallen into the trap of idolizing African culture in an uncritical way. African theology, as I understand it, seems to be mainly concerned with the "culturization" of the gospel. Because African theology starts from the context of African culture, which is patriarchal (in the static sense), it runs the risk of being party to the legitimization of the domination of women. We need to find out to what extent African theology has addressed the question of the oppression of women specifically. Is it not just another male theology? Is it not part of the conspiracy to continue oppressing us as women?

A further complication in South Africa is the racist apartheid system, which fosters the static culture of the patriarchal system in order to legitimize itself and to divide and oppress people in a society where racism is used to benefit capitalism. Racism, which is built on an ideology that claims one race is superior or inferior to another,[1] is here used to justify profit-making for one race at the expense of other races. In South Africa, racism coincides with sexism, which discriminates on the basis of sex. In the racist apartheid system, black men and women are exploited jointly in the labor market, but the women are paid less than the men. This exploitation is even worse for rural women working on farms. They are the most exploited of all workers, having few rights and almost no legal protection against harsh working conditions and starvation wages. Women are forced to accept these conditions because of a high rural unemployment rate, unreliable remittances from male migrant workers, and no rights to any land. According to the terms of the Land Act of 1936, about 80 percent of the blacks are confined to 13 percent of the land in South Africa.

Pass laws and influx control, both aimed at monitoring and controlling Black movement, have been successful in making it impossible for Blacks to work in many areas. Marriage also contributes to women's oppression. Women married in the "community of property" situation bind themselves to their husbands and are classified as minors, making them inferior to men. Capitalism uses sexual reproduction and the masculine-feminine socialization of children in such a way as to make women more exploitable, rather than to satisfy human needs. This is a special oppression of women as women, as well as of women as workers.

Women and Men in the Church

There can be no argument that the church is one of the most oppressive structures in society today, especially in regard to the oppression of women. The church is almost always a mirror of society. You need only look at the Roman Catholic Church to see elements of the Roman empire. It is not difficult to see elements of the British empire in the Anglican Church or the apartheid system in the Dutch Reformed Church in South Africa and other related churches there. Those South African churches, for instance, talk about white churches, which are the real churches to them, as mother churches; and the so-called Indian, Coloured, and African churches are called "daughter" churches. This is a reflection of the white government, which rules everybody, with Bantustans as their "babies."

About three-quarters of the people in the church are women, but decisions affecting the church are made by men alone (with very few exceptions). Women are treated as minors, inferior to men, just as they are in society. Only men are assigned to lay positions of leadership, with powers of control; women are looked down upon. On the issue of the ordination of women, for instance, the matter is still being discussed in some churches. It is men who still decide whether women should be ordained or not. Women are talked *about*, not *to*. They are regarded as minors who are not to be trusted with the sacramental offices of the church.

On the other hand, Jesus treated women in a remarkable way. He was a symbol of what equality means insofar as men and women are concerned. Jesus did not see a woman's place as in the kitchen. He allowed women to sit at his feet. He mixed with the prostitutes. Jesus encouraged women like Mary to participate in his work rather than just prepare meals (Lk.10:48). He was often in the company of women (Mk.15:40). They followed him to Galilee and helped him in his work and were also present at his crucifixion. Women were the first to announce his birth (Lk.1:26–56) and they were with him to the last to witness his death. They were also the first to witness his resurrection and bore witness of it to the other disciples.

Even though Paul was a person of his times and conformed to the sexist tendencies of that society, he does talk about women preachers and co-workers. He talks of mutual and equal love, of respect between women and men. All this was against the traditions of his time.

This church, the male-dominated church, *wants* women but does not *need* them. Women are wanted because they are workers (cleaning the church, making cakes, fund-raising, etc.) for the comfort of men. Men are like Pharaoh, who wanted the children of Israel as slaves, but did not need them as people. This feeling of not being needed is expressed by a woman, a former member of the Gereformeerde Kerk (Reformed Church), who said:

In the Dopper Church I feel irrelevant; the reason why I have no qualms about leaving the church is that I know I will not be missed, as I was never needed. It is difficult as a lay person to play any part in a Church which defines itself, not in terms of a body with members with gifts but in terms of functions and positions. So women assume an inferior position and never take responsibility for anything more consequential than baking for functions. If I attend Sunday service, keep the children quiet and do not concern myself with matters that are too high for me, take no responsibility for what happens to the congregation as a body nor for what I read in the Bible, if I pray for the congregation without being allowed to know what is happening in the congregation, then I can be a suitably submissive, passive and slowly dying feminine member of the reformed church.[2]

The Bible tells us that the church is the body of Christ (Eph. 4:16). We are supposed to be embodied in this church, which has its wholeness (1 Cor.12). But the present church recognizes only men as members of the church, if it is "church" at all. I wish to argue that in its present form the church is not the body of Christ, but it is *like* the body of Christ. Therefore this type of church cannot be "improved" but must be "born again." We create a "new" church, which shall be the real body of Christ. I propose therefore that we change the theme, as given to me, from "Women and Men Building Together the Church in Africa" to "Women and Men Re-creating a New Church Together in

Africa"—a church that will be a source and agent of liberation, justice, and peace in all respects.

TOWARD A NEW CHURCH AND A NEW SOCIETY

The women are the church and have been the church of Christ since its beginning. However, they have found themselves playing a marginal role and generally being regarded as misfits. It is therefore imperative that in this process toward building a new church in Africa, women should face more seriously the task of their liberation. It is here that feminist theology comes in. *By feminist theology I understand the act of reflecting on the significance and influence of our faith on the experiences of women with a view to making women fully human.* Women need to emerge as full human beings, liberated from all forces that have kept them in slavery for the past years. The Christian faith should be the great motivating force in this movement toward self-fulfillment.

The liberation of women for meaningful participation in the church also means that the power of women should change the society and the economic structures that have been exploitative. The struggle of women to be human beings also means that they will fight all oppression: they will fight oppression and exploitation by their husbands; they will fight racism and other forms of discrimination; they will fight apartheid together with its evils such as forced removals, influx control, pass laws, and ethnicity. Feminist theology wishes to remind women that their role in the church is not that of slaves, but of partners with God.

There are evidently structures oppressive of women inherent in both the Black Community and the Church. This situation is regrettable and calls for our serious and urgent attention.

We affirm that there can be no genuine National Liberation Struggle as long as the cry for the liberation of women is relegated to insignificance or to the post-liberation agenda.

We note that Jesus, in his teaching and by his example of human relations based on equal dignity of all, is opposed to oppression founded on sex. [3]

Women cannot build the church with men, however, until men have been liberated to accept women. Feminist theology, therefore, aims to challenge men about their views of women, about their treatment of women, and also to question whether that treatment does not thereby make them oppressors. It is in this respect that black theology has come to realize that there can be no liberation from oppression by whites while women's oppression is not addressed. This self-criticism by black theology is also a challenge to women to step up their struggle. The following excerpts from the Final Statements of two theology conferences show this growing realization:

Although the Conference castigated itself for the poor representation of women it was acknowledged that the true measure of liberation in any Society is the extent to which women are liberated. For this reason Black Theology cannot be a Theology of Liberation unless feminist theology is a fundamental part . . . of a Black Theology of Liberation.[4]

Whereas women form the majority of the oppressed we note with regret that Black Theology has not taken women seriously, but has seen theology as a male domain.

We, the participants of this conference, feel that there is no way that Black Theology will be a meaningful liberation force if it does not allow women to participate as equals.

Any struggle which does not take the oppression of women seriously, cannot be an authentic revolutionary force. . . .

We, the participants of the ICT [Institute of Contextual Theology] Women's Conference acknowledge the part that Black Theology can play within the liberation struggle in South Africa. We are . . . , however, concerned that women have not been included in this domain right from the conception of this programme, in spite of the fact that we do have Women Theologians' Conferences.

We believe Black Theology cannot exist as a liberatory movement without the participation of all theologians striving for a non-sexist, non-racial, democratic South Africa.[5]

Men and women need to cooperate on the basis of mutuality. God's plans of differentiation of God's creatures was not meant to be a disadvantage to others, but was meant to enrich one another. Mutuality is relevant only where partners recognize and respect each other; mutuality does not recognize paternalism.

Once women are seriously acknowledged as partners, as the body of Christ, we can build a new church. I say a "new church" because the church as we have it today is a creation of male persons. As women, we have always felt like strangers in this male church. We have been given concessions and permissions like children. We have always had to ask permission and be apologetic. The new church we want to build should be nondiscriminatory. It should be a church where all human beings are regarded as equals.

One of the tasks of this church is to examine all the symbols of Christianity and check to see if they are polluted by a male-dominant culture. This means examining the Bible itself, theology, and church history or traditions. It is important that women reread the Bible, because the Bible we have now has been edited with the influence of male domination. It is men who composed it, and it used male symbols.

In the Final Statement of the Black Theology Conference in Cape Town in 1984, the participants made the following recommendations:

We . . . regard it as belonging to both the nature and task of a Black Theology of Liberation to embrace in its programme the question of the liberation of women and we call upon all to:

1. Embark on definite educational programmes directed to both the male-dominated Church leadership who are the victimisers and the women who are the victims.

2. Transform those social and economic structures of society which are unjust and oppressive and not simply substitute women for men in them.

3. Encourage those cultural patterns and customs whose function promotes equally the interest [and] well being of all members of the community and to eradicate those that dehumanise women or serve the interests of men at the expense of women.

4. Encourage and facilitate the meaningful involvement of women in Church life and in community and women's organizations.

5. Challenge ecclesiastical oppression against women, e.g., the reluctance or absolute unwillingness of some Churches to accept full ordination of women to the ministry of the word and sacraments.

We also express our concern about the need for more critical analysis of the cultural and economic forces that serve to reinforce the ideology of male dominance and humbly call upon feminist theologians to inform Black Theology and forge an alliance with it.

Our task is not only to build a new church but also a new society. Cooperation in building a new society is needed because the society we presently have denies the full humanity of women. In this project, God is with us because God came to create a new society. If we are to establish a new economic order, upon what principles would it be based? To delineate its chief elements is one of the many tasks that lie ahead of us.

CONCLUSION

Empower women. Women need to retain their singularity and distinctiveness in order for their contribution to be vital and lively. The life that women are looking for and are now rediscovering will become each one's concern if women continue to make it their cause. It would not be easy for women to accept it, however, because they have grown used to sacrificing themselves readily and always taking back seats. Men also need liberation from their prejudices of masculinity.

In summary: There can be no cooperation in building the church while women are still being oppressed and exploited and treated as minors. What we need is not improvement or development of the present church, but its renewal, its complete change. Feminist theology is an important step in this task, for it will pave the way for mutuality, for full participation of women in building a new church and a new society.

NOTES

1. In 1983 the following allocations were made as subsidies per child for education:

Whites	Indians	Coloureds	Africans
R1221	R798	R286	R165

This subsidy for each white child is more than seven times that of Africans. The average household income per month in 1983 was:

Whites	Indians	Coloureds	Africans
R1390	R819	R548	R204

From the few examples given we find that resources are shared very unequally. Africans, Coloureds, and Indians make up 85% (more than four-fifths) of South Africa's population, yet they receive only about 20% (one-fifth) of the country's resources.

2. D.M. Ackermann "The Role of Women in the Church: Certain Practical Theological Perspectives," in *Sexism and Feminism in Theological Perspective*, ed. W. S. Vorster (Pretoria: Unisa, 1984).

3. From Final Statement, Black Theology Conference, Cape Town, South Africa, 1984.

4. From Final Statement, Black Theology Conference, Welgespruit, South Africa, 1983.

5. From Final Statement, Feminist Theology Conference, Hammanskraal, South Africa, 1984.

3

The Christ-Event from the Viewpoint of African Women

I. A Catholic Perspective

Thérèse Souga (Cameroun)

MY ACT OF FAITH

Jesus Christ means everything to me.

As an African woman, a Christian, one consecrated to the service of God in God's church and in the world, I believe in Jesus Christ: for me, Christ is the true Human, the one who makes it possible for all persons to reach fulfillment and to overcome the historic alienations weighing them down. For me, that faith entails unconditional adherence to the God revealed in Jesus Christ, the one whom God has "highly exalted above every name, so that at Jesus' name, every knee should bend, in the heavens, on earth, and under the earth, and every tongue should proclaim that Jesus Christ is Lord in the glory of God the Father" (Phil. 2:9–11).

For me this unconditional belonging to the God of Jesus Christ means entering into the paschal mystery: it is a desire, growing deeper within me each day, to know Christ, to commune with his sufferings, to open myself to the power of his resurrection, to be open to the action of the Holy Spirit, who builds the church and the history of human beings. This is a matter of deep attitudes, and of motivations, and of operative meanings.

The realism of the cross every day tells me, as a woman of the Third World, that the laws of history can be overcome by means of crucified love.

Translated from French by Phillip Berryman.

JESUS AND WOMEN THROUGHOUT THE GOSPEL

The gospel leads me to discover that Jesus bears a message of liberation for every human being and especially for those social categories that are most disadvantaged. Since in Jewish society during Jesus' time women did not enjoy a high status, as we have been told, women are by that fact a category that will attract Jesus' attention.

In His Ministry before the Resurrection, Jesus Reveals Himself to Women

In the story of *the Samaritan Woman* (Jn. 4: 1–42), it is in her daily activities, "drawing water," that she meets Jesus, whose first word to her is "Give me something to drink." This request sets in motion a dialogue between Jesus and her, and through this dialogue Jesus gradually reveals himself to this woman. For her part, little by little, she opens herself to the word of Jesus and asks herself who he is. Somewhat reassured, she becomes a messenger of the Good News among her neighbors.

This woman carries out her role as apostle so well that those who believe in Jesus tell her, "We no longer believe because of what you say, but we have heard for ourselves and we know that he is truly the Savior of the world."

Thus Jesus reveals himself to this woman, and this encounter with Christ makes her a messenger of the Good News.

The Women Who Follow Jesus Are Genuine Disciples of Christ

For us it is important to discover that women occupy an important place in the group of the disciples—they are among those who follow Christ—and their role is not simply one of taking care of housekeeping duties, but also one of receiving the Master's teaching. Nowhere in the Gospels does it say that they were excluded when the Master delivered that teaching.

In the Acts of the Apostles (Acts 1:12–14) they are devoted to prayer along with the other disciples as they await the Holy Spirit. In the account about Martha and Mary where tradition shows us two kinds of women, one active, the other contemplative, we note that Mary's position at the feet of Jesus is that of the disciple at the feet of the Master, which reminds us of Paul's position at the feet of Gamaliel (Acts 22:3). Nevertheless, it should be noted that in order to bring women into the group of his disciples, Jesus assumes an attitude that is both very sensitive to them and yet does not rule out strictness and does not excuse them from the demands of the new alliance. Jesus is the friend of Martha and Mary, Lazarus' two sisters. It is from within this relationship of friendship that he reveals himself to them and to all the people around them. Martha's confession of faith calls to mind that of Peter in Caesarea Philippa:

"Yes, Lord, I believe you are the Christ, the Son of God who comes into the world" (Jn. 11:27).

Jesus does not shrink from establishing friendship with women, nor from challenging them deeply, but he does so to reveal who he is and to bring them into his mission.

Jesus Heals Women as a Fulfillment of the Kingdom

In the Gospels, we see women suffering from many evils. For them, Jesus is the one who delivers them from their physical, moral, and spiritual miseries.

a) The woman with the hemorrhage (Mt. 9:18–22) had an illness that not only brought her a long period of bodily suffering (twelve years) but is considered shameful and placing her among those who are impure (cf. Lev. 15: 19–32) and cutting her off from life in society.

She discreetly slips through the crowd, since she is unable to express openly her plea to be cured. Nevertheless, she is moved by a great desire to be cured and a deep confidence in this man, whose goodness she has no doubt heard praised. Thus she comes from behind and does not touch Jesus' body (like the public sinner who moistened Jesus' feet with tears and covered them with kisses) but, rather, the fringes of his garment, for she says to herself, "If I only touch his garment, I shall be made well" (v.21).

Jesus turns around, sees her, and says, "Take heart, daughter! Your faith has made you well." This poor woman is raised to the rank of a daughter of God, and Jesus takes her out of the isolation in which her illness had confined her, setting her back into society and among the daughters of Israel. This is not only physical healing. Jesus confers on her more than she expected, since he restores her dignity.

b) The Canaanite woman (Mk. 7: 24–30; Mt. 15: 21–28) is a pagan, a Greek, of Syro-Phoenician origin, as Mark specifies. She is suffering with a mother's love; her daughter's illness wrenches from her cries of pain: "Have mercy on me, O Lord; my daughter is severely possessed by a demon" (Mt. 15:22). This woman is pouring out her suffering so much that she is disturbing the people around Jesus. The disciples tell him, "Send her away, for she is crying after us" (Mt. 15: 23).

Jesus' first response is silence. Is he insensitive to the distress of this woman who is not a Jew? But in the end the woman's persistence brings him to engage in dialogue with her. He probes her faith, and seeing how deep it is, he grants the cure.

Thus, in the Gospels, Jesus is the one who delivers women from every infirmity and suffering. Prostitutes, excluded from life in society, emerge from that situation and, having been relieved of their misery, they are purified and even come to enjoy intimacy with God. Mothers see their children cured or returned to life (cf. the widow of Nain). The kingdom of God has come for them as well. They share in the messianic signs just as much as others, and Jesus is especially sensitive to their situation.

Women Are Associated with Jesus' Passion and Resurrection

Present throughout Jesus' whole public life (many follow him from Galilee), they are also there during his passion and resurrection: on the road to Calvary, women weep and lament him (Mt. 23:37); they are at the foot of the cross (Jn.19:25-27); they watch when he is laid and prepare for his anointing (Mk. 15:47-16:1); they go to the tomb at early dawn and are the first to know that he has risen (Lk. 24:1-10); it is the women who announce the news of the resurrection to the apostles and "the rest"(Lk. 24:1-11); and it is to a woman that Jesus first appears after his resurrection (Jn. 20:11-18). Women are thus the first to live the reality of the resurrection, this new humanity that emerges from the cross and life. They are involved in the whole mystery of Christ.

Women Witness to Jesus Christ in the Church from Apostolic Times

During the apostolic period recounted in the Acts of the Apostles, we discover that women are involved in the birth of the church. They go along with the apostles and play an important role in the life of the incipient church. Thus, in Acts 9:36, we read that in Joppa among the disciples was a woman named Tabitha, or Dorcas in Greek. Similarly we hear of Priscilla and Damaris, and there are many others who play a very important role in the life of the community. Furthermore, the Eucharist is celebrated in Christian families, but we shall not go any further into this aspect, since there will be a presentation, at this conference, on women and the church.

RELATING JESUS TO OUR AFRICAN CONTEXT

Jesus and Today's African Woman

Is this Jesus whom we find to be full of concern for the women of his own time also today standing with African women in their particular context? Can African women understand Jesus Christ and understand themselves in relation to Jesus of Nazareth? Doesn't the concrete historic situation of African women challenge the theology that we would like to live in the churches of Africa? This modest work can only discern some leads to be pursued in further research.

To begin with, we realize that we must improve our present situation: false images of women persist in the church in Africa and in turn produce certain negative kinds of behavior. Should not Christology question these images in order to question the real situation of African women and subject it to a critical examination in the light of Jesus Christ?

The Attitude of the African Church towards Women

Except for the Blessed Virgin, the church, which has often forgotten the role of women in the Gospels, has been the bearer of an image of women likening them to Satan. Thus in the missionary context there has developed an attitude of mistrust toward the black woman. We find that at a deeper level this mistrustful attitude comes from a vision of human beings in their relationships: the notion is that people from hot countries are incapable of continence. Such colonial prejudices, nourished by a pseudo-ethnology, amount to an ideology, the ideology of black Eros.

In addition, some of the missionaries who evangelized our countries were marked by an asceticism that led them to take a harsh attitude toward women. Some of them came from families where even a remote Jansenist influence left its mark and strongly characterized their attitude toward women.

Moreover, a popular exegesis of the Bible narratives (e.g., Gen. 3:6, Eve offering to Adam the fruit God has forbidden) has the effect of linking in people's imaginations women's intentions with those of the devil. Even today in conversation one can hear it said that the woman is "the devil's tail." Such images reveal a vision that is foreign to the light of revelation. We Africans have to make a break that involves going from ideology to a Christian theology of woman, going from imagery to an intellectual practice that entails reflecting on the situation of African women, so they may discover their place in the churches and occupy it.

Guideposts for a Faith Reflection

We also ask whether or not, in a Christian context, women can come to understand themselves without understanding what they have received from Jesus Christ. Are not the theological question about women and the Christological question closely bound together?

We situate the problem in the horizon of the relationship to be discovered between women and Jesus Christ in an African context. "Woman, what is there between you and me?" (Jn. 2:4). What is there between Jesus Christ and the African woman?

Cannot what we strive for in faith be rooted in the context of a people, of the Third World woman? In Accra, in December 1977, African theology opted to be a theology of liberation and not of adaptation.* Insofar as we are conscious that we must free ourselves from a threefold captivity—cultural, spiritual, socioeconomic—should not what we strive for in faith take this specific context as its starting point? Hence to begin with, we are going to examine the solidarity existing between Jesus and African women in the situations they experience.

Certain Problematic Aspects of African Women's Experience

There seems to be a deep bond, even a complicity, between Jesus of Nazareth and African women, a bond due to the fact that the women are among those

---

*The Pan-African Conference of Third World Theologians. See *African Theology En Route*, ed. Kofi Appiah-Kubi and Sergio Torres (Maryknoll, N.Y.: Orbis Books, 1979).

who are most marginalized in our society. In order to realize this, we are going to invoke some of our proverbs and certain sayings about women:

Ye mininga a kad kobo ai bod? Does a woman speak in public?

Ye ba laiñ mininga ai tañ bod? Is the woman considered a person?

Wa yi ma bie mon abod afé (mon fam)? When are you going to make me a baby (child)?

Women themselves seem to accept this situation. When there is an unidentified noise and someone asks, "Za a duñ?" (Who's there?) a woman answers, "Seki mod, ma" (It's nobody, just me). Thus, from the moment she comes into the world, woman is a problematic being: she is not regarded as being fully a person.

Certainly one can respond that African society recognizes the woman's role as mother, wife, educator, and nurturer. But it is clear that all these roles are utilitarian, so much so that a childless woman is generally not highly regarded by those around her, and indeed may be regarded as having failed in her calling. How can one be fully a woman without being a mother?

In order to understand all this, ought not our contact with the gospel aid us to question ourselves about Jesus Christ as we experience our condition as women in this particular context? Is it not by taking this experience and this relationship into account that we may begin gradually to move forward in theology? It seems to us that there can be no understanding of Jesus Christ outside of the situation in which we seek to understand ourselves.

Even a glance at our society leads us to conclude that the lived experience of African women is not always taken into account. Everything is in the hands of men: they have the power; it is they who have the right to speak, who enjoy respect, who have the right to take initiatives, and they are often favored by the law. Being a woman means silence, being brushed aside, suffering, weakness.

Certainly there are women who have stepped forth, who have claimed their right to speak, and who command respect. Indeed, these women have to have manlike qualities to get ahead so they can be taken seriously.

Are women, who make up a larger group than men in the population, benefiting from a more just situation? They are often overworked both in the city and in the countryside. They have to worry about feeding the family, taking care of the children, and paying for their education. The many hardships and sufferings they undergo, and the burden of their work and of childbirth, make them age more quickly than men.

Politically speaking, it is true that recently a great effort has been made to involve women in the advance of the nation and to bring them into decision-making circles. But this effort is still not very satisfactory. The representation of women in political affairs remains insignificant when compared to their numbers, and thus their political weight is practically nil.

In the professions, where there are women doctors, lawyers, teachers, and engineers in many areas, it also remains true that illiteracy is a mass phenomenon in our Third World countries. Moreover, certain prejudices remain very much alive, and certain individuals who even have public posts can advocate revolutionary viewpoints in their official speeches, and yet show their inconsistency in their behavior toward women. Thus the deputy Henri Lopez, in his book *Tribaliques*, says to his daughter, "Don't forget that you are a woman. A woman's primary work is work in the home." And, speaking about his daughter, he says to his wife, "And do you think she'll keep her husband at home with her graduation certicate? She'll keep him home with good meals, and something else besides" (Henri Lopez, *Tribaliques*, Yaoundé: Ed. Cle, 1982). Nevertheless, this deputy was applauded for the very revolutionary stands he took at the inauguration of a congress of the avant-garde National Federation of Women in his country.

The Correlation between Women's Experience and Liberation in Jesus Christ

Sensitive to the misery and oppression of the weak, Jesus Christ in his incarnation takes on all these situations of weakness and of injustice. This weakness is found in the life of Jesus: Jesus at birth is laid in the manger meant for animals (Lk. 2:6–7); at his presentation in the temple, his parents' offering was a modest pair of turtledoves (Lk. 2:22–24); a carpenter's son, he is from Nazareth, and "can anything good come out of Nazareth?"(Jn. 2:46). It is by way of these situations that Jesus bears in his person the condition of the weak, and hence that of women.

In the light of Christ, if Jesus is the God who has become weakness in our context, in his identity as God-man, Jesus takes on the condition of the African woman. The African woman can tell herself: Christ has been concerned with, and has been touched by, the situation that I am living. The situation of the African woman in society reflects the condition of the peoples of the Third World. That is why it is legitimate to strive to live out faith starting from the situation of African women.

Christology is intended as discourse about Jesus. But during his ministry, in his passion, and after his resurrection, Jesus shows a great deal of interest in women and they are very interested in Jesus. Thus the question of the relationship between women and Jesus leads us to discover that Jesus reveals God in the various kinds of bonds connecting him to women throughout the Gospels.

We must never forget that it is a datum of revelation that "when the times were fulfilled, the Son of God was born of a woman." With this phrase, Paul is deeply Christian in emphasizing the realism of the incarnation, especially when we take into account the lot of women in the Jewish world. It is of one of them that the Son of God is born. In this fashion God wants to confound man by choosing to come into the world by way of woman. "What is weak in the eyes of the world" has delivered us from our prejudices, and Jesus has chosen this way for coming into the world. From the vantage point of the Third World, and without forcing anything, Jesus is truly Good News for the women of Africa.

CONCLUSION

Christ is in solidarity with women, for they incarnate the suffering of the African people. It is within this situation that he liberates them and entrusts them with his message of life for both men and women today.

The resurrection of Christ has overturned the religious world of the ancient church and has liberated women from all situations that exclude them. It has changed the lot of women and has ensured them a place in the world of faith.

While under the domination of the male side of humankind, the universe tends to be harsh, closed, aggressive, and even unjust. The Christian woman, following Christ, is the bearer of harmony, sweetness, justice, and understanding. Through the initiatives that she will be emboldened to undertake, she is responsible for inviting the man to have a different vision of reality, to wake him up to the situation of the little ones and of the weak who are likely to be crushed. In an aggressive situation, where one might think she would be annihilated, as she takes on this situation with faith in Christ, she grows. Like the church, which sings about the happy fault that brought us such a Savior, the woman can see her situation of weakness as a treasure that opens her up and sensitizes her to situations of injustice and oppression. Her belonging to Jesus Christ increases within her this thirst to know him, to live from him, to work to make the gospel take root in this society of hers.

We need a Christology that takes into account the situation of women in the African world. Christology cannot be reformulated without taking into account women and their place in church and society in Africa.

A Christology certainly exists already, but at our own level we want to try to reappropriate faith in Christ within our context. This Christology thus becomes open to questions coming from African women, and African women will then have to take an active role in the Christological debate. This will undoubtedly enhance the face of the church and will contribute to the rooting of the faith in our culture and in our continent.

II. A Protestant Perspective

Louise Tappa (Cameroun)

Before getting into the heart of the matter, I believe one issue must be raised in the discussion. We are Christians, that is, disciples of Jesus Christ. We are not disciples of Peter, or of John, or of Paul. John, Peter, James, Paul and so forth were disciples of Jesus just as we are, and in their communities they sought to recall the story of Jesus and to live it in those communities. That is why, for example, we cannot speak of a Christology in the New Testament: there are different Christologies. John's Christology is not Matthew's Christology, or that of Luke or Mark. On this point I would like to state that when we speak about women's place in the early church, we should be aware that our debate today has been around for a long time. In John's Gospel, as many have noted, women—Martha and Mary—occupy the position that Matthew, for example, would prefer to give to Peter. The one who first confesses Christ in John's Gospel is a woman, and not Peter, as is the case in Matthew. One has the impression that already at this point in the early church there is a conflict, and I would even say a competition, between communities, between those who do not accept women as apostles on the same plane as men, and others who do not allow themselves to be enslaved by the patriarchal system of the age. With regard to the formation of the biblical canon, it is clear that the books we have today and that make up the canon are only a portion of the Christian experiences of the early church, and that many writings were excluded from the canon, not because they were heretical from the viewpoint of the teaching of Jesus, but because at that time, theology was already being formulated in the perspective of the dominant class of the age, the perspective of the class of conquerors. The writings that gave women leadership positions in their communities were eliminated.

I would now like to cite a passage from the Gospel of Thomas to illustrate what I am saying. The Gospel of Thomas is an apocryphal book, written around A.D. 140. The passage I want to draw your attention to is the following, which I have freely translated:

His disciples will say to him: when will the Kingdom of God arrive? [Jesus says]: It will not come when one expects. One will not say, Here it

---

Translated from French by Phillip Berryman.

is! or There it is! Rather, the Kingdom of the Father is spread over the whole earth, and men do not see it. Simon Peter said to him: Let Mary go away, for women are not worthy of life. Jesus said: I will lead her so she may become a male, so that she may thus become a living spirit, similar to you males. For every woman who becomes male will enter into the Kingdom of heaven.

I imagine the term "male" might shock many, but I do not think Jesus intended to change Mary's biology, not at all. What Jesus said—and we have no reason to doubt that he did—is that in the society in which he found himself, woman had no voice, and was not a person (as has been noted over and over). Only a man could be the master of his own destiny. Thus I understand and translate the text in the following sense: "Jesus said: I am going to lead Mary, if she accepts my teaching, so she will take charge of history, so she will take part in the building of history just as much as men."

The point is that the history of our (institutional) church is a history written from the angle of the victors and it has very little room for the struggles waged by women within the early church to live truly the gospel of Jesus Christ.

What is Christology? The task of Christology is to work out the full meaning of the reality of the Christ-event for humankind.

We have many methods at our disposal for working this out. But it can be said here that the prevailing method within the churches is always the doctrinal approach. We are supposed to adhere to the "articles of faith revealed by God" if we are Catholics, and to take the whole Bible as "word of God" if we are Protestants. Unfortunately, this often means that Christ is reduced to a sublime abstraction. Always a positive abstraction, of course, but one that can still be ignored when the time comes to translate it into the life of our communities. That is why even to the present it has been possible to interpret the doctrines of the incarnation (liberation) and of expiation (reconciliation) in terms that leave intact the social structures and models of our communities, including the church.

I would propose to you another procedure, one that is much simpler but not less Christological. It simply amounts to contemplating and thinking of Christ in relation to our situation and our praxis. To do that I am going to put more emphasis on the praxis of Jesus himself, even though I shall occasionally also refer to his teaching. It seems to me that the fundamental question we must answer is the following: In the sociopolitical, socioeconomic, sociocultural, and socioreligious context of Third World countries in general and of Africa in particular, what does confessing Christ mean for the African woman? As I emphasize below, it is a matter of the Christ of history and not the Christ of dogma. The Christ of history is the one who defined his mission as a mission of liberation. There is a consensus that in the text of Luke 4:18-19 Jesus presents the content of this liberation: "The spirit of the Lord is upon me," he says, "for he has anointed me to announce good news to the poor. He has sent me to proclaim liberation to the captives and to the blind, the restoration of their sight, to set the oppressed free, to proclaim a year of favor for the Lord."

The liberation Jesus brings is thus a total liberation. One cannot speak of physical liberation separated or divorced from spiritual liberation. Indeed, after this text of Jesus, the spiritual encompasses the physical. The truly spiritual is that which embraces all the material and physical life of the human being and our communities. On this level, I suggest to you that we look into the concrete to see what we have been saying abstractly thus far.

There is a model of liberation that Jesus proposes and which is, unfortunately, not interpreted as it should be. The text has already been mentioned several times, but I do not think it is a bad idea to look at it again. The text is Mark 5:21–34: the daughter of Jairus and the woman with the hemorrhage. We are going to emphasize this text somewhat, for it is crucial for our understanding of the liberation Jesus wishes to bring to humankind, not only to women. The scene presented to us here is that of two persons who come to Jesus and who ask him for the same thing. In the biblical narrative, the woman has no name, whereas Jairus, a man, a well-known dignitary in the synagogue, is named. The woman goes to Jesus asking for life, while Jairus is likewise asking life for his daughter who is sick. Often those who speak of or comment on this text of Jairus deal with the incidents separately. It is hard to see the relationship between Jairus and the nameless woman. Yet the two incidents go together and one cannot do justice to what is happening here unless they are treated in this manner.

The situation of the woman in Jewish society has been commented upon. Imagine a little what could have been the condition of this woman during that period. She is afraid to approach Jesus. Why? Because between her and Jesus, in accordance with the ideology that she has internalized, between her and Jairus, there are unbreachable barriers: social barriers, since, as someone who is afflicted by hemorrhaging, she is impure, which from a religious standpoint means she is an outcast. From that angle, she is socially dead. We are told that over a period of twelve years, she has spent all her money seeking help. She is poor, she has nothing left. In short, she is outcast not only socially, but also economically and religiously as well. She has no right to touch Jesus. In reading the book of Leviticus one can find all kinds of taboos that were in effect during that period. A woman like her is dead socially, and therefore politically she does not exist. These are the barriers that she has to cross in order to be able to meet Jesus. For that reason, we must form an idea of Jairus, who in the Jewish community is the one who must make sure that this woman stays where she is. He is a Jewish dignitary and it is precisely his task to make sure that this person who is socially dead stays in her place. Thus between her and Jairus there is an abyss. Between these two, however, stands Jesus. I think one cannot ignore the model of liberation of the message we find here. It is a model applicable not only to women's liberation, but to the liberation of all the oppressed among the poor of the land.

The woman touches Jesus cautiously because she is afraid. When men preach on this text they often stress Jesus' magical power, but I do not think that is the essential point. When Jesus turns around, he says someone has touched him, but that is not to show his power, since the disciples have already decided to believe in him. (How could you know some individual had touched you in the middle of that crowd?) No. Finally Jesus stops, addresses the woman, and his message is, "My daughter, you have no reason to hide when it is a matter of pleading for the life God has given you. You have no need to plead in secret." To me, this means that when you are a disciple of Christ you ask as a child of God. Confessing Christ necessarily entails affirming oneself as a child of God.

Self-affirmation is very difficult in our context today, especially for women, since, in our context, women have so interiorized the ideology of self-denial that they feel it is illegitimate and presumptuous to demand things for themselves! It is on this point that we should focus when we hear arguments such as "The women's liberation movement is not a response to a genuinely African need" or "The African woman has always been one to give of herself" (the romantic image of women). The implication is that those who make such arguments are not willing to accept that the kind of contextualization demanded by male theologians for themselves can be employed by African women for their own particular life experience. On this point, I would like to say that we cannot be authentic disciples of Jesus Christ unless we acknowledge that we are children of God, called to share in the mission of liberation initiated by God. That is why women's liberation can be viewed only in the context of the liberation of all the oppressed of the earth.

Before concluding, I would like to say a word about contextualization. I believe that today it is impossible for African theology, as it has been called, to emerge and to bloom unless both the African churches and African theology start out from, and develop around, the situation of women in Africa. Africa will be great if African women are willing to make it great. I believe that because the African woman is at the bottom of the scale. She is oppressed by her African brother; she is oppressed by other women who are not African; she is oppressed by non-African men. Especially when the hierarchical scale on the international level is taken into account, the African woman is at the very bottom of that scale. She incarnates the mass of the poor and the oppressed. Thus I believe that when this woman has really come to understand the message of liberation that Jesus bears, she will be able to take her brothers by the hand and lead them to the way of liberation that is ours.

Let us not forget that the principle that makes it possible for someone to profess Christianity while being a racist is the same principle that enables one to profess Christianity while keeping women in a lower position than men. As long as our view of God is nourished by, or reflects, the belief that it is God who from the beginning has created social inequality, or that it is God who from the beginning has created one human category inferior to the other, we have no right to demand the liberation of our black brothers in South Africa, for example. The principle of apartheid is the same one that our brothers and colleagues preach in churches today when they say that women are not worthy to enter God's ministry. On the basis of the teaching of Jesus Christ, we can say quite confidently that the practices, teaching, and structures of our church are the product of a kind of idolatry whose effect is that it is no longer the human being who is created in God's image but, rather, it is God who is created in human image. I believe Christology is really at the center of this discussion, for Christ is the source of our faith, Christ is the norm of our faith, Christ is the content of our faith.

As African women who have accepted Christ as our liberator, are we ready to affirm ourselves as children of God so that our participation in the building of Africa may be truly effective? Unless we make that affirmation, it will not be possible; unless we make that affirmation, we shall never be independent beings; unless we make that affirmation, the countries of the Third World will continue to be dependent on the industrialized countries; unless we make that self-affirmation, the church of South Africa will continue to preach a God who is an oppressor God.

I am convinced that Jesus died so that the patriarchal God might die and that Jesus rose so that the true God revealed in Jesus might rise in our lives, and in our communities. It is our duty to live and reflect that resurrection in our everyday lives.

4

The Christ for African Women

Elizabeth Amoah (Ghana) and
Mercy Amba Oduyoye (Ghana)

INTRODUCTION: CHRISTOLOGY AND WOMEN

"Christology" is a familiar word among Christian theologians and one that is quite able to stand by itself and be explicated as a theological issue and concept. The curiosity that arises—if any—will be in relation to the word "women" and the conjunction "and." The import of the conjunction is to my mind that of a question, which could be stated in various ways: What have women to do with the concept of Christology? What do women say about Christology? Is there such a thing as a women's Christology? Do the traditional statements of Christology take into account women's experience of life? What we shall do here is to share some thoughts on the Christ from the perspective of African women.

To do this, however, it is undoubtedly of use and interest to begin with what African men say about Christ, since they have dominated the field of written theology. This will necessitate taking a look at scriptures and church history, alongside African Christianity and traditional religions, before coming to what the women of Africa wish to say about Christ.

THE CHRIST OF SCRIPTURES AND TRADITIONS

Most Christians refer to Scripture as meaning the Hebrew Bible and its Christian supplement, the New Testament, but we would like to start with a reference to the "unwritten Scriptures" of the Fante of Ghana. When the Fante were journeying to their present home in southern Ghana, they crossed vast tracts of waterless plains and they thirsted. Such was the agony of a people on the move, but their leader, Eku, the matriarch, did not despair. She spurred them on. They were to press forward until they came to a place where they could settle in peace and prosperity. Following her encouragement, they dragged their weakened legs along. They then came to a pool of water. Having suffered much treachery on their journey, none dared to salve the parched throat with the water now presented invitingly before them. It could have been poisoned by their enemies. Matriarch Eku took her life into her hands, drank from the pool, and gave to her dog to drink. The people waited. They peered at the woman and her dog with glazed eyes. Neither human nor animal had suffered from drinking the water of the pool. All fell to and drank their fill, shouting "Eku aso" (Eku has tasted). And so the place where this happened is to this day called Ekuaso. Eku has tasted on our behalf; we can now drink without fear of death.[1]

All human communities have their stories of persons whose individual acts have had lasting effects on the destiny and ethos of the whole group. Such are the people remembered in stories. Not all are Christ-figures; only those whose presence has led to more life and wholesome relations are commemorated as having been "God-sent." In the Hebrew story, the idea of the "God-sent" figure crystallized into that of the Messiah, the anointed of God. The Messiah was expected to be a male figure of power, as a ruler of God's people and a prophet called by God to guide the people. Much else accrued to the figure of the Messiah as the lot of the people passed through political changes. One such metamorphosis taken over by Christians is the Messiah as the Suffering Servant of God. But even cast in this lowly mold, the figure of the Messiah remains powerful and victorious and male. Messiah is a servant who suffers but one whose presence always tells the people how God's future for humanity stands inviolate in spite of all appearances. As Jesus of Nazareth and most all who fell into his way of life and thinking were Jews, they had been brought up on the various images of the messianic figure and had prayed for the timely arrival of the anointed one of God, who was being expected by the whole nation.

We are not aware of the concept of the expected one in African mythology. However, deliverers abound; some are memorialized in legends, but they are not always male. The folk etymology of the name of the village of Ekuaso illustrates this. There have also been instances of "innocent" persons, women as well as men, who were being sacrificed to bring peace and prosperity to communities. One such legend will suffice for illustration.

A feud arose between two Nigerian communities as a result of adultery. In those days, the offense was punished by the execution of the man involved. In the case under review, the man was from an ethnic group that did not execute adulterers. After long periods of struggle, a compromise was reached. A nameless woman was sacrificed to "atone" for the man's infringement of the adultery taboo.[2] Such an event cannot be reckoned as vicarious suffering, and contemporary African women must resist such a model.

There are also instances of persons who are made scapegoats and who suffer the fate of "the goat of Azazel" in the Hebrew atonement ceremonies. They are banished from their communities, carrying the sins of the whole people so that the community may live more fully in the coming years.[3] But the myth of a future utopia to be ushered in by "One Who Is to Come" is a rare one among Africans. African myths tell of a past of perfection in primeval times, not of a future of plenty and bliss. The individual, however, lives in hope, almost a certainty, that tomorrow will be better. The immediate morrow that those who are alive now may hope to see is the immediate concern of prayer in the traditional religion.

The Christian religion raised in Africa the hope of a future when all things would be righted and be "gathered up" in Christ. Classical Christologies that have been taught in Africa include that of the Christ enthroned in glory, who, as a magnanimous potentate, oversees all and orders all according to the will of God. The imagery is that of Luke's Jesus of Nazareth, whose central concern was the kingdom of God. The royal Christ fitted into the colonial ambiance of the propagation of Christianity as well as the missionary's self-image of a benevolent paternal figure who knows what is best for African converts. The need for a conqueror to overcome the evil forces that cross the way of the African was brushed aside as superstitious fear. The classical Western Christologies have been appropriated by the Western churches in Africa, which are faithfully carrying on the legacy of the Western missions. "Jesus is Lord" remains the keynote of this Christology—"Lord" in terms of a benevolent ruler.

Christ has also been preached in terms of the one who is sacrificed to wipe away inauspiciousness and free us for a new beginning. The eschatology that accompanies this Christology has, however, focused almost entirely on "the end of the age" and often on a supramundane realm where all is well. African Christians have had to support this Christ with spiritualities from their own traditions, which assure them of immediate well-being in the *now* and in the near future. The inadequacy of the received Christology with its emphasis on the end of the age is part of the reason for the rapid growth of the African charismatic churches that offer a Christus Victor.

The predominant myth of Christianity in Africa, however, remains the paradise to come: the messianic hope of a golden age has even begun to surface in political terms as "African unity." In the church, it is stated in terms of a single unified church. As these ideals retreat or, rather, tarry long, people either buy deeper into the apocalypticism of the "Coming One," and therefore of Christ the King who sits in judgment of his subjects to reward faithful Christians with bliss and unbelievers with torment, or they simply give up.[4] This Christology, we suggest, is not up to the task of empowering Christians for life in Africa today, with its material and spiritual demands. It masks the relevance of Christ in the business of living today and in the immediate future.

Africans require a holistic view of life. This demands a Christ who affects the whole of life and demonstrates that there is nothing that is not the business of God. The need to rewrap Christology in African leaves may be illustrated by questions that African students often raise concerning sacrifice. We read in the Old Testament that God does not approve of human sacrifice, so why does God use the cross as the means of salvation, they ask. If Jesus of Nazareth, the Christ-figure, represents "the right and good way of being human,"⁵ what does that say to human suffering and especially voluntary acceptance of limiting conditions? What are the implications of the Christian affirmation that the anointed one of God, the Christ-figure, is anointed of God to bring victory over all the powers that seek to alienate us from this road to true humanity? Are there other Christ-figures apart from Jesus of Nazareth?

Johannine Christology has established a firm principle that there is no other name. If this is so, then the One Name ought to cope efficiently with the whole life of the whole people, *all* the "people that on earth do dwell," and therefore all of Africa and the life of all who live in Africa as Africans and not as bleached into anything else. The whole business of the whole of Africa is God's business and therefore demands a Christology that explicates how that business is Christ's business.

AFRICA'S BUSINESS

The devil is a reality in Africa; witches actually operate to release life-denying forces into the world. Individual people may be possessed and used by negative forces to prevent life-affirming and life-giving environments and activities. Evil is real, and evil is embodied in persons as well as unleashed on people by spiritual forces. Further, the spirit world is a powerful reality in Africa. God created not only the palpable world but living spirits whom we do not see but whose presence we certainly feel and who, we believe, definitely impinge on our lives for good. They are the servants of God, a sort of intricate administrative and executive service managing God's business in God's *oikos*. Such a cosmology calls for a Christology that consciously deals with the relation of Christ to God, the relation of Christ to the spirit world, and how the Christ, in the context of the belief in spirits, stands in relation to Africans in their dependence on God. Is the Christ the "chief executive," giving us confidence that, however precarious our circumstances, all is in fact under control?

The theology of the people sees the Christ in this role. At a recent performance by the Dwenesie Singers of Ghana, the lyricist, weaving her words from the event of "the stilling of the storm" produced a tapestry with a picture of the Christ as the one who brings under control all that would have brought us death. She gave a vivid description of a life in which nothing holds together! "When we try to hold onto poles, they break. When we try to hang onto ropes, they snap. You who speak to the tumultuous sea, still our world, control the elements, direct our ways, and aid our efforts." The Christ of the theology of the people is the Christ who breaks the power of evil and empowers us in our life's journey.

In Africa, where one's forebears retain an ongoing interest in one's affairs and continue to be involved long after they have departed to join their forebears; precedence has a strong hold on the regulation of ethical life. Is Jesus our ancestor, the quintessence of a life of faith? If so, then one begins to formulate Christology in terms of mediation and of participation in the divine-human axis that links humanity to divinity. In Jesus of Nazareth we see the return to earth of the Divine Spirit of God, the source of life, as an individual—just as in African tradition the ancestors return in the birth of new babies. This would, of course, imply that there can be many Christs as the spirit of a grandmother returns to grandchildren in perpetuity as long as such children are named after her, that is, called by her name.[6]

Does Christianity have room for the concept of many Christs, persons in whom the Spirit of God dwells in all its fullness? Has history seen many "Christs" and will such Christ-figures continue in perpetuity? These would be legitimate questions for a Christology that focuses on Jesus of Nazareth as our ancestor in religious obedience.

In Africa, where physical suffering seems endemic, where hunger and thirst are the continuous experience of millions, a suffering Christ becomes an attractive figure. However, Jesus of Nazareth is seen more as a comrade who did not accept deprivation as the destiny of humanity but, rather, demonstrated in his dealings with people that such suffering is not in the plan of God. You cannot be sad when Jesus is around; you cannot fast. Healing and eating and drinking were the experiences of those who were with him, and when they told their story they did not neglect to say so. In fact, they assigned large portions of their stories to the telling of these experiences. They were as impressed by these as by his death and resurrection. They did not report only what Jesus said, for they saw what he *taught* as made up of both what he did and what he said. His presence saved situations. This is another one of the reasons for the growth of African charismatic churches, whose prophets and healers are seen as mirroring the Christ. Jesus Christ in his life enhanced life where it had been overshadowed by death, even bringing life where physical death had arrived prematurely. Christ, the great Healer, is seen as the center of the Christology of these charismatic churches.[7]

The Christ who is on the side of life is seen as being on the side of God. He not only taught that laws which frustrate and stifle life are to be scrapped; he himself did that, healing on the Sabbath and defending his disciples against the scruples of religious legalism. Even his acceptance of death can be read as the outcome of love for life, since the will of God can only foster life, even if the path has to be through death. Africa's business has to be that of turning death into life.

WHAT AFRICAN MEN SAY ABOUT CHRIST

It is from this background that we turn to African men's writing. John S. Mbiti expresses clearly the fountainhead of African spirituality when he writes: "To live here and now is the most important concern of African religious activities and beliefs. There is little concern with distinctly *spiritual welfare of man* [sic] *apart from his physical.* No line is drawn between the spiritual and the physical. . . . This is an important element in traditional religions, and one which will help us to understand the concentration of African religiosity."⁸ Any Christology that aspires to meet such a spirituality must have a Christ that stands for spiritual-physical welfare. Disinterested religious zeal or one aimed at extraterrestrial well-being is not an indigenous African spirituality. Spirituality in Africa is one of struggle that enables persons to live a good life here and now that they may die "a good death" and join the ancestors.

According to Emmanuel Milingo, Africa needs a Christus-Victor Christology, because "the people are ready to seek help from any source. Despair and disappointment drive people to all who claim to have the power to conquer evil." Milingo is not exaggerating when he adds that people "seek gifts of wealth and prosperity from the devil and make pacts with the devil." This is a clear demonstration that a Christus-Victor Christology is what Africa demands. Is this Victorious Christ, God? Victory over Satan, the embodiment of the forces of death, is what Africans pray for, and "Jesus precisely came to fight Satan and win us back from him. Jesus assures us that death, sin and Satan have been put down by him." Following Jesus' example and seeing the need for exorcism in Africa, Milingo felt called to a "ministry of deliverance."⁹

Milingo also deserves special mention among the African Christians who have offered the ancestor motif as a possible model for Christological construction, for it is he who says, "Jesus fits perfectly into the African understanding of ancestor." He describes Jesus as an ancestor in the community, intercessor between God and our human community, possessor of ethereal powers that enable him to commune with the world above and with the earth, being a citizen of both worlds. In this way Jesus is taken into the African cosmology in much the same way that Emperor Tiberius (A.D. 14–37) wanted to add him to the pantheon of the Greco-Roman world of the first century of the Christian era.¹⁰ As a universal ancestor, Christ is made available to all who call the name of Jesus. Jesus, says Milingo, does not replace the ancestors of the individual family; he stands for all as the ancestor of the whole human family. In Milingo, Jesus replaces not only the ancestors but the gods and their priests, working only through those who cooperate in the quest for life and "neutralizing" the power of those who work for death. Milingo states categorically: "We are marrying Jesus with our ancestors . . . [not] merely making a comparison between the two and leave it at that." It is the *midzimu* or the *nananom*¹¹ who, together with Jesus, are the protectors and guardians of each and every family. There are several *nananom*, but one Christ.

Kwesi Dickson, in his *Theology in Africa*, devotes a chapter to the cross, and through a skillful discussion of the meaning and place of death in the African community he underlines the salvific nature of the cross, showing it to be a most potent symbol for Christology in Africa. Death, he says, is "an occasion for seeking more life."¹² The willingness to suffer that others might have more life is entirely consonant with the African communal ideology. This calls all baptized persons to Christ-like sacrifice.

The theology of sacrifice does have deep implications for Christology. Africans who first became Christians did so not for the reason that the blood of animals was "ineffective, but that the blood of Christ has much greater efficacy."[13]

Burgess Carr and Gabriel Setiloane join Kwesi Dickson in highlighting the cross. Carr associates it with "redemptive violence" that was necessary for the political freedom of much of black Africa and that continues to rage in apartheid South Africa where the forces of life and death have locked horns in what appears to be a last-ditch battle to settle the affirmation that there is only one human race.[14]

Setiloane's theology of the cross focuses on God's preferential option for the poor to the end that they may be led out of the captivity of dehumanizing conditions.[15] His poem "I Am an African" is now a well-known contribution to Christology in Africa.[16] For him the crucified Christ is the Christ of Africa, and the cross is the basis of hope in Africa. Carr reinforced this when he advocated support for the liberation movements of Africa "because they have helped the church to rediscover a new and radical appreciation of the Cross." Violence, when sanctified by God, becomes redemptive.

John Pobee has suggested the ruler-image,[17] Christ the King, a latecomer in Christological imagery, does pose problems. The human experience of this hierarchically organized system with its legalisms and usually patriarchal structures does not commend itself to the oppressed and marginalized of this world. Patriarchal/hierarchical structures have little room for the participation and inclusiveness that those whose humanity is being trampled upon yearn for. Christ for this situation is the prophetic figure of a Moses sent by God to stand up to the Pharaohs of our day. The reason for the royal imagery stems from the African system of rule in which the ruler is seen as the one who speaks the mind of the community and ensures its well-being. The traditional ruler in Africa is usually a constitutional monarch with limited powers, who is aware that power derives from the people. Pobee, however, reserves the ruler for God and makes Christ the *okyeame* (go-between) through whom the ruler speaks and through whom the people's voice reaches the ruler—often in more felicitous language than the original word of the people. The *okyeame* is not simply a mouthpiece, but also an interpreter. The *okyeame* is an ambassador and represents the ruler in "foreign courts and is treated as the ruler when holding the staff of office (*akyeampoma*)."

WHAT AN AFRICAN WOMAN SAYS ABOUT CHRIST

Though most of the published studies on Christ in Africa are by male theologians, nonetheless there exist reflections by women, which are virtually unknown. Among these are the reflections, stories, and prayers of praise of Afua Kuma of Ghana.

Afua Kuma lives and works in the tropical forest of Ghana, a farmer and midwife from the Kwawu area. She belongs to the Church of the Pentecost. When in church, she is called Christiana Afua Gyane. She has had published prayers and praises to Jesus that capture vividly the language, culture, proverbs, folk tales, and court poetry of the Akan. Afua's theology and precisely her Christology—as most of her words refer to Jesus—is one that comes from the interplay of faith and life.

From Afua's words one gets some insight into what Christ means for the many in African churches to whom the word of God comes as a story, and who then make their own connections with Christ as they go about their daily routine, as well as in the high points of life. Some of Afua's "Praises" follow:

Yesu who has received the poor and makes us honorable, our exceedingly wise friend, we depend on you as the tongue depends on the jaw.

[You are] the rock. We hide under you, the great bush with cooling shades, the giant tree who enables the climbers to see the heavens.

Yesu, when you walk in the darkness you do not need a lamp. When you step out the sun goes before you and the lightning comes behind you.

He hangs out cloth on the sea to dry, and we are able to wear it. It dried.

Let us hear one wonderful story. There were bullets, and he used kapok to kill the elephant! When he was turning round, he stepped on a buffalo and it died.[18]

All one needs is a few gospel miracles to produce Jesus the wonder-worker among a people whose folktales, folklore, and legends are replete with the miraculous; where the elements are hostile and the forest full of animals that could become food if only they could be hunted with a minimum of danger. A Savior is one who can kill an elephant for the whole village to live on. Jesus, the enabler and friend, becomes a truly great and wise friend. "When we walk with him and meet war, we have no fear."

Afua uses much contemporary imagery as the rural and the urban are linked together when relations move to and fro. Her imagery of Jesus can be that of the ordinary folk, like teachers who influence the society for good. She even describes Yesu as the "Pensil" with which teachers teach knowledge to children. In the stanza following, Jesus is the enabler of a variety of people: he is the spokesperson for lawyers, the helper of the police, the one who gives victory to soldiers and food to prisoners. Because Jesus is all this, women praise him and Afua Kuma blesses people in the Holy Name of Jesus, promising them his gifts: "The kind one who gives to thousands, Yesu, has come. He has brought gifts for his people. This morning, what you are looking for your hands will touch." The needs of the people include food and shelter. She refers to Yesu as having a great hall that can accommodate all who come. Children, who usually occupy a large proportion of African prayers, appear only once, when she refers to Yesu as the one who makes the sterile give birth to twins. But she is preoccupied with the difficulties of clearing the forest and of meeting wicked people in the forest. In all this, one thing is clear: with Jesus, difficulties are bound to melt away. "We do not need guns and bullets, and the enemies disappear."

THE CHRIST FOR AFRICAN WOMEN

Much of what Afua Kuma has said about Christ sounds similar to what the male theologians of Africa who were quoted in the preceding pages have said. The Christological images of most Christian women in Africa will likewise have a familiar ring. This causes no small wonder, as the men and women of Africa share the same reality and tradition and learned their Christianity from the same Western, male-centered, clerically minded missionaries.

African women, however, have a different experience and interpretation of this common reality and of lived Christianity. For example, when Pobee suggests that Christ is the *okyeame* of God the ruler, to him the *okyeame* can be nothing else but male. Whereas in the Akan system of rule the *okyeame* can be either a man or a woman. Another example is the significance of the cross in the Christologies. In the Christological statements of the male African theologians, the cross, which looms so large in the theologies of Western-trained academics and preachers, gets very scanty treatment in Afua's theological reflections. The cross, she says, has become the fishing net of Jesus. It is also the bridge from which Christians can jump into the pool of saving blood that leads to everlasting life. Here is a perception of the cross that demands not only that we admire what Jesus has done and allow ourselves to be caught in the net, but that we too stand ready to jump into the pool of blood through which we shall reach the life that is life indeed.

Though, in general, the women affirm the Christological position of the African men, at times they go beyond it or contradict it altogether. This can be gleaned not so much from the writings of African women as from the way they live and from their Christianity—their very spirituality, their witness to what Christ means for their lives.

The Christ whom African women worship, honor, and depend on is the victorious Christ, knowing that evil is a reality. Death and life-denying forces are the experience of women, and so Christ, who countered these forces and who gave back her child to the widow of Nain, is the African woman's Christ.

This Christ is the liberator from the burden of disease and the ostracism of a society riddled with blood-taboos and theories of inauspiciousness arising out of women's blood. Christ liberated women by being born of Mary, demanding that the woman bent double with gynecological disorders should stand up straight. The practice of making women become silent "beasts" of societies' burdens, bent double under racism, poverty, and lack of appreciation of what fullness of womanhood should be, has been annulled and countered by Christ. Christ transcends and transforms culture and has liberated us to do the same.

Jesus of Nazareth, by counter cultural relations he established with women, has become for us the Christ, the anointed one who liberates, the companion,

friend, teacher, and true "Child of Women"—"Child of Women" truly because in Christ the fullness of all that we know of perfect womanhood is
revealed. He is the caring, compassionate nurturer of all. Jesus nurtures not
just by parables but by miracles of feeding. With his own hands he cooked that
others might eat; he was known in the breaking of the bread. Jesus is Christ—
truly woman (human) yet truly divine, for only God is the truly Compassionate
One.

Christ for us is the Jesus of Nazareth, the Servant who washed the disciples'
feet, the Good Shepherd who leads us only to "green pastures," to the kingdom
of God, who in fact comes after us to draw us back to God. Christ seeks to
save. Jesus Christ is "Lord" because Jesus of Nazareth was a servant, meeting
the needs of humanity in obedience to the will of God even to the point of dying
that we might be freed from the fear of physical death.

The Christ for us is the Jesus of Nazareth who agreed to be God's "Sacrificial
Lamb," thus teaching that true and living sacrifice is that which is freely and
consciously made; and who pointed to the example of the widow who gave all
she had in response to God's love. Christ is the Jesus of Nazareth who approved
of the costly sacrifice of the woman with the expensive oil, who anointed him
(king, prophet, priest) in preparation for his burial, thereby also approving all
that is noble, lovely, loving and motivated by love and gratitude.

Jesus of Nazareth, designated "the Christ," is the one who has broken down
the barriers we have erected between God and us as well as among us. The
Christ is the reconciler, calling us back to our true selves, to one another and to
God, thereby saving us from isolation and alienation, which is the lack of
community that is the real experience of death.

In Christ all things hold together. The integrity of the woman (a person) as
born into a particular culture, and yet belonging to the community of Christ-
believers, is ensured. The integrity of the woman (a person) as body/soul is
ensured, recognized, and promoted by the way Jesus of Nazareth lived and
interacted with women and with persons handicapped by death-dealing cultural demands and by physical and material needs. The Christ has held body/
soul together by denouncing oppressive religious practices that ignored
well-being. It is this Christ who has become for us, for African women and for
Africa, the savior and liberator of the world. This Christ dominates the
spiritual churches of Africa such as the one to which Afua Kuma belongs. The
women give expression to a spirituality that enables them to face human
struggles and problems. In fact, women have founded some of these churches
and within them exercise their spiritual gifts of healing, solving marital problems, and so forth. God wears a human face in Christ. God in Christ suffers
with women of Africa.

CONCLUSION

An African woman perceives and accepts Christ as a woman and as an
African. The commitment that flows from this faith is commitment to full

womanhood (humanity), to the survival of human communities, to the "birthing," nurturing, and maintenance of life, and to loving relations and life that is motivated by love.

Having accepted Christ as refugee and guest of Africa, the woman seeks to make Christ at home and to order life in such a way as to enable the whole household to feel at home with Christ. The woman sees the whole space of Africa as a realm to be ordered, as a place where Christ has truly "tabernacled." Fears are not swept under the beds and mats but are brought out to be dealt with by the presence of the Christ. Christ becomes truly friend and companion, liberating women from assumptions of patriarchal societies, and honoring, accepting, and sanctifying the single life as well as the married life, parenthood as well as the absence of progeny. The Christ of the women of Africa upholds not only motherhood, but all who, like Jesus of Nazareth, perform "mothering" roles of bringing out the best in all around them. This is the Christ, high priest, advocate, and just judge in whose kingdom we pray to be.

This has serious consequences, for Jesus of Nazareth has pointed out the Christ-figures among us. Whatever we do or do not do to the least of these figures, we are assured that we are relating to the Christ through our interaction with, or avoidance of, such people by the contribution we make to the oppression they live.

Finally, the only way we can convince Africa that Jesus of Nazareth is uniquely the Christ of God is to live the life we are expected to live as Christ-believers. Do not call "Lord, Lord" while ignoring the demands of God.

Christology down the ages, though derived from the experiences of the early companions of Jesus of Nazareth and those of their immediate associates, has been formulated in response to the actual historical realities of each age and place. Persons have contributed by the way each perceives and experiences Christ. "Christ" has *been explained* through imagery, cosmology, and historical events understood by both "speakers" and "listeners." This process continues in Africa. One thing is certain: whatever the age or place, the most articulate Christology is that silently performed in the drama of everyday living.

NOTES

1. Narrated by Graecia Adwoa Asokomfo Tewiah, a specialist in children's education and a collector of Fante legends.

2. J. O. Awolalu, "Aiyelala, a Guardian of Social Morality," *Orita Ibadan Journal of Religious Studies* 2 (Dec., 1968): 79–80.

3. See *The Carrier*, in Wole Soyinka, *Three Short Plays* (London: Oxford University Press, 1969), pp. 79–120.

4. J. S. Mbiti, *New Testament Eschatology* (London: Heinemann, SPCK, 1971), pp. 57–61.

5. Leonard Swidler, ed., *Consensus in Theology? A Dialogue with Hans Küng and Edward Schillebeeckx* (Philadelphia: Westminster Press, 1980), p. 19.

6. In the naming system of the Akan, my family name, Ewudziwa (and its masculine form, Ewudzi), returns several times among cousins, having been handed down by fathers who name their children after their own fathers. It is men who hand down these names; among the Akan, women do not name their progeny or anybody else, although their names may be "immortalized" as much as men's by their sons.—M.A.O.

7. Worship in the African charismatic churches is heavily punctuated with prayers that are a call for life. See A. Omoyajowo, "Prayer in African Indigenous Churches," in *The State of Christian Theology in Nigeria 1980-81*, ed. Mercy Amba Oduyoye (Ibadan: Daystar Press, 1986).

8. J. S. Mbiti, *African Religions and Philosophy* (London: Heinemann, 1969; New York: Doubleday, 1970).

9. Emmanuel Milingo, *The World in Between: Christian Healing and the Struggle for Spiritual Survival* (Maryknoll, N.Y.: Orbis Books; London: C. Hurst & Co., 1984), pp. 5, 31, 54.

10. Tertullian, *Apology* 5.

11. "Ancestor" in Akan is *nana* (pl. *nananom*). *Mudzimu* (spirit) is "ancestor" in Shona (quoted by Milingo, p. 83).

Attempts to explain the Christ in terms of African cosmology have at times cast him in the mold of the ancestral mediator. Since Harry Sawyerr's *God: Ancestor or Creator?* (London: Longman, 1971), and his *Creative Evangelism: Towards a New Christian Encounter with Africa* (London: Lutterworth, 1968), there have been several attempts by Africans to formulate theological statements that show an understanding of Africa's value system. See also J. S. Mbiti, *New Testament Eschatology in an African Background* (London: Oxford University Press, 1971), pp. 187–88. See also John S. Pobee, *Towards an African Theology* (Nashville: Abingdon, 1979), chap. 5.

12. Kwesi A. Dickson, *Theology in Africa* (Maryknoll, N.Y.: Orbis Books, 1984), pp. 185–99.

13. Milingo, *The World in Between,* p. 82.

14. Burgess Carr, "The Engagement of Lusaka," in *The Struggle Continues* (report of All Africa Conference of Churches Assembly, Lusaka, 1974), pp. 73–81. Carr's statement that "In accepting the violence of the cross, God, in Jesus Christ, sanctified violence into a redemptive instrument for bringing into being a fuller human life" raised much dust among the ecclesiastics who had gathered in Lusaka for the assembly and generated a lot of debate in the plenary discussion.

15. Edward H. Schroeder, "Lessons for Westerners from Setiloane's Christology," *Mission Studies: Journal of the International Association for Mission Studies* 2, no. 2 (1985).

16. See Setiloane's poem, "The God of My Fathers and My God," *South African Outlook,* October 1970.

17. John S. Pobee, *Towards an African Theology,* pp. 94–98.

18. The rendering here is by Mercy Amba Oduyoye. Only selected lines from stanzas are given here. The entire work is available in English translation under the title *Jesus of the Deep Forest,* transl. and ed. Peter Kwasi Ameyaw, Fr. Jon Kirby, S.V.D., et al. (Accra: Asempa Publishers, n.d.).

5

Women in the Bible

Teresa Okure (Nigeria)

INTRODUCTION

The issue of women in church and society constitutes, perhaps, the single most important theological question of our century. Indeed, some scholars have compared it to the Gentile question in the early days of Christianity. Not surprisingly, as arguments rooted in Scripture were used to sustain the practice of forcing Gentiles to undergo circumcision as a condition of salvation, so too today scriptural arguments are advanced to justify the age-old practice of excluding women from certain leadership and ministerial roles in church and society. The Bible as the embodiment of the revealed will of God thus plays a decisive role for Christians in their approach to the women issue today, including in the Third World, to seek to understand correctly what the Bible actually says concerning the divine will for women.

Fortunately for the Gentiles, Paul, a God-inspired leader and scholar, was able to demonstrate on the same scriptural grounds that the law-inspired impositions laid on the Gentiles were in fact opposed to the universal will of God contained in the promise to Abraham (Gal. 3:16–18). Today, if the women issue is to receive its true understanding from God's perspective, as the Gentile question did, then it too will need God-inspired leaders and scholars who, like Paul, will be able to demonstrate truthfully, objectively, and convincingly on the same scriptural grounds that the sustained practice of excluding women is in truth opposed to the expressed will of God revealed in the Scriptures and in Jesus of Nazareth, the Son of Mary.

This task calls for a close rereading in their literary and cultural contexts, Jewish and patriarchal (cf. *Dei Verbum,* 12), of those passages that deal with women, particularly those that are said to embody the eternal and divine will for them in creation. It also calls for a close observation of the way in which God actually relates with and uses women to effect the divine plan of salvation for humanity. From God's own actions revealed in the Scriptures, it should be possible to discern correctly what God's will for women really is.

The reflection by African women theologians on women in the Bible took place in three different stages: first at the Nigerian National Consultation held in Ibadan (July 26–29, 1985), then at the Continental Consultations held in Yaoundé, Cameroun (August 4–10) and Port Harcourt, Nigeria (August 18–24) for the French and English speaking countries, respectively. I presented the initial paper on the subject at the Nigerian Consultation in Ibadan entitled "Biblical Perspectives on Women: Eve, the Mother of All the Living (Gen. 3:20)." This paper was subsequently published in *Voices from the Third World,*[1] and appears to have served as the basic inspiration for the second paper on "La femme et la bible" presented by Soeur Juliette Ekemela (Fille de Notre Dame du Sacré-Coeur) at the Francophone consultation in Yaoundé. I presented a third paper on "Women in the Bible" at the Anglophone Consultation in Port Harcourt.

This present paper offers a synthesis of these three presentations and the discussions which they inspired; it also embodies additional insights by the panelists. In all the discussions, efforts were made to reread the biblical stories concerning women from African women's perspective. The paper discusses, first, the constitutive significance of Eve for a study of women in the Bible, then the liberative and oppressive elements in the Bible with respect to women, and, finally, new hermeneutical principles for reading the Bible as a patriarchal book and their pastoral implications.

THE CONSTITUTIVE SIGNIFICANCE OF EVE

The story of Eve, the first woman created by God (Gen. 2:22) and named "mother of all the living" (Gen. 3:20), constitutes a natural starting point for a study on women in the Bible. Throughout the centuries, and in the Judeo-Christian traditions in particular, the story of her creation and fall has been used as the divine norm for determining the role and status of women in church and society. Traditional and popular belief views Eve, woman, as a being inferior to Adam, man, physically, socially, morally, intellectually, and spiritually. Details of this inferiority are meticulously worked out by the rabbis and by the fathers of the church, whose teachings have formed and nourished centuries of opinion concerning women.[2]

The reasons offered for this belief are that the man was created first, the woman second, out of the man's rib, and so destined to serve merely as his helper (Gen. 2:7, 20–22). Accordingly, the woman is said to have no identity of her own, but to derive her being from the man and exist only for him, to serve his personal and domestic needs (cooking, cleaning, washing) and bear and rear *his* children. Her formation from the man's rib, rather than from his head, for instance, is seen by the rabbis as symbolic of her essentially inferior status, lest she be proud or "that she should be modest."[3] On the evidence of 1 Corinthians 11:7–9, and contrary to Genesis 1:26–27, it is emphatically maintained that only the man is in the image of God, while the woman is merely the image of man.[4] Finally, it is observed that as the morally weaker sex, Eve, not Adam, succumbed to the devil's deceit and so became the cause of sin and death in the world.[5] All the ills of humanity, including the sinfulness of the man himself, are thus to be blamed on the woman.

Obviously this belief in the innate inferiority of the woman and in her exclusive instrumentality for sin and death is based on a misreading of the Genesis accounts of creation and the fall (Gen. 1:26-2:4a; 2:4b-4:2; 5:1-2) and on failure to discern the distinctive purpose of each of these narratives.[6] For the creation accounts taken at their face value furnish no grounds whatever for this belief. Rather, they make fundamental statements concerning the nature of humanity in relation to God and the rest of creation, and concerning the personal relationship between man and woman.

The first creation account (Gen. 1:26-2:4b; 5:1-2) makes the theological statement that the human species is composed of male and female; that it is a unity in nature and a diversity in sex; and that as an entity it was created in the image and likeness of God. The term ādām in this narrative is clearly a generic term for humanity defined as male and female (5:2). Conjointly created in the image and likeness of God and conjointly given dominion over the rest of creation (1:28), both the male and the female stand equal in honor and dignity. It is also conjointly as male and female that both can carry out the divine injunction to be fruitful, multiply, and fill the earth (1:28), contrary to some rabbis who held that this command applied only to the male.[7]

But while the first creation account defines the human species as composed of male and female who stand equal in dignity and honor before God and are given co-mastery over creation, the second creation account (Gen. 2:4b-24) emphasizes the identity in nature of male and female as a species distinct from the rest of the animal species. Second, it underlines that this male and female were destined by God to belong to each other as husband and wife (Gen. 2:23-24). As I indicated in a previous article, the main point of this second account is to be found in verses 23-24.[8] In other words, the first unit in human society is that of husband and wife, and it is from this unit that the family, inclusive of children, develops. The visual imagery of the creation of the woman from the man's rib vividly illustrates both their identity in nature and their destined union as husband and wife in "one flesh" (vs. 24). It can even be said to symbolize their equality, since, according to Augustine, they were thus intended to "walk side by side" and "together look where it is they walk."[9]

If these are the different thrusts of the two creation accounts, then these accounts cannot be cited in support of the belief that woman is by nature inferior to man. Such a belief arises, rather, from the sociocultural practices of the sinful world in which the biblical authors and their subsequent interpreters lived. Jewish patriarchal society, as we know, was one in which the woman had no legal status, except insofar as she was an object of marriage and divorce.[10] She could not, for instance, testify in court or inherit property; nor was she expected to keep all the 615 precepts of the Torah. Her sole raison d'être was the husband; she was his "home,"[11] and her duty was to secure his happiness and serve him in the meaner and menial aspects of life. In short, the woman was de facto if not de jure the property of the husband, for he could acquire her like a slave by money or sexual intercourse and divorce her if she caused the slightest "impediment" to the marriage, like spoiling his food or growing old.[12] The wife was also held responsible for the husband's piety or wickedness.[13] Women in general were believed to be "gluttonous, eavesdroppers, lazy and jealous,"[14] devoid of intellectual capacity, and living only for self-ornamentation.[15] Given this prevailing attitude toward women, one understands why a man who allowed himself to be ruled by a woman was to be held in contempt, why Qoheleth finds woman "more bitter than death" (Eccles. 7:26), why Sirach regards the birth of a daughter as "a loss" (Sir. 22:3), and why the Jewish male counted it a daily blessing that God did not make him a woman.[16] Arthur Cohen's attempts to explain away this latter attitude on the grounds that women did not have the privileged duty of keeping the Torah [17] only serve to accentuate the exclusion of the woman from the rare blessings that accrued to one who kept the Torah, blessings that Psalm 119 so eloquently celebrates.

Perhaps the most conclusive evidence for the poor standing of women in Jewish society is that they are classified in the Mishnah as objects, along with such topics as "feasts," "seeds," and "damages."[18] Of course, the Jewish attitude toward women is not exclusively negative, but the negative one dominates the literature and has exercised the greatest formative influence on society's attitude toward women. Even the positive evaluations of women in the biblical and rabbinic literature are made from the standpoint of their usefulness to men, as, for instance, the valiant woman in Proverbs 31:10-31. The patristic attitude toward women offers no improvement on the Jewish one. The woman is said to be of "small intelligence" and, as a wife, to exist for "just one purpose: to guard the possessions we have accumulated, to keep a close watch on the income, to take charge of the household."[19]

Clearly this prevailing negative assessment of women is a far cry from the status accorded them in Genesis 1:26-27. How did it all come about? Genesis 3 attempts an explanation. Taken at its face value, the account of the fall in no way attributes to Eve the sole responsibility for the entry of sin in the world. If anything, as I have illustrated in my earlier analysis of the passage,[20] the whole movement of the narrative indicates that the biblical author imputes greater blame to Adam, a term reserved here exclusively for the man; he personally received from God the prohibition against eating the forbidden fruit (2:16-17), hence his is the climactic punishment, which has a universal scope—the earth is cursed because of him (3:17), and death is pronounced as part of his punishment (3:19). Had Eve alone been guilty, as the church fathers and 1 Timothy 2:24, for instance, maintain, Adam would not have been personally punished, since God is a just judge.[21] Moreover, given that nothing happened till Adam, allegedly the morally and intellectually superior sex, took and ate (3:6b-7), one cannot help concluding that the sequel of the story and the fate of humanity would have been different had he not eaten.

Strikingly, the woman is given the promise of salvation through her "seed" even before she receives her punishment (Gen. 3:15–17).[22] The punishment of her subjection to the husband is clearly a description of the sociocultural reality that obtained in the author's patriarchal society briefly described above. By viewing this subjection as a punishment for sin, the biblical author rejects the idea that this state of affairs could have been the created order willed by God. The divine promise of salvation in Genesis 3:15 was ultimately fulfilled when Jesus, the seed of the woman, Mary, conquered sin and death on the cross and made us all God's children (cf. Gal. 4:4).

Thus, as Eve, after the fall, became physically "the mother of all the living" (Gen. 3:20), thereby playing a role akin to that of God, the source and giver of life (Ps. 36:9; Job 33:4), so, at the annunciation and at the foot of the cross, Mary became spiritually the mother of God's children in Christ (Cf. Jn. 19:25–27). Revelation 12, which is applied to Mary at the Feast of the Assumption, portrays the church, mother of God's children, as woman, just as in the Old Testament Zion was called "mother" (cf. Ps. 87:5). Hence motherhood, the bearing and bringing forth of life, remains a prerogative that God shares exclusively with the woman.

Strikingly, Eve receives the name "mother of all the living" from Adam after the fall. It is as if henceforth all hope of life depended on her. For if death entered the world through one man (Gen. 3:19; Rom. 5:5), life was to be restored to humanity through the seed of the woman (Gen. 3:16; Mt. 1:21). And if mythologically the woman was formed from the man's rib (Gen. 2:21–22; 1 Tim. 2:14; 1 Cor. 11:8), ontologically every man is born of woman (Mt. 11:11; 1 Cor. 11:12). Furthermore, in the Christian tradition all human beings are Mary's children insofar as all are Christ's brothers and sisters "according to the flesh" (*Humani Generis*). For it must not be forgotten that Mary was the only human agent who cooperated with God in the incarnation and birth of Christ. This is a foundational doctrine of our faith. Rightly, then, does the church attach great importance to Mary's role in the work of our redemption. But it needs to be remembered that however filled with grace Mary was, she was and remains biologically a woman. In the order of creation, the woman is named Eve (from the root word meaning "life") because she brings to birth all the living. In the order of redemption, it is fittingly said that they found the child "with Mary his mother" (Mt. 2:11).[23] The woman's role in God's scheme of creation and redemption is of paramount importance for humanity. The treatment of her as inferior or of no consequence finds no basis whatever in this scheme.

Recognition of the woman's role in God's scheme of creation and redemption does not, however, imply a denial of the woman's share in the sinfulness of the world. What is contested here is the traditional belief that all the sufferings of humanity are to be attributed to the woman as the sole cause. As Adam sinned against God, so did Eve. But unlike Adam she was humble enough to admit that she had been deceived. Thus women in the Bible exemplify the two faces of Eve: on the one hand, Eve, the instrument of life, exemplified in such women as Judith and Esther, God's instruments of salvation for the nation; and on the other, Eve, an agent of sin and death, exemplified by such women as Jezebel (2 Kgs. 21:5-16) and Athaliah (2 Kgs.11:1-3, 13-16). The former compare with male figures like Joseph and Moses, the latter with Herod (Mt. 2:16-18). Thus, whether as instruments of life or of death, both the man and the woman stand united in their common fate and destiny.

It has been noted that both the male and the female were created in the image and likeness of God. Yet over the centuries, the male image of God has been well recognized, developed, and projected into the human psyche; not so the female image. The treatment of woman as an inferior being goes hand in hand with the playing down or even conscious denial of the feminine attributes of God. In a male-oriented society, God is Father, not Mother, King of kings, not Queen of queens. And while God is readily feared as powerful, almighty, and possessing all authority, qualities usually associated with the father, God is not readily loved as humble, self-sacrificing, tender, and compassionate, virtues generally associated with the mother (cf. Hos. 11:1-11; Isa. 49:11-15). God's fate thus proves to be very closely bound up with that of the woman insofar as a denial of the woman's ability to image God means a denial of God's own feminine attributes, hence a distortion of the divine image itself. Only when the woman is granted her full honor and dignity in society will God also come fully into his/her own. Then humanity will no longer be ashamed to recognize and celebrate the womanliness of God. Thus will our knowledge of God also be enriched, and we shall come to relate to her/him more as the giver and fosterer of life (cf. Jn. 10:10) than as law and order or a power and authority to be feared.[24]

LIBERATIVE AND OPPRESSIVE ELEMENTS

Our foregoing analysis of the Bible has revealed the fundamental truth that the Bible and its interpretations embody both a divine and a human element with respect to women. The liberative elements in the Bible with respect to women stem from the divine perspective, the oppressive ones from the human perspective. The latter are socioculturally conditioned and, in the last analysis, sinful. The liberative elements emphasize the woman's equality with the man, her being made conjointly with him in the image and likeness of God, of equal dignity and honor, and her being given the special privilege, akin to God's, of bearing, mothering, and fostering life. The oppressive and sinful elements, on the contrary, portray her as an inferior being, subjected to the man, having no identity of her own, and ultimately the cause of sin and death. Throughout the Bible, we meet side by side the divinely liberative and the humanly oppressive elements concerning women.

On the liberative side, women serve throughout the Bible as God's co-workers and agents of life. In other words, God did not simply create the woman to be the mother of all the living and leave her at that. Rather, in keeping with his distinctive gift to woman of motherhood, God consistently involved women in the divine activity of giving, preserving, and redeeming life. A few examples will suffice; first Rebekah. We are all familiar with the story of how Rebekah helped Jacob to steal the paternal blessing from Isaac (Gen. 27:1-29, 41-28:5). Seen from the twentieth-century perspective, her action is not to be condoned, but in the moral code of the time, she would be praised for her ingenuity, which parallels that of Abraham in Egypt when he gives out Sara, his wife, to be his sister and so brings disaster on innocent Egyptians (Gen. 12:10-29).

In Rebekah's case, her ingenuity was not directed toward her personal gain. Even before the children were born, God had taken her, not Isaac, into his confidence by revealing to her the destiny of the two children in her womb (Gen. 25:23). When, therefore, Rebekah secures the paternal blessing for Jacob in place of Esau, she is cooperating with God in her own way to bring about the realization of the divine plan. In this she compares well with those Israelites who, from our perspective, abused other people in order to enhance their divine election (cf. Judg. 18:21-31; 21:16-24). Not only did Rebekah secure Isaac's blessing for Jacob; she also saved him from Esau's destroying anger by sending him to his uncle, Laban, where he won wives from among his own kindred as well as abundant wealth, both important considerations in those days.[25]

Just as Rebekah served as God's instrument at a decisive moment in Israel's history, so did the women at the time of Moses, in a crucial stage of Israel's history, namely, the exodus. This group of women worked concertedly with God in preserving both the life of Israel as a nation and of Moses as God's instrument of liberation for the nation (Exod. 2:1-11). While Pharaoh and his officials are bent on exterminating Israel lest the Israelites become their enemies, the Egyptian midwives, though of Pharaoh's own camp, refuse to comply with his orders to kill every male child of the Hebrews; as a result, Moses is kept alive at birth. Moved also by the maternal instinct to preserve life, Moses' mother devises a means of hiding the child. He is eventually rescued by Pharaoh's daughter who, unlike her father, is moved with pity for this "Hebrew" boy (2:6). Moses' sister then sees to it that the boy is brought up for Pharaoh's daughter by the boy's own mother. Thus through the concerted efforts of these women Moses is not only kept alive but also given the best education in the land. Later on, when he flees from Pharaoh, it is Zipporah who first provides a home for him as his wife, then saves him from God's destroying anger on account of his failure to circumcise his son (Exod. 2:15-22; 4:24-26).

When we come to the final and greatest stage in salvation history, we meet again another great woman, who cooperated singlehandedly with God in conceiving and giving birth to the author of our salvation, namely, Mary, the mother of Jesus and of the church, Mary who is both virgin and mother.

In all these instances, God manifests a deep respect for the women by treating them as individuals in their own right. God deals directly with them instead of first passing through their husbands. Mary's case is particularly striking. We recall that in Jewish society the consent of the woman in marriage was not normally sought, except as a matter of formality. Yet at the annunciation, God respectfully asks a maiden from Nazareth for her consent to be the mother of God's Son and waits for her reply (Lk. 1:26–38). The next person to know of this event is Elizabeth, while Joseph is kept in the dark for a long time. Jesus' deep respect for women is also well known. We may, for instance, recall his compassion for widows, the most pitiable group of women in Jewish society (Lk. 7:11–17; 21:1–4; Mk. 12:40; Mt. 23:14), his respect for sinful Jewish women (Lk. 7:36–50; Jn. 8: 1–11) and, in particular, for the Samaritan woman (Jn. 4:1–42). In this last case not only does Jesus dialogue publicly with a woman whom any decent Jew would have shunned like the plague (Samaritan women were regarded as a permanent source of contamination; cf. Jn. 4:27), but he also turns this notorious sinner into his effective missionary to the Samaritans (4:28–30, 39–42).[26]

These few examples will suffice to illustrate how God worked with women as co-partners in giving, fostering, preserving, and saving life. There is no paternalism whatever in God's or Jesus' treatment of women. For in Jesus' teaching, women as well as men constitute possible objects of God's judgment (cf. Lk. 17:34–35).[27] In Judaism, too, although the wife was subjected to the husband in most matters, even with respect to the vows she had made to God (cf. Num. 30:3–13), her individual rights were recognized insofar as she could not be barred from participating in feasts on account of the sinfulness of the husband. Seen aright, that is, from the divine perspective, the Bible embodies nothing but liberative elements with respect to women.

The oppressive elements in the Bible, as we have said, stem from the sinful human perspective. At this point we can cite only two key areas where this oppression is most operative, namely, the institution of marriage and the concern for ritual purity. Cohen rightly observes that the Bible as a patriarchal book means that the husband had "absolute authority over his wife."[28] Indeed, if the books of the Bible can be said to agree on any one issue with respect to women, it is that the woman suffers her greatest humiliations and subjection to the man in the institution of marriage. This is true not only of the foundational statement in Genesis 3:16, but of subsequent biblical traditions right up to the New Testament (cf. 1 Cor. 11:2–12; 14:33b–36; 1 Tim. 2:11–12; Tit. 2:2–3), where subjection to the husband is inculcated as a virtue to be performed "in the Lord" (Col. 3:18; Eph. 5:22).[29] In marriage, the husband claimed absolute rights not only over the wife as a person, but over her very sexuality. We may, for instance, think of the humiliations to which the woman was subjected before marriage to ensure that she was a virgin (Deut. 22:13–21) or the most pitiable treatment of the suspected adulteress prescribed in the Mishnah (see under *Nashim*). The wife had no corresponding rights or sanctions over the husband.

This phenomenon is not peculiar only to Jewish society but appears to be universal. For if the verdict of the wife's subjection to the husband was attributed to God (Gen. 3:16), it was left to the man to work out the details of this subjection through laws enacted concerning marriage, betrothals, adultery, and divorce.[30] Wisdom literature is particularly rife with stereotyped tirades against wives, and Sirach in particular extends this against women in general: "Better the wickedness of a man than a woman who does good" (Sir. 42:14).[31] This universal phenomenon of the plight of the woman in marriage deserves special study, for the present breakdown in the marriage system all over the world may not be unconnected with the refusal by wives to allow themselves to continue to be treated as the property and slaves of their husbands. Often this legitimate reaction is wrongly interpreted as the woman's rejection of her maternal role. Yet no sane woman, and certainly no African woman, would see anything belittling or derogatory in motherhood per se.

Another important area of women's oppression in the Bible is that of cultic purity. Jewish laws concerning ritual purity were particularly biased against women. Since women were menstruants by nature, they could not be relied upon at all times to be ritually clean. For this reason they were barred, as a sex, for life from sacred places and ministries in Judaism.[32] In the Temple, women had their special court, next to that of the unclean Gentiles, beyond which they could not pass. In my view, this concern for ritual purity constituted the single most important factor in the exclusion of women from the ministerial priesthood in Judaism. This point is worth remembering in the current debate on the admission or nonadmission of women to the ministerial priesthood.

We know from the New Testament what Jesus thought of ritual purity or of that concept of holiness that emphasizes external cleanliness. We think, for instance, of the woes uttered against the scribes and the Pharisees in Matthew 23:25-27; or of those instances where, contrary to normal Jewish practice, Jesus touched and allowed himself to be touched by those who were legally classified as unclean, such as the woman with the issue of blood (Mk. 6:25-34). To continue to exclude women from certain Christian ministries on the basis of reasons inspired by outmoded Jewish taboos is to render null and void the liberation that Jesus won for us, and which allows of no social and ritual distinctions between male and female, Jew and Gentile, slave and free, since all constitute one person in Christ (Gal.3:26-28).

As in the area of marriage, so in that of ritual purity: the oppression of women appears to be universal, especially in Africa. But in whatever way we look at it, no oppressive element in the Bible can be attributed to God's will. God is by nature the liberator of the oppressed; God cannot ipso facto be an oppressor in any form of the word. Recognition of this truth has deep pastoral and hermeneutical consequences for our reading of the Bible, which we shall now briefly consider.

NEW HERMENEUTICAL PRINCIPLES AND THEIR PASTORAL IMPLICATIONS

The foregoing study of women in the Bible was necessarily restricted to an examination of a few key areas. The hermeneutical principles and pastoral considerations that this study inspired must also of necessity be limited to a few key areas. First, in examining the story of Eve, we discovered that certain elements in the biblical accounts had been either misinterpreted over the centuries or simply ignored. For the Bible is a patriarchal book not only because it was written by men (and for the most part for men), but because over the centuries it has been interpreted almost exclusively by men. Yet the human race is composed of male and female, each with its own distinctive way of perceiving reality. There is therefore an urgent need to correct the imbalance and impoverishment of Scripture caused by this one-sided interpretation by bringing to bear a feminine perspective in the interpretation of Scripture.

Creation of humanity as male and female has consequences that extend beyond the purely biological. It demands that both men and women be involved in every sphere of human endeavor. Nowhere is this more needed than in the theological and scriptural fields where humanity most lives out its likeness to God. Women must therefore be encouraged and enabled to undertake the study of Scripture up to the highest level. It is a singular tribute to EATWOT that from its very inception it recognized the need for, and welcomed the involvement of, women in the doing of theology. Women themselves have a duty to humanity to make their contribution felt in this area.

This provision for feminine hermeneutics will, among other things, help to ensure that those dimensions of God's word that can be properly understood only by women are brought to light for the benefit of all. Particularly affected will be those stories that concern women and God's relationship with them, as Elizabeth Fiorenza has amply shown in her book, *In Memory of Her*. Equally, it will ensure that the much neglected feminine aspects of God are acknowledged and celebrated by all God's children. Humanity stands to gain, not to lose, from the involvement of women in the study of Scripture.

Second, rereading the Bible as a patriarchal book demands that sustained efforts be made to discern between the divine and the human elements in it.[33] For while the former embodies timeless truths for our salvation, the latter inculcates practices that are socioculturally conditioned, hence inapplicable universally. In what Origen calls the principle of accommodation, God puts up with our imperfect knowledge of divinity and divine ways while leading us progressively to an ever fuller or more perfect knowledge. The women issue is clearly an area where God is leading us today to a more perfect knowledge of the divine will. As humanity once cooperated with the old sinful order by belittling the status and significance of women in society, it now has a corresponding duty to cooperate with God in making concrete and visible the reality of the new order restored by Christ (Gal. 3:26–28). This demands that serious efforts be made to translate into programs of action within our ecclesial structures our theological belief in our oneness in Christ. In this respect, it is not only the woman who needs to be liberated from subjection and oppression; the man needs to be freed from his evil tendency to lord it over women and treat them as inferiors, a tendency that is fundamentally unchristian (cf. Phil. 2:1–12).

Third, and most important, the rereading of the Bible demands that emphasis be placed on the vocation of woman as mother, God's privileged instrument for conceiving and bringing forth life. In the past, insufficient recognition has been given to this singular role of woman in society. This emphasis will go hand in hand with sustained efforts to develop and celebrate the motherhood of God. For though in the last analysis God is neither man nor woman, the human categories we use to express our knowledge *of* God help us in our relationship *with* God. Our celebration of the motherhood of God will help us to approach God and Jesus as compassionate, merciful, and tender givers of life and refuge of sinners rather than as mighty lords to be feared and appeased. In general, children (African children in particular) fear and obey their fathers, who have power and authority. But they love and feel most secure with their mothers, who enable growth in them. Let us allow God to be our mother, as well as our father: the gain will be wholly ours.

As to the pastoral implications of all this, women need above all to develop a better image of themselves and of one another. For often women are their worst enemies in this respect. They need to recognize that it is no honor to God to deny or play down their own God-given dignity and place in society. If they do not lay hold of their destiny, that destiny will never become theirs, and humanity as a whole will continue to be impoverished by it. As *Pacem in Terris* rightly declares, those who know they have rights have the responsibility to claim them. This is a challenge to women.

In struggling for their God-given rights, women must reject all measures that contradict their divine vocation as agents of life or that give the impression that they wish to lord it over men. That would mean simply replacing one sinful system with another. The struggle for the liberation of women can be genuine only if it is liberation in Christ, in whom men and women form one body and where each party is called upon to study and promote the well-being of the other, thereby sharing in God's own life-giving activity.

Sustained efforts must be made to educate both men and women, through Bible study groups, in a proper understanding of the Bible. There is obvious need to awaken and free people from centuries of sociocultural and theological conditionings based on a false understanding of the teaching of the Bible concerning women. Only in this way will humanity come to know that truth in Christ which sets us all free (cf. Jn. 8:31–36). Only in Christ can men and women be truly free to attain to their full destiny as people created in the image and likeness of God.

The efforts made in this present study to highlight the teaching of the Bible concerning women are in effect a contribution toward the attainment of this liberating knowledge. It is hoped that the study will stimulate further research, reflection, and discussion on this all important subject, and that this in turn will lead to appropriate action.

NOTES

1. Philippine Edition 8 (2, 1985) 17–24.
2. See, e.g., Arthur Cohen, *Everyman's Talmud* (New York: Schocken, 1975), pp.

160–61, and Elizabeth Clark, *Women in the Early Church,* Message of the Fathers Series, vol. 13 (Wilmington: Michael Glazier, 1983),pp. 27–76.

3. Genesis Rabba 18:2; Cohen, *Everyman's Talmud,* p. 160.

4. Cf. John Chrysostom, *Discourse 2 on Genesis, Series Graeca* (PG). 54.587; Clark, *Women,* p. 35.

5. Irenaeus, *Against Heresies* 3.22.4, PG. 7.958; Tertullian, *On the Dress of Women* 1.1.2., *Corpus scriptorum ecclesiasticorum . . .* (CSEL) 70.59; Augustine, *Literal Commentary on Genesis* 9.42, CSEL 28.1.376; and Ambrose, *On Paradise* 12.56; 14.72, CSEL 32.1.316, 329; cf. Clark, *Women,* pp. 39–41.

6. In fairness to the church fathers, it must be noted that source and redaction criticism that attribute the two creation accounts to different authors (Gen. 1:26–2:4a; 5:1–2 to the Priestly author, P; and Gen. 2:4b–4:2 to the Yahwistic author, J) are modern developments in biblical science. Even if the validity of the customary authorship designations, J, E (Elohistic), P, and D (Deuteronomic) are today contested, the fact remains that each of these creation narratives has its own distinctive focus, which requires recognition from the exegete.

7. M. Yebamoth 6.6; T. Yebamoth 56b.

8. See Okure, "Biblical Perspectives," *Voices of the Third World,* 20–21.

9. Cf. Augustine, *On the Good of Marriage* 1, CSEL 41.187; Clark, *Women,* pp. 28–32; and Ambrose, *On Paradise* 10.48. Unfortunately, these fathers did not always follow to its logical conclusion their insight into the basic complementarity between husband and wife.

10. See the whole section on *Nashim* ("Women") in H. Danby, *The Mishnah: Translated from the Hebrew with Introduction and Brief Explanatory Notes* (London: Oxford University Press, 1938), pp. 217–329, esp. pp. 307–21; Cohen, *Everyman's Talmud,* pp. 159–70; cf. Lev. 20:10–21; Deut. 22:22–28.

11. Yoma 1.1; Shabbath 118b; Cohen, *Everyman's Talmud,* p. 162.

12. Gittin 9.9; cf. Deut. 24:1.

13. Genesis Rabba 17.17.

14. Genesis Rabba 45.5.

15. Kethubboth 65a; Cohen, *Everyman's Talmud,* p. 161.

16. B. Menahoth 43b.

17. Cohen, *Everyman's Talmud,* p. 159.

18. See, e.g., Danby, *Mishnah,* pp. ix–x.

19. Augustine, *On Genesis* 11.42; Clark, *Women,* p. 40; and Chrysostom, *The Kind of Women Who Ought to Be Taken as Wives* 4 (cf. Clark, *Women,* p. 36).

20. Okure, "Biblical Perspectives," *Voices of the Third World,* pp. 22–23.

21. Noticeably, Adam's punishment extends for three verses (vss. 17–19) in contrast to Eve's one verse (vs. 16).

22. Strikingly, the word "seed" is here used of the woman, whereas in other parts of the Bible and in general usage it is reserved almost exclusively for the man; cf. Gen. 9:9; 12:27; 15:5, 8, 13; Exod. 32:13; Lev. 22:4; Josh. 24:3.

23. As at Bethlehem, so on Calvary (Jn. 19:25–27). We recall, too, that the sign of hope given to fear-stricken Ahaz was that of a maiden with child, Emmanuel, God with us (Isa. 7:14). The Bible is consistent in portraying the woman as the symbol of life and hope.

24. In the view of the church fathers, the main reason why the woman cannot image God is that "image" "has to do with authority, and this only the man has" (Augustine, *On Genesis* 2, PG. 54.589; cf. Clark, *Women,* p. 35).

25. I treated this and the next two passages in a paper on "The Role and Contribution of Women in the Bible," delivered at a seminar on "The Role and Contribution of Women in Church and Society," Catholic Institute of West Africa, Port Harcourt, Nigeria, June 1985.

26. A detailed analysis of Jesus' encounter with the Samaritan woman is given in my doctoral thesis, *The Johannine Approach to Mission: A Contextual Study of John 4:1-42*, in particular, chaps. 4 and 5 on the exegesis of 4:1-42.

27. Ben Witherington III (*Women in the Ministry of Jesus*, SNTSMS 51 [Cambridge, Eng.: University Press, 1984], pp. 44-52) discusses in detail this aspect of Jesus' attitude toward women as illustrated in his teaching and parables.

28. Cohen, *Everyman's Talmud*, p. 167.

29. Similarly, slaves were exhorted to be subject to their masters as to the Lord (cf. Eph. 6:5-8). Yet today, the church regards slavery as an abuse of human rights, a degradation of human dignity. The church has yet to take a similar stand with regard to the subjection of wives to their husbands.

30. See Danby, *Mishnah*, pp. 217-39.

31. Sirach's attitude toward women is phenomenally negative. See further, Sir. 9:1-9; 23:22-27; 26:5-12; 35:13-16; 42:9-13.

32. For laws on ritual purity affecting women, see in particular Lev. 12:1-8; 15:19-30.

33. Cf. *Dei Verbum*, no. 12.

6

Final Statement

I. Recommendations

Yaoundé, Cameroun, Women's Meeting of Francophone Africa, August 3-9, 1986

We African women recommend that all biblical texts be read and presented as they are, even if they challenge our mental, social, or economic structures—as they undoubtedly did at the time they were first written and made known.

According to the account of the creation in Genesis 1:26-28, man and woman are responsible together for dominating the earth and for making it fruitful. We recommend that African women be aware of this in educating their children, both boys and girls. We recommend that they search together to conquer famine by exploiting the potential of our African soil for the well-being of the African people.

According to Galatians 3:26ff., man and woman are equal in Christ. We ask the churches to give women their rightful place.

The wives of the Hebrew slaves in Egypt saved their people by preventing the extermination of their sons. We recommend that the African woman today save her children from the three forms of alienation (cultural, socioeconomic, and spiritual) which weigh on Africa today.

We recommend that the African Christian woman place a new value on hospitality, as did the widow of Sarepta.

We recommend that the African Christian woman become the guarantor of the spiritual life of the home and keep alive the flame of faith, as did the five wise virgins in Matthew 25:1-13.

Translated from French by Susan Perry.

We recommend that the churches support the creation of small communities centered around the word of God where human and Christian solidarity are possible.

We recommend that the churches be present in all ceremonies marking the life of individuals and communities and in all rituals pertaining to them so that the life of Christ overcomes these circumstances (purification, widowhood, funerals, etc.).

We recommend that the churches study the deep significance of African rituals and search for new ways of expressing them in the initiation to Christian life in Africa. This will require that the churches train Christian animators inspired by mature faith and capable of being witnesses of the Good News of the liberating power of Jesus Christ.

It would be good, for example, to study a method of initiating young people into a harmonious but responsible integration with the life of modern society. This could be done by creating youth hostels, effectively enlivened by the church (priests, pastors, and committed Christians).

We recommend that churches support the creation of training centers for Christian women, thus placing them in direct contact with the word of God. As a means of sensitizing them, we propose that the women themselves make use of mass media.

We recommend that the churches and committed Christians participate responsibly in drawing up laws concerned with the condition of women.

We recommend that the churches recognize the celibate life, not only traditional religious celibates, but also a celibate life freely chosen by certain individuals, for the service of the church and of society. This position presupposes, certainly, great conviction and maturity on the part of those interested.

We recommend that the churches include the members of the two families as well as the future man and wife in the preparation for Christian marriages.

We recommend that the churches support the creation of groups of Christian households who can reflect together on their problems in the light of the gospel of Jesus Christ.

The African woman is the soul of the society and thus the initiating teacher in spiritual and divine matters. Concerning the formation given to religious and lay women, we believe that the churches must prepare women to be capable of preaching the word of God, of directing retreats and study groups, of taking responsibility for the formation of pastors, evangelists, lay leaders, apostolic workers, priests, and other ordained persons. We recommend that women be equally present in the teaching of Christian doctrine, not only as female catechists, but also as professors of theology.

In the process of evangelizing Africa, women have always been in the vanguard in hospitals and in educational, social, and cultural institutions. They should also be given the responsibility for direction of these projects.

As women, we hope the churches will seriously study how women in our countries can participate in the administration of salvation through the sacraments.

In the government and administration of the church as well as in the management of its resources, it is necessary to reserve for both lay and religious women, not only positions as secretaries, assistants, or observers, but also responsible positions where they will be able to share with officials the right to decide how best to carry out the gospel.

We hope that EATWOT will organize a pan-African meeting between African women theologians and those of the Coptic and Ethiopian Orthodox churches so that we may better understand the role played by African women in the transmission of the gospel of Jesus in those parts of Africa.

We recommend that the churches have the humility to recognize that their mission has not been all that it could have been. Consequently, they must seriously study these new forms of spiritual life in order to use them to restructure themselves.

We recommend that the churches engage in a meaningful and sincere dialogue with the leaders of groups to achieve mutual knowledge of each other.

We recommend that the churches support and promote the theological formation of members of these groups.

We recommend that the churches begin to play a prophetic role in our societies and in our countries and that they move toward those people who are thirsty and marginalized.

Finally, the experience of spiritual life shows that God speaks to all people without discrimination. Is this not an invitation issued to the churches to give women their rightful place within these structures?

CONCLUSION

The experience of spiritual life shows that God communicates with all people without discrimination.

The proclamation of the resurrection begins with the announcement of Mary Magdalene to the apostles, who are not yet enlightened. Then they emerge from their fear and become a community of disciples and missionaries of the gospel of the liberation of Christ.

This mission is the same for women today: to be witnesses of the resurrection of Christ in our lives and to be open to the spirit of the gospel.

Is this not an invitation issued to the churches to give women their rightful place within these structures?

As women, we are ready to receive the rights we claim and to use them meaningfully.

At the end of these days of reflection and of shared life, we want to underline the exceptional importance of this meeting. This is the first time that French-speaking African women theologians have met under the auspices of our Association. This has allowed us to know ourselves, to pool our experiences, our doubts, our hopes. Although we have only begun to explore these themes, we are convinced of their importance. Also we dare to hope and to believe that our reflection will deepen in our future meetings.

We hope that this meeting awakens the conscience of each African woman and leads her to actions which are more motivated and more engaged in the service of our society, our church, and our continent.

We cannot end this report without once again thanking all those who contributed to the success of this meeting. We thank the Executive Committee of EATWOT and in particular Mrs. Rose Zoe-Obianga, coordinator of the African women of EATWOT.

II. Communiqué

EATWOT Continental Consultation of Anglophone Africa on Theology from Third World Women's Perspective, Port Harcourt, Nigeria, August 19–23, 1986

An international meeting of African women was held at CIWA [Catholic Institute of West Africa], Port Harcourt, Nigeria, from August 19 to 23, 1986. The theme was *Doing Theology from the Third World Women's Perspective*. The countries represented were Cameroun, Ghana, Kenya, Nigeria, and Sierra Leone. Delegates from these countries were joined by an enthusiastic group of women participants from the Rivers State, and most especially from the Port Harcourt diocese of the Roman Catholic Church. The meeting was sponsored by the Ecumenical Association of Third World Theologians, which seeks to broaden the scope of Christian theology by developing it from the perspective of the Third World and making it address the Third World Reality, inclusive of women.

In this meeting we, the women participants, aimed at broadening our understanding of women's situation: economic, political, cultural, and religious. Through the discussion of women's experiences of God, we were able to understand the spirituality out of which women struggle for the liberation of the peoples of Africa. Through working together we deepened our commitment and solidarity for full humanity for all. The Consultation gave us new spectacles with which to re-read the Bible. This re-reading of the Bible gave us new insights which we hope will lead to a holistic understanding of what it means to be church in Africa today.

We affirm that:

1. Men and women together image God and that *neither* is complete without the other.

2. In Christ we see the fullness of true humanity; therefore, Christianity in

Africa should be a force for full human development.

3. Women have a vital contribution to make in God's project of bringing all God's children to full humanity.

In view of this, we, the women who met at Port Harcourt, are committed:

1. To participating fully as women in the holistic human development that will enable us to realize our goals and eliminate all life-denying forces in church and society in Africa, especially those rooted in ritual.

2. To working toward the elimination of racism, abject poverty, and the neglect of rural areas. We want to break the silence that has led to the minimal and inadequate participation of women in decisions that affect their lives and that could lead to the church's fulfillment of its mission in Africa with respect to women.

3. To working together with other women and cooperating with all who seek to promote Christ's message in all its fullness; Christ who came so that all may have life in all its fullness (Jn.10:10) and who said:

I will wipe away all tears from their eyes.
There will be no more death, no more mourning or sadness.
The world of the past has gone . . .
Now I am making the whole of creation new (Rev. 21:4–5).

We, therefore, call upon all people of good will to join forces with us in working for the total liberation and transformation of African men and women through the power of that gospel which is Jesus Christ.

Part Two

ASIA

7

Women's Oppression: A Sinful Situation

Aruna Gnanadason (India)

In the Indian epic *Ramayana,* the sage Vishwamitra is at one point in deep penance—so deep and intense is his penance that it shakes the whole universe, including the heavens and the throne of the Lord of lords, Indra himself. In order to break Vishwamitra's penance, Indra sends to the earth the beautiful Menaka to dance her way into the soul of the devout sage. Menaka dances around Vishwamitra. Ultimately she touches the sage seductively, wakes him out of his trance to take her into his arms. The penance is broken, the heavens stop shaking, and Indra is at peace.

Male mythology all over the world makes woman responsible for the advent of evil in the world. As Rosemary Ruether observes, "It also translates female evil into an ontological principle. The female comes to represent the qualities of materiality, irrationality, carnality, and finitude, which debase the 'manly' spirit and drag it down into sin and death."[1]

Many more examples can be quoted from Hindu mythology to show how man "falls" from his higher spiritual principle and is entrapped in the lower female material principle. This thesis forms the basis of much of Indian literature, art, and culture. Male/female, spirit/body, human/nonhuman dualism is extended to the good/evil (sin) dualism. What is more clearly indicated is that in these polarities of human existence, the "evil" side is scapegoated as female.

To overcome her latent evil nature, woman is socialized into submitting to certain accepted male-determined norms or she is punished and "put in her place" for what is actually a sin committed against her. Therefore Sita, the great heroine of the *Ramayana*, is not accepted by her husband, Rama, who says, "Whatever I did was for the sake of avoiding scandal in every way, for clearing the name of the reputed dynasty. . . . You have been looked at by Ravana with his vicious eyes and have been molested on his lap. How can I accept you as such and sully my great family?"[2] Sita then enters into the fire to prove to her husband her purity and adherence to the code of chastity.

Based on this episode a contemporary Tamil novelist, Jayakantan, wrote a story entitled *Agni Pravesam* ("Entering the Fire") in 1966. A girl, in Jayakantan's story, while waiting for a bus on a rainy day, accepts a lift from a man who is driving by. He seduces her. She narrates this incident with fear and tears to her mother on her return home. The mother at first is shocked, but after that she bathes her daughter in water, telling her that the water is the fire that will purify her. I add here a comment of the writer and literary critic C. S. Lakshmi: "Whether by water or fire, that the episode called for a process of purification itself was an evidence that the umbilical cord with tradition was not cut off."[3]

In spite of the fact that Jayakantan could go that far and no further, as far as women's rights were concerned, the novel whipped up strong protests from writers and the public. Many of the voices of censure were, unfortunately, from women. They were enraged that the heroine was alive after the incident. Such characters are usually killed or are maimed in some way. It was considered an outrage against Tamil culture that Jayakantan had allowed the woman to go scot-free. Many counterstories were written almost as if in an attempt to blot out from the readers' minds the shameless episode. This is just one example to show how the myth of the inherent evil in women is sustained in the Indian psyche.

In the Bible, too, the myth of Eve as causing the fall of "man" and the loss of paradise has been reinforced by the strict adherence to the earlier Yahwist account of the creation of man and woman (Gen. 2:7ff.) and the downplaying of the later Priestly account (Gen. 1:26ff.). In this latter account there is no hint in the description of her creation that woman had a subordinate status. Humanity is created male and female. There is no suggestion that one of the two sexes is evil because of gender.

But such myths have formed the theological basis of the church's denigration of women for centuries. The early church fathers were vocal in their pronouncements to exclude women from all ecclesial leadership:

Woman, you are the devil's gateway. You have led astray one whom the devil would not dare attack directly. It is your fault the Son of God had to die; you should always go in mourning and rags [Tertullian].

Adam was led to sin by Eve and not Eve by Adam. It is just and right that woman accept as lord and master [the one] whom she led to sin [Ambrose].

Among all savage beasts none is found so harmful as women [John Chrysostom].

Woman is a sick she-ass. . . . a hideous tapeworm. . . . the advance post of hell [John Damascene].

. . . Woman is indispensable for the task of procreation; but for all other spiritual tasks, another male is to be preferred [Augustine].[4]

This kind of pomposity and arrogance, cited by a feminist theologian as "evidence of a deep misogynist contempt and fear of woman,"[5] can be discerned even today when church leaders make categorical statements like "The question of the ordination of women is against the will of God, and therefore cannot be discussed" and "Women's primary task is to pray for the church—not to get involved in administrative or ministerial roles," and so on.

Male mythology and the gradual patriarchalization of the church and society have associated woman with "sinful nature" and have systematically caused and justified the oppression of women.

OPPRESSION OF WOMEN: A SYSTEMIC SIN

When speaking of the systemic causes of women's oppression, it becomes imperative to reflect briefly on the state of India's economic, political, social, and cultural environment because the situation of women is inextricably linked with the situation of all oppressed groups within the context of a crisis-ridden Indian society. India faces deepening economic crisis. The economy is rapidly getting sucked into world capitalism. There is also an increasing authoritarian trend, seen in the building up of a sophisticated surveillance machinery and of police and paramilitary forces to surpress internal dissent. The latest policy has been to go in for high technology and heavy industrial investment, which only intensifies India's dependence on Western powers. Now, with the alleged Pakistani threat, India seems to be heading for an atomic-bomb program.

Women, no doubt, are the worst sufferers within the shaky economic scene and the militaristic culture. It is becoming more and more clear that violence against women whether in the family or in the society is political in nature. It is just a symptom of the militarism that pervades society. Women in India do not have access to nutritional, educational, or other facilities that are available. In the article "Girls Inside, Boys Outside," Kalpana Sharma makes some startling, statistically supported statements to prove this point.[6]

The basic reality is that women in India have somehow to survive discriminatory practices all through their lives. Some are lucky to be admitted into school, but the majority of those who do enter drop out in a couple of years, as a girl's access to education is quickly curbed by demands on her time for household chores. The negative values perpetuated through our educational system contribute nothing toward increasing the self-esteem of women. Neither the educational system nor media is neutral. They have a markedly male bias.

Women in India have not come very far from Judaic times—when a woman's primary role was that of wife and mother. The laws were promulgated largely in the male gender so that the people were addressed through the men. Many specific examples can be given to substantiate the low status of women in that society. Perhaps the most powerful examples are those of a concubine's rape and ultimate dismemberment (Judg. 19) and Lot's offer of his two daughters to the men of Sodom and Gomorrah (Gen. 19:4–8). We also recall the story of Jephthah's sacrifice of his daughter, to save face. All these speak of the powerless, nameless, voiceless women in Judaic times. Wives are seen as property of their husbands, as was established by the curse on women in the Garden of Eden, "and he shall rule over you" (Gen. 3:16). Wives were made sexually available to others so that the men could protect their own lives (Gen. 12:10–20; 20:1–18; 26:6–11; Judg. 19:1–29).

RAPE AS A POLITICAL WEAPON

Woman is trapped within a vicious circle of violence that constantly seeks to exploit and destroy her being. In the Indian context, rape is a political weapon used to suppress a rebellious woman:

A complex interplay of the forces of an unequal socio-economic system and the institution of patriarchy generates an ideology and value system which seeks to propagate itself through an invidious process of socialization and structural forms of violence in institutions such as the law, media and family, which reinforce social and economic relations and roles. Personal violence against women, like rape and dowry deaths, therefore only reflect the systematic violence of our society that creates conditions which are in themselves destructive. This understanding should prevent us from viewing acts of physical violence against women as isolated incidents attributable mainly to individual aberrations. Oppression of and violence against women has, very definitely, a cultural, psychological, material and sociological base.[7]

The oppression of women is to be understood not simplistically but as a systemic sin rooted within the context of well-organized and established structures of oppression, which grind to dust the aspirations of large sections of workers, peasants, tribal groups, *dalits* (a movement among the Untouchables of India), and particularly women, who are, in the words of a peasant woman, "slaves of slaves" to be found at the lowest depths of caste and class hierarchy.

So as to maintain the status quo, the dominant group in any society controls the lives of the majority and keeps them in a position of subservience by perpetuating inequalities. As *Manushi*, a radical women's magazine, puts it: "In this game women are special targets because the subjugation of women is the primary precondition for keeping hierarchical, exploitative social structures intact." This is done by basing all customs and habits on religion and the country's cultural heritage, giving the most heinous crimes against women a quasi-divine legitimation.[8]

Women have therefore a low image in society and none in their own estimation, and often support and uphold patriarchal norms and follow those very customs and traditions that oppress them. The suppressed group, to some extent, internalizes the dominant ideology, which shapes its own socialization, and so becomes filled with fear and ambiguity about its own humanity. Thus we must see two interconnected but distinguishable aspects to the ideology of the "other" as of lesser value: projection and exploitation. Projection externalizes the sense of inadequacy and negativity from the dominant group, making the other the cultural "carrier" of these rejected qualities. The dominant group can then rationalize exploitation as the right to reduce the other to a servile condition, abuse, and even kill them on the ground of their lesser value.[9]

Feminists in this century have analyzed this desire to dominate "the other" as the basis of the class/patriarchal society we live in. In its most direct form it manifests itself as war, internal repression, growth of authoritarianism, salvaging operations, genocidal campaigns—and also in direct forms of violence against women: dowry deaths, rape, battering, and so forth. Sin comes about precisely by this distortion of the self/other relationship, basing it on domination and control. It can also be seen in women's passive acquiescence before such distortions. Therefore *sin* must be seen not merely as one individual personal straying away from the values of justice and peace but as a collective, systematic destruction of the community that is at the foundation of God's good creation. To restore community, to create a new world would be the task to which we as Christians are called.

TOWARD A NEW DAY

In Asia the structural violence against women and such patriarchal institutions, such as family, marriage, Christian personal laws, sexist liturgical practices, and low participation of women in the church and its ministry and in the society, have not yet been adequately analyzed theologically, nor have they been recognized as "sins" against half the people of God. Theologians (particularly male theologians in this context) who have been able to recognize the structural forces that dehumanize people in general are unable to point specifically to the institutionalized discrimination and violence against women as being untenable to our faith commitment. This reality restricts Asian theological growth. There is an urgent need to listen and learn from the voices of women in struggle, who search for their humanhood.[10]

Women have begun their walk toward the sun, toward a new day. The women's movement, its spread and growth all over Asia, is an expression of hope. The women's movement is increasingly being recognized as a political force that can have far-reaching consequences on movements for change in Asia. The women's movement has had its impact on the theological efforts of the church too. A small but committed group of women within the church in India, and in other parts of Asia, have begun a "rereading of the Bible in a scientific way informed by a commitment to women's liberation and to human liberation in general."[11] This experience is the basis for the development of consciousness. Added to this, Asian women have to understand the Bible in their own consciousness of oppression as Asian women or as Third World women. This makes the task doubly difficult, but also challenging.

Translations and interpretations of the Bible have been done in the andro-centric mindsets of Western culture, and this has had its own impact on the pressures against the participation of women in leadership roles in the early church and in the church of today. The androcentric language of the Bible, particularly in the naming of God in purely masculine terms, legitimizes the sexist language and symbols used in the church today and goes a long way in restricting women's full participation in ministry. The language by which we name God is important because God is really beyond human conceptions. "God is indescribable. We cannot know God fully, for God is a mystery, not an object of knowledge but an object of faith. Language, though it is an indis-pensable tool for expressing thought, is yet a very limited and imperfect tool to speak and write about God. Most of the religious language is figurative, analogical, and metaphorical."[12] Naming God in purely masculine language is a matter of concern because this has formed the basis of the entire structure of divine-human and human-human relationships, which are understood in a patriarchal framework.

Asian theologians have to discover new concepts of the face of God from their cultural heritage and traditions. The synchronizing of the female and male principles in the half God-man, half God-woman concept of *Ardhanariswara*,[13] is a case in point. In Asia the face of God can be discovered in many images, even in the image of a slum woman who holds her newborn baby in her arms and stares with brave eyes into an empty future with a determination that she and her child will live.

IN CHRIST: A NEW WOMAN

To women theologians a rediscovery of their biblical heritage has led them to draw strength from the Jesus community, which was an egalitarian, non-hierarchical community. Sinners, prostitutes, beggars, tax collectors, the ritu-ally polluted, the crippled, and the impoverished—in short, the scum of Palestinian society—constituted the majority of Jesus' followers. These are the last who have become the first, the starving who have been satisfied, the uninvited who have been invited. And many of these were women.

Jesus does not waste his time trying to upgrade the feminine role by giving new dignity to the old task. On the contrary, he creates an alternative. A woman's freedom in Christ therefore includes, at the core, her freedom from the system of dominance that diminishes her personhood by imprisoning her womanhood. The Christian feminist viewpoint automatically leads to a cri-tique of historico-cultural traditions that have given women a distorted image of their bodies, their abilities, their roles, their responsibilities, their dignity, and their destiny. Each woman is called to be transformed as person and as woman, not in such a way as to become a "happy slave" seeing blessedness in the subservience demanded by society, but as an individual gifted with human dignity and salvific splendor, no less than her male counterparts.

Women have realized that they derive power from a God who has a definite preference for those who are discriminated against. In a story in the Old Testament (Num. 27:1-8), we see the courage and commitment of five women, the five daughters of a man called Zelophehad who, when their father died, stood up in front of the leader of the Israelites, Moses, and the other leaders of the community and demanded their right to the name and inheritance of their father. Moses, the one in whose hands lay the scales of justice, did not make an arbitrary judgment; he took the case to the Lord (the Bible tells us). And the Lord said that the women were right in their demand! The word of a just God transcended the social and legal practices of those times. Many other examples both from the Old Testament and from New Testament times can be given to show how God intervenes on behalf of the oppressed and changes the course of the traditional practices and laws of the time.

Women's role in church and society is therefore not merely to participate within patriarchal structures of church and society or to perpetuate them (sometimes inadvertently) but to reinterpret the critical-liberating tradition of Christianity, which is the axis on which the prophetic messianic line of biblical faith revolves. Women can participate creatively only when they break through the sinful patriarchal structures (in the family, church, and society) so as to transform relationships based on a subordination/domination ideology into one based on the freedom promised in Christ. In this effort we draw inspiration from Jesus' radical attitude toward women. For eighteen years, the bent-over woman in Luke's story was weighed down by the sinful structures around her but was able to overcome her bent-over state and was recognized as a "daughter of Abraham" by Jesus. To be the daughters of Abraham is to discover the power we derive from Christ.

NOTES

1. Rosemary Radford Ruether, *Sexism and God Talk: Towards a Feminist Theology* (London: SCM Press, 1983), pp. 168-69.

2. Ramayana Valmike, *Yudha Kand.*

3. C. S. Lakshmi, *The Face behind the Mask: Women in Tamil Literature* (New Delhi: Vikas Publishing House, 1984), p. 141.

4. As quoted in *Wina Vani* (newsletter of the Women's Institute for New Awareness), Mangalore, Mar. 23, 1984.

5. Elisabeth Schüssler Fiorenza, *In Memory of Her* (New York: Crossroad Publishing Co., 1983), p. 55.

6. Kalpana Sharma, *Sunday Express* (magazine supplement of the *Indian Express*), Oct. 27, 1985.

7. Madhu Bhushan, "Women and Violence," *Sangarsh* (magazine of the women's group Vimochana), 1985.

8. "The Media Game," *Manushi,* no. 5 (1980).

9. Rosemary Ruether, *Sexism,* p. 162.

10. Aruna Gnanadason, "Doing Theology with Asian Resources—from the Perspec-

tive of Women in Struggle," paper presented at a workshop on Doing Theology with Asian Resources of the Association of Theological Education in South East Asia (ATESEA), Kyoto, Japan, May 1985.

11. Gabriele Dietrich, in a paper on "The Origins of the Bible Revisited: Reconstructing Women's History," presented at the National Consultation "Towards a Theology of Humanhood: Women's Perspectives," sponsored by the All India Council of Christian Women (AICCW), Association of Theologically Trained Women in India (ATTWI), and Catholic women, Bangalore, November 1984.

12. Sumathi Iswaradevan, in "God Talk and Women," paper presented at the National Consultation "Towards a Theology of Humanhood," Bangalore, November 1984.

13. *Ardhanariswara* (Sanskrit, "the lord who is half woman"), a composite male-female figure of the Hindu god, Siva, together with his consort, Parvati. The symbolic intent of the figure according to most authorities is to signify that the male and female principles are inseparable in the universe and are always found together. (Explanation extracted from the new *Encyclopaedia Britannica,* 15th ed., 1976, vol. 1, Micropaedia Ready Reference and Index.)

8

Emerging Spirituality
of Asian Women

*Mary John Mananzan (Philippines) and
Sun Ai Park (Korea)*

INTRODUCTION

Spirituality is a very interesting and important topic to tackle. However, it is a subject that many have yet to explore and articulate, at least in the Asian context. We shall start with "What Is Spirituality?" and then discuss the Asian situation that is the context of the spirituality of Asian women. It is also important to treat the "Framework and Nature of Asian Women's Spirituality" and "Interfaith Dialogue and Asian Women." We shall conclude with a theological reflection.

WHAT IS SPIRITUALITY?

Spirituality is not a simple concept. It is used to describe different realities that have converging elements. The totality of the elements may differ from one understanding to another. Christians or theistic people, for example, may not be able to understand how nonbelievers could have a spirituality. And yet self-proclaimed atheists may be deeply spiritual people.

What then is spirituality? In Christian theology and practice, an old understanding of spirituality would more or less describe it as theology applied to daily life—to one's personal life of prayer and asceticism, to be more precise. There is, however, an emerging understanding of spirituality as the inner core made up of all the experiences and encounters one has had in one's life and out of which come the motivations, inspirations, and commitment that make one live and decide in a particular way. One might say, it is the shape in which the Holy Spirit has molded herself into one's life.

Donald Dorr [1] writes about the center in a person, which is partly influenced by one's genetic heritage and environment but is largely shaped by one's gut-level experiences and major options in life. It is also this center that is the focus of our "experience of God." It is here we allow the Holy Spirit to move us, to act in us, to assimilate the major experiences we encounter in our lives, especially the new and unpredictable that might totally contradict the accumulated experiences that through the years have shaped our core. This is where the phenomenon of conversion, metanoia, may be realized. Meditation, prayer, and asceticism enable individuals to integrate these experiences into their inner core or to revise it partially or completely.

Modern-day prophetic theologians, especially Latin American liberation theologians and feminist theologians, come out boldly on the holistic liberation message that the Judeo-Christian religion has in its core, and point out errors and misunderstandings that traditional church theology has woven into the Christian understanding of spirituality. One of the most serious errors is the dualism that separates the spiritual from the bodily and material realm, intellectual from emotional expressions, concerns of the other world from those of this world, and that subsequently divides men from women. Feminist theologians attribute the last division to patriarchy.

Gustavo Gutiérrez expresses the holistic nature of spirituality in a rather pointed way: "When one is concerned with one's own stomach, it is materialism, but when one is concerned with other people's stomachs it is spirituality." [2] Both are concerned with the stomach, but one is called materialism and the other spirituality. Christian spirituality deals with this fine distinction, which can be summed up as the unity of self and others, the material and the spiritual, love and justice, community and individuals, religions and politics, peace and struggle toward holistic salvation.

Women's struggle is part and parcel of the historical struggle for the holistic salvation of all humanity. Women can make a unique contribution toward this goal based on their spirituality, which is formulated throughout their concrete pro-life way of living and experiences. All the disastrous dimension of patriarchal culture is typically exemplified in its demeaning, ignoring, and despising the very spirituality of women that is oriented toward and sustaining life in love. The spirituality affirming womanhood, reaching out for liberation of all women and all humanity, is emerging in all parts of the world, and Asia is not exempt.

ASIAN WOMEN'S REALITY

The spirituality of women has its context in the situation of oppression in which they live. It is therefore necessary to describe the Asian situation in order to understand the emerging spirituality of women in the continent.

Asian women share the domestic, economic, political, and religious oppression that their sisters all over the world suffer. However, the concretization of the oppression varies. The image of the subservient, servile Asian woman is behind the varied forms of trafficking of Asian women ranging from mail-order brides to prostitution. Because of the economic crisis, women in Asia suffer a double burden in the work situation (low wages and sexual harassment) and a triple burden in the case of rural women (field work, domestic work, and marketing of goods). Because of political repression, Asian women have also been raped, tortured, imprisoned, and killed for their political beliefs.

Specifically, Malaysian women suffer the resurgence of religious fundamentalism and worsening communal relations; Korean women suffer from the division of their country into North and South and from the oppressive Confucian family law; Indian women suffer from the caste system and the dowry system—and Muslim women in some Asian countries have to submit to female genital mutilation. Sri Lankan women are torn by the ethnic struggle. Although Japanese women belong to a First World society, they also suffer from the male-oriented emperor system, the tragic experience of the nuclear bomb, and the hazards of a highly technological society.

In Asia, as well as in other parts of the world, there is the problem of "tokenism." Some women are given a status of equality and privilege as an excuse to perpetuate the general structure and patterns of society. "Token" women are not oriented into the new vision of human relationship and community that the alternative feminist ideology offers; therefore, they are not committed to the work of renewal. Instead they ape the old pattern of individualism and dogged competition for self-glory. That is the reason why this present dialogue on Asian women's spirituality provides a very important groundwork. If Eve is as equally responsible as Adam for "the fall," she also needs repentance and conversion to be accepted into the reign of God. This honest admission of shared responsibility in sin, but with hope and faith in the grace of God, which brings wonders and new creation, is the starting point of an emerging Asian women's spirituality that motivates their actions and reflections. Aggravating the situation is the division and misunderstanding among women because of differences in perception regarding oppression. In fact, in Asia there is a real oppression of women by other women, evident in the caste system and in the practice of having domestic servants.

It is these complex and varied forms of oppression that Asian women are struggling against, and in the process of the struggle they are giving birth to a spirituality that is particularly woman's and specifically Asian.

FRAMEWORK AND NATURE OF ASIAN WOMEN'S SPIRITUALITY

External and internal exploitation and oppression in the sphere of politics and economics do not exclude women. On the contrary, in their powerlessness they are more severely victimized than their male partners in their particular class, race, and caste. This is the result of patriarchal domination. Women's oppression comes in different combinations of political, economic, and religio-cultural oppressions within the underlying patriarchal domination.

Therefore, in Third World countries, dealing only with women's issues cannot uproot all the problems women face in their societies. It is obvious that the emerging Asian women's spirituality longs for freedom and exploitation—a free society for themselves as well as for the men and children. The liberation framework of Asian women includes, and is included in, the overall people's movement to be free. It brings a qualitatively different vision and interpersonal relationship from the traditional male ways of constructing communities.

In the Philippines, women are involved in national liberation struggles; they were alongside the men in the anti-Marcos-dictatorial-regime movement. Filipino women are still committed to the struggle of the people in the economic, political, and cultural movements of liberation, which have not ceased even after the February 1986 event. They see this struggle toward societal transformation as a necessary though not sufficient condition for their own liberation. As they go through the crucible of suffering, they experience significant changes in their understanding and practice of religion and in the manifestation of their religiosity. We see that the spirit of protest against domination, whether it be the social, political, economic, ecclesial, or domestic order, has correlation with the spirituality of the Asian women's overall struggle for liberation. The general tendency of this spirituality is the search for human dignity and self-determination toward holistic liberation.

The February 1986 event in the Philippines—the demonstration of people power that negated the dictatorial oppression of Ferdinand Marcos—has not solved the basic problems of the country. There is still the unequal distribution of land and capital, with 2 percent of the population owning and controlling 70 percent of the resources; and the Philippines continues to be exploited by the United States through the International Monetary Fund/World Bank and the transnational corporations. Thus massive poverty is still widespread, and prostitution remains a very big problem.

As the women take up the prostitution issue in the Philippines and in other countries like Thailand, Korea, India, and Sri Lanka, they are dealing with the question of the human dignity and self-determination of these innumerable victims who are pushed into the degrading situation by force of circumstance. And they are fully aware that the problems are structural and systemic. Asian people everywhere are coming to this realization and various types of protest movements are occurring. They are protesting against the control of the big powers and their own exploitation, which deprives them of their right to self-determination and human dignity. A few examples are Korea, India, and Sri Lanka.

Let us turn to Korea. The division of the country was decided by the superpowers at the end of World War II. This decision was imposed on the Korean people by the two competing ideologies that exist in today's world. Did Koreans have the time or the opportunity to make their own choice? See what has happened there ever since.

These two tiny countries are used as buffer zones by the two ideological powers and are the frontline of their warfare. The Korean War in 1950–53 was an example. At the expense of millions of lives, and grave human and economic casualties, the war gained nothing but deep-rooted enmity and increasing militarism. It is said that the two Koreas now rank as fifth and sixth in military might in the world, with nuclear weapons in stock to be used at any time.

The intellectuals and workers in South Korea see clearly the foreign and local exploitation that accompanies political oppression. The protest demonstrations have continued ever since student power toppled the American-backed dictatorial regime in 1960. Thousands of students have been tortured and imprisoned. What do they want, risking so much? They want to have a truly independent and unified democratic country where the rights of the people for self-determination, and their participation in building a political and economic system for the people and of the people, will be a reality and not mere lip-service.

If Koreans are protesting against the arbitrary division of the nation and its consequences, in the Indian subcontinent the protest is against the colonial policy or the arbitrary bringing together of different ethnic, linguistic, and religious groups to form a nation. The communal conflict in Sri Lanka and India has this factor. Of course, other factors such as the discriminatory economic and educational policies of the two governments are also responsible. The struggle of the Tamils in Sri Lanka, the Punjabs in India, the ethnic minorities in Japan—all have the same spiritual traits. They all want equal and just treatment and a full share of human dignity. And in all these, the women are the most affected and are therefore correspondingly militant in the struggle for the liberation of their people.

In an atelier of Japanese women artists, Tomiyama Daeko has a large picture depicting her eschatological vision. As in Isaiah, babies are playing with wild beasts, and flowers and plants are all around, growing in peace. In the center is a house in which a woman is giving birth to a child.

For Ms. Tomiyama, female sexuality is sacred. It is in the center of the universe. For her, depicting it in a meaningful way is important so that it does not become pornographic. It is reminiscent of the fertility cult of ancient times where birthing was the center of worship, and goddesses and priestesses were the free expressions of matriarchal ideology.

Modern-day feminist theologians give new interpretations to female sexuality. For example, Phyllis Trible explores the original Hebrew meaning of the word "womb" and associates it with compassionate spirituality.[3] Carol Ochs develops the spirituality of women in their motherhood function.[4] Dorothee Sölle emphasizes the life-giving aspect of women to choose life amid the nuclear devastation threatening today's world.[5]

The experience of motherhood must be incorporated in the process of marching toward a new society, which feminist women and men envision. The nature of this new society is feminist. Feminism promotes the equality of all human beings, and the ideology is derived from the experiences of women giving birth, and caring, and nurturing their children and family to the extent of denying themselves in the highest spirituality of love. The women do this in order to give life and to provide for others so that all may live. Here the self and the community are one. The extreme individualism we see in the Western societies cannot have its way.

However, there can be a danger of condoning the traditional self-effacing masochism of women reinforced in the glorification of motherhood, keeping them in the depth of despair and resignation. This is so if motherhood is used for exploitation, by an individual man, of one or more women where nothing is questioned and no meaning is given. However, when conscientized women and men act and live out this supreme spirituality toward the goal of a new heaven and new earth in concrete models, it is liberational.

A woman worker in Korea, Soon Ock Lee (pseudonym) was trained in the urban and rural mission program when she worked for a textile company in Seoul. She organized a workers' union and faced police violence. After a year in prison, her name was put on the list of people not to be hired by any other company. She had to struggle for survival. After several desperate attempts for a job she was hired by a bus company as a ticket girl, using her relative's identity card. It was a very tough job.

About seventy girls working for the company lived in a longhouse, which was fenced with barbed wire to prevent any of them from running away. They were awakened at 4 A.M. to get ready to go to work at 5 A.M. The day's work was tiring and heavy. They had to swallow insulting words from customers and had to face occasional bodily search on suspicion of embezzling bus fares. When they returned to the house after 11 P.M., everybody was tired and cross. They had to queue up for the shower. There was only one running-water faucet. They had to sleep in indescribable conditions.

Soon Ock hated the whole situation. But eventually she thought of the reasons why the girls were the way they were and decided to help them. When everybody went to sleep she collected all the handkerchiefs and socks, which were thrown about everywhere in the room. She washed all of them and tidied them when they were dry. For the first couple of days, the girls did not notice, but eventually they began to appreciate and trust Soon Ock. When she won their confidence, she organized a strike to demand better working conditions, humane treatment, and overtime pay (which was not provided for). She booked a motel room, which was several miles away from the house. She woke up all the girls one night and took them out of the house and to her motel room. The next morning, the bus company found no ticket girls. The authorities started to investigate. Soon the police were mobilized in the vicinity of the motel, but the girls refused to come out for three days, until their demand was considered. The girls' working conditions improved a bit, but Soon Ock was again dismissed and her name continued to be on the list.

In this story we see a similarity to the Exodus-event. The women, coming from different situations, the mother, the sister, the midwives, and the Pharaoh's daughter, all acted in saving and preserving a life, which became the mighty undercurrent of the historical liberation of the exploited and oppressed

Hebrew people. Soon Ock's action for justice was motivated by the love of neighbor. Her sacrificial act of protest against injustice and dehumanization of her sister workers made them experience a glimpse of liberation and solidarity of sisterhood. The individuality of Soon Ock is unified with the collective destiny of her colleagues, culminating in a perfect unity of love and justice, self-assertion and service for others, a quality of spirituality blended with spontaneous actions, where the material concerns became transformed into purified spirituality.

As women, we experience regular and everyday discrimination: the limiting experiences of housewives confined to the home, as society assigns them, the despair of the wives who are beaten but who cannot separate from their husbands "because of the children" or because of social disapproval or because of their own emotional and psychological dependence on their husbands. We defy the exploitation and discrimination and sexual harassment of our sisters who work either in the rural areas as an invisible contribution to agricultural production or in the urban setting as factory workers. We defy the continuous insult to our womanhood in the mass media and advertisements and the more blatant exploitation of our sisters through prostitution, mail-order brides, and so forth.

But aside from these regular, day-to-day experiences, we have our own private hell, which we experience at crisis points of our lives as women and to which each one of us could relate with poignancy and anguish and from which we emerge either triumphantly with inner liberation or with bitterness and resentment, crushed and mortally wounded in the depth of our being.

A Filipino prostitute, who was a guest in an alternative tourism seminar, is still struggling to find meaning in her life of prostitution that began when she lost her virginity at the age of fifteen to get money to pay the hospital bills of her tubercular mother. She struggles with the hate that wells up within her as she tells of how a policeman, Mang Apeng, threatened to arrest her and her American companion. After being paid 150 pesos (approximately $7) by the American, Mang Apeng still waited for her at the hotel to rob her of the 200 pesos that she earned after the exhausting and degrading evening with her companion. In despair, she shared with us the fact that she is two months pregnant, and exclaimed, "Lord, forgive me, I have to abort it if I have to continue earning my living."

We feel there is a growing awareness among Asian women of the ramifications of the women's question. The personal and social experiences of women as well as their common struggle have shaped the particular form of spirituality that is emerging among them. This spirituality is nourished by their growing understanding of their self-image, which has been obscured by the roles that have been assigned to them by patriarchal society. It in turn influences not only their interpersonal relationships with the significant people in their lives, like their husbands, but also their relationship with men in general. This also forms the collective consciousness that is growing among women as they struggle against the exploitation and discrimination against them, and as they experience the triumph and victory they have achieved in this struggle. It is therefore not just a vertical relationship with God but an integral spirituality that is shaped by prayer and also by relational experiences and struggle—personal, interpersonal, and societal.

The emerging spirituality of women is characterized by an inner liberation from the internal and external slaveries they have struggled to break. Militant women are one in the experience of this sense of liberation coming from their development in self-knowledge and self-acceptance and in their growth in self-esteem.

Christian women involved in national struggles have begun questioning the traditional teachings of the church, especially those that justify the subordination of women. They are slowly getting a clearer self-image and are experiencing a process of inner liberation from the abiding guilt feelings induced by religious doctrines and ethical teachings of the church. Women are less and less inclined to pattern their life after the impossible model of virgin-mother of the domesticating Mary-cult imposed by foreign missionaries. They are questioning the interpretation of St. Paul's "wives, obey your husbands" when it comes to the use of their body in the frequency of pregnancy or in submitting to their husbands everytime the latter claim their marital rights. Although the Catholic church has never budged from its insistence on the natural method of birth control, about 90 percent[6] of Catholic Filipino women quietly contravene this Catholic position and use other forms of contraceptives. Not a few have had themselves ligated after the birth of their third or fourth child.

Among middle-class women, who more than their lower-class sisters are devastated by broken relationships with men, there has been an acceptance of single parenthood. Women are learning to face life alone, conquering their emotional and psychological dependency, finding a meaning in life apart from their estranged male partners. The growing organization of women among the urban poor and in labor unions has resulted in a sense of sisterly solidarity that strengthens the women in their struggle against the discrimination and oppression they experience both in their homes and in their work places.

INTERFAITH DIALOGUE AND ASIAN WOMEN

Interfaith dialogue is an important part of the discussion of the emerging Asian women's spirituality. Ecumenical spirituality seeks unity of humankind in humility and reverence toward all life and all belief systems. Christian triumphalism, which is the spirituality of colonialism and neocolonialism, is judged here. A Hindu has this to say regarding Christian missionary endeavor:

Look at what Christian civilization has done to the life in the world. There is merciless exploitation of natural and human resources, which has brought ecological crisis and suffering and the misery of millions of workers and peasants in Asia. There is the nuclear threat, which can annihilate more than twenty times over the total life on the planet. And still you want to make us Christians?[7]

How are we going to face this accusation of non-Christians who are seriously concerned with the well-being of all humanity? As Christian women, can we condone all the structural and systemic evils Christian civilization has brought, and concentrate only on securing privileged posts in a rotten structure? While it is important to fight for power positions when one is discriminated against for being a woman, it is as important to be committed to bringing about radically new values that are people-oriented, concerned for life and for a truly humane community. This goal is a double task for a better society with women leaders. But if we women claim to be the hope, we must carry out this task. There is no easy way out. The story of Esther has a profound message. Esther went through a highly competitive screening test, but she hid her identity until it was time to reveal it. She used strategic actions, all carefully planned in order to save her people from imminent schemes of peril. Her action was founded on total commitment. She said: "If I must perish, I must perish!" (Esther 4:17). She was ready to give her own life for the many; Christian women leaders must be accountable for the faith of their sisters and brothers. For this, a consciousness-raising education that would awaken the awareness of Christian women to this task is of utmost importance.

This search for the wholeness of life that is the core of the emerging women's spirituality is further underlined in the statement of the Urban and Rural Mission of the Christian Conference of Asia on the occasion of the Bhopal, India, tragedy in 1986:

Christian: Biblical faith, spirituality and religion have centered on liberation/salvation. Salvation means wholeness . . . meaning whole, entire, complete or uninjured, unimpaired, unbroken. . . . Wholeness suggests all that the Hebrew word *Shalom* conveys. *Shalom* is a comprehensive word for prosperity and well-being, peace, harmony, happiness of the people of God in [God's] presence and company. SHALOM.

Buddhist: The key word for the affirmation of wholeness of life is to walk on. When one is a weakling, one is afraid of death and suffering and cannot walk on. Once we understand the Dharma, then we can adjust our inner condition to have a detached view of the world, less greed, hatred and delusion.

Islam: All creation and humankind is one single whole, living through genesis, leading to the perfection of the person, i.e., the complete expression of one's creativity in terms of reaching towards two essential arms (*a*) the relation between person and environment, and (*b*) the relation between person and God, i.e., the inner being.

Hindu: That which holds is Dharma, i.e., the order. It is a totality, a holistic point of view towards life. . . . It is a question of an order, a complete, total view of things in which things have to fall in place. . . . When we talk of the so-called Hindu, in fact, we are talking of civilization and not of religion or faith.

This statement represents the common views of these four major religions in Asia as they seek the holistic salvation of humanity. However, knowing that deep-rooted misogynous ideologies and practices are the reality in all the existing major religions and cultures in Asia, one cannot help but raise a burning question. No matter how beautiful the idea of wholeness might be, can a patriarchal culture be inclusive of women's aspirations?

What Elisabeth Schüssler Fiorenza says about feminist suspicion in hermeneutics[8] is echoed by Asian women as we open our eyes to the reality of discrimination against women in the name of respect for the traditional culture and religions. Women find themselves very often excluded even by the ideology of wholeness and holistic salvation. It is because patriarchy can never be holistic. Patriarchy is basically androcentric, and it can never include women and children in the center of its world as equals. Even love for women and children is for men's own selfish needs. That is the reason why women and children are put perpetually on the periphery even if mechanisms of make-believe are woven into their emotional and financial dependency.

In the coming reign of God, Christ will put children in the center (Mt. 19:13–15). In Jesus' life and mission of counterculture, he befriended all the downtrodden, including women. If a growing people's movement all over Asia is a sign of our times, demands made in the various women's movements are the torch lighting the way toward the true wholeness of life.

Having pointed out the need for feminist critics, what do we do with our traditional culture? On the one hand, the women of Asia are rediscovering their history and are resurrecting their women leaders, heroines, and saints of their particular tradition as sources of cooperation and strength for their struggle. The Filipinos enshrine Princess Urduja and Gabriela Silang, the Indians Mira Bai, Panditta Rama Bai, and so forth. Realizing that the Bible, in spite of all reinterpretations, remains a book written in a particular society, and fully aware of a necessary cultural critique, Asian women are delving into their own traditions, myths, and legends to provide them with the insights, values, and inspiration in their effort toward the full flowering of their womanhood. On the other hand, there is also need for women to undertake a critique of culture. They must actively participate in the interfaith dialogue to give feminist input, sorting out what are the really liberating elements and what are the oppressive elements in them. This kind of cultural analysis in the search for an alternative culture from the feminist perspective is another aspect of the emerging spirituality.

CONCLUSION

From the foregoing reflection we can glean the characteristics of the emerging spirituality we have appropriated as "feminist." In this spirituality, God is one who unites—not one who divides people by creedal dogmas. This spirituality discloses a very liberating portrait of Jesus. The image of the human being transcends the dualistic body-and-soul relationship and has an optimistic view of the possibilities of personhood. Faith is not a security in being saved because of legalistic obedience but is an exciting dimension of radical openness. Salvation has a communal historical and cosmic dimension and is integral and total. The emerging spirituality is active rather than passive, expansive rather than limiting. It celebrates rather than fasts, it surrenders rather than controls. It is an Easter rather than a Good Friday spirituality. It is creative rather than conservative.

Our understanding of salvation that emerges is one worked out by a God of history with the people, and results in a liberation that is total and concrete: total in the sense of the whole person being saved, body and soul, in the context of a social milieu; and concrete in the sense of being a liberation from concrete evils such as slavery, as well as bringing about concrete blessings like land. Throughout salvation history, this was the experience of the people of God. The emerging spirituality of women shows the characteristics of the original meaning of salvation, namely, its totality and concreteness. The release of women's creative energy and new insights have resulted in a refocusing of the different elements of spirituality, which tend to converge in a certain trend that draws its vitality from creation as contrasted with the traditional spirituality that focuses on the fall and redemption.

Spirituality is a process. It is not achieved once and for all. It does not become congealed. It is not even a smooth, continuous growth. There can be retrogression or quantum leaps. It has peaks and abysses. It has its agonies and its ecstasies. The emerging spirituality of women promises to be vibrant, liberating, and colorful. Its direction and tendencies seem to open up to greater possibilities of life and freedom, and therefore to more and more opportunities to be truly, intensely, and wholly alive!

NOTES

1. Donald Dorr, *Spirituality and Justice* (Maryknoll, N.Y.: Orbis Books, 1984), p. 20.

2. In a conversation Sun Ai Park had with Gustavo Gutiérrez when she visited him in his parish house in Lima, Peru, in 1980.

3. Phyllis Trible, *God and the Rhetoric of Sexuality* (Philadelphia, Pa.: Fortress Press, 1978).

4. Carol Ochs, *Women and Spirituality* (Totowa, N.J.: Rowman & Allanheld, 1983).

5. Dorothee Sölle, *Choosing Life* (London: SCM Press, 1981).

6. As reported in a random study made in a women's studies course in a leading women's college in the Philippines.

7. From a conversation Sun Ai Park had with Dr. Stanley Samartha when he was in Singapore to prepare an Interfaith Dialogue Consultation in 1986.

8. Elisabeth Schüssler Fiorenza, "The Will to Choose or to Reject: Continuing Our Critical Work," *Feminist Interpretation of the Bible,* ed. Letty Russell (Philadelphia, Pa.: Westminster Press, 1985), p. 130.

9

New Ways of Being Church

I. A Catholic Perspective

Christine Tse (Hong Kong)

INTRODUCTION

When I accepted the invitation to present this paper here in Oaxtepec I was fully aware that I am not a trained theologian in the academic sense of the word. I am more qualified, perhaps, as one who is involved and concerned with developing a process of theologizing in Hong Kong and, to a certain extent, in the countries of Asia, which I frequently visit.

Since I am to speak for Asia, my first response was to interview people who are in touch with and have knowledge about women in Asian countries. My desire to begin with the experience of Asian women was greatly enhanced by the country reports presented at the Seventh Asian Meeting of Religious (AMOR VII) in Korea in 1985. These reports were given by women religious from Japan, Korea, Taiwan, Hong Kong, Thailand, Philippines, Indonesia, Sri Lanka, Bangladesh, India, and Pakistan, in consultation with religious in their own countries. So the reports can be seen as fairly representative of the views of the religious in their respective countries. In the background, there is also my involvement in EATWOT's national and Asian theological meetings.

Having said this, however, it is important to remember that religious women are but a minority of the women of Asia. They are not representative of women in Asia as a whole, except insofar as they are part of the women in the church. Religious women, in fact, have a closer working relationship to the institutional church in administering its religious institutes than to grassroots communities.

My approach is similar to a community model of theological reflection presented by a Catholic feminist theologian, Dr. Mary Hunt, whose course I attended in New York in the summer of 1986. According to Mary Hunt, "theology emerges basically from people's sharing of their work, their faith and their lives." She defined the process of theologizing as the "organic and communal sharing of insights, stories and reflections on questions of ultimate meaning and value." This process is what the meetings of AMOR are promoting and is the basis of the reports I have been using for my own discussion here.

KINDS OF PARTICIPATION OF WOMEN IN THE CHURCH

Women have always participated in the activities of the church. Research has shown that the early Christian movement included women's leadership and could therefore be called "equalitarian." Elisabeth Fiorenza found that women played a very important role in the history of the church by participating in and influencing the spread of Christianity. She thought that Galilean women were decisive not only for the extension of the Jesus movement to Gentiles but also for the very continuation of this movement after Jesus' arrest and execution.[1]

Nowadays, the presence and coordination of a great number of women religious and committed lay women, both single and married, who are working at various levels of church activities, have become essential to the vitality of the Asian church. According to the reports presented at AMOR VII, women religious are active in pastoral work such as teaching catechism, family visits, hospital ministry, and assistance to parish groups and activities. They are respected by the laity as well as needed by the priests in the parishes. Therefore we cannot ignore their participation in, and contribution to, the church in Asia.

In the area of formal education, it is invariably true that lay women and women religious have played a leading role in running Catholic nurseries, health activities, primary and secondary schools, and colleges. Not only do sisters head these educational institutions, they also supervise and train leaders through them. These leaders become a driving force in the church. One modern criticism is that these institutions catered to the elite and didn't change their values. Did we really educate with leadership as a goal?

At the same time, relatively few reports have mentioned the involvement of women religious in justice and peace activities, which have become an important development in Asia. There may be several reasons for this: first, most women religious in Asia are still not aware of justice and peace work; second, justice and peace work is done more as part-time work and does not therefore enter the mainstream of activities mentioned above; and third, justice and peace work is more comfortably done outside the church structure to avoid possible confrontation with the hierarchy or the bishops' conferences which might hurt them.

HOW DO ASIAN WOMEN SEE THEMSELVES IN THE CHURCH?

In the AMOR reports, it is commonly seen that women believe that they exert a basic, motivating power, that they are an invisible force that continually sustains the life of the Christian community. There is a marked divergence in how they feel about their participation in the church. Some are rather happy because their contribution is much valued within the church; they see this as a step forward from the dependent position that has been traditionally allocated to women. In all Asian culture, except a relatively few tribal matriarchal cultures, there is the stereotypical female who is expected to be silent, passive, and submissive in the patriarchal family and religious system.

Women do not take part in basic policy decisions; their decision-making power is limited to the practical implementation of plans. Women religious are feeling, in various degrees, that their role is secondary in a male-dominated church where the hierarchy assumes the right to decide the role of sisters in the church, their suitability for sacramental ministry, the dress they wear, and the organization of their community life. This is even more true for local religious congregations.

In several dioceses within some Asian countries trends are emerging toward greater collaboration between sisters and priests in different fields of ministry. However, some can question whether the inclusion of women in ministries is just a form of tokenism or is a real step beyond the narrow cultural and social barriers, enabling the women and the priests to work as partners in a team-spirit. For example, the permission given to some lay women and women religious to distribute Holy Communion can be just a means of lessening the burden of some of the parish priests, in the absence of male religious or suitable laymen. It is not necessarily a recognition of women's worth or participation in ministerial work.

PATRIARCHY LEGITIMATES HIERARCHY

What has happened to cause and strengthen the patriarchal structure in the church today?

The origin of patriarchy in the church is believed to be related to the apologetic writings of the post-Pauline and Petrine periods which sought to limit women's leadership roles in the Christian community to merely supplementary roles. This ignored the attitude of the evangelists John and Mark, who were both seen to accord women apostolic and ministerial leadership. Susan T. Foh has a more detailed interpretation of Paul, which I am not going to elaborate here. Paul seems to contradict himself when, in Galatians 3:28, he says, "There is no such thing as Jew and Greek, slave and freeman, male and female, for you are one person in Christ," for in other of his epistles he legitimizes submission of women by adapting it to the Greco-Roman patriarchal structure.[2]

Augustine of Hippo (fourth century) promoted the idea that woman is created to help man, on the assumption that Eve's body is made from the side of Adam, even though the formation of both of their bodies flows from a divine act. In other words, the person of Eve takes her existence from the person of Adam, since she depends on him for the matter of her body.

Augustine's theory on the formation of Eve from the side of Adam establishes a relation that has served as rule for the relationship of man and woman in general. For Augustine, the ideal society demanded a harmonious order established by a hierarchical relationship between a superior and an inferior, and he identified femininity with inferiority, and maleness with superiority. Thomas Aquinas reinforced this in the thirteenth century, and since then the exclusion of women in the hierarchy has been strongly rooted within the church.[3]

Up to today, despite new biblical studies and new interpretations on and about the Christian community as a discipleship of equals (equality in sharing goods did not last long—not for any theological reason but simply because of human nature), the church is still holding a very rigid position regarding the type of ministry women can exercise in the church. This is clearly seen in an exchange of letters between the Vatican and the Anglican Archbishop of Canterbury. The exchange was specifically over the right to change a tradition that has been unbroken throughout the history of the Catholic Church Universal, in the East and in the West.

The Archbishop of Canterbury wrote in a letter to Cardinal Willebrands (Dec. 18, 1985) about a conviction expressed synodically by a number of provinces of the Anglican Communion that "on the Anglican side there has been a growing conviction that there exist in Scripture and Tradition no fundamental objections to the ordination of women to the ministerial priesthood."

Willebrands's reply (June 17, 1986) leads us very much to think about the Augustinian connection. He wrote:

> We can never ignore the fact that Christ is a man. His male identity is an inherent feature of the economy of salvation, revealed in the scriptures and pondered in the Church. The ordination only of men to the priesthood has to be understood in terms of the intimate relationship between Christ the redeemer and those who, in a unique way, cooperate in Christ's redemptive work. The priest represents Christ in his saving relationship with his Body the Church. He does not primarily represent the priesthood of the whole People of God. However unworthy, the priest stands *in persona Christi.*

Of course, let us not forget that earlier Pope John Paul II had already pointed out to the Archbishop of Canterbury in a letter (Dec. 20, 1984) that "In those same years the increase in the number of Anglican Churches which admit, or are preparing to admit, women to priestly ordination constitutes, is in the eyes of the Catholic Church, an increasing obstacle to that progress."

Interestingly enough, the studies of an internationally known psychotherapist[4] show that the very structure of most theological assumptions results in a dominance-submission scheme. In this scheme, power is at the top and total powerlessness is at the bottom.

Ann Wilson Schaef has made studies in numerous workshops conducted with women. She explored how these women see God, and humankind in relation to God; and how male and female relate to each other. The results may be tabulated thus:

GOD	HUMANKIND	MALE	FEMALE
male	childlike	intelligent	emotional
omnipotent	sinful	powerful	weak
omniscient	weak	brave	fearful
omnipresent	stupid or dumb	good	sinful
immortal	mortal	strong	like children
eternal			

These findings led to the conclusion that, in people's minds, Male is to Female what God is to Humankind. The myth of the domination of man over woman is supported by our theology to sustain a hierarchical structure. In this structure, God dominates over men; men dominate over women; women dominate over children; children dominate over animals; and animals dominate over the plants and earth.

THE ASIAN SCENE

To the surprise of our sisters in the West, what they have been saying about male domination in society and in the church is not only true of their sisters in Asia, it is even more cruel in form.

Asia has a long history of its own. This has been continuously enriched by its various and long civilizations, rich cultures and traditions, eventful historical, social, and political changes throughout the centuries. However, among the variety of differences, one common feature that emerges all through Asia is the subjugation of women to men, both at home and in society at large. Matriarchal societies were short-lived, and those rare matriarchal societies that still exist today are to be found mainly in tribal communities.

Our sisters in the West might be shocked even at the thought that some women are still being burned alive in India today for failing to satisfy their husbands with the amount of dowry demanded, that the evidence law in Pakistan (*Diyat* and *Qasas*) virtually reduces a woman to half a human being since the testimony of two women is needed to equal that of one man. *Qasas* debars women from evidence in case of murder, sexual offenses, theft, and drinking; even when the husband is murdered in the presence of his wife, her evidence has no value at all. *Diyat* (blood money) rules that when a woman is murdered, the compensation awarded the unfortunate family of the woman is half that awarded when the murdered person is a man.

Women in China or in countries whose cultures and traditions are influenced by Confucian thought are used to considering themselves virtuous if they accept everything with passivity and quiet resignation. A woman is subservient to her father before she is married, to her husband after marriage, and to her oldest son when she becomes a widow. Education is either denied to girls or given first to boys in the family.

Chinese women in the past had to endure the torturous practice of foot-binding. Muslim women have suffered the inhuman practice of circumcision so that they can never enjoy sex. In general, most women of all religions in Asia, except Christianity, have had to tolerate some forms of legalized polygamy. Even today, many of these cruel treatments of women continue.

It is against this background that Christianity came to the East. Hence the patriarchal structure became even more deep-rooted. Furthermore, since the church is the religious minority in most of the countries in Asia, the church cannot make itself totally free from Islamic influences or Confucian traditions even if it would like to.

THE ROLE AND CONTRIBUTION OF WOMEN IN NEW WAYS OF BEING CHURCH

New ways of being church are *(a)* returning to the spiritual kingdom of Isaiah (11:6–9) wherein different categories of creatures are depicted as living together peacefully: the wolf and the lamb, the calf and the bear, the sucking child and the asp; *(b)* returning to the teaching of Paul, who wants no more division, for "you are one in Christ" (Gal. 3:28); *(c)* returning to the teaching of Vatican II that the church is a mystery, a sacrament of union with God and of union with persons, a people related to God through Christ, an ever new responding in the spirit to the signs of the times (Constitution on the Church in the Modern World, nos. 1, 4); *(d)* returning to the 1971 Synod of Bishops' document, "Justice in the World" (chap. 3), which says: "we also urge that women should have their own share of responsibility and participation in the community life of society and likewise of the church." In new ways of being church, women can make many contributions.

Conscientization

Women have to go through a process to break the mindset that induces them automatically and spontaneously to assume an inferior role to men. Paolo Freire would call this a "culture of silence." In this respect, I am fortunate to have the chance to visit many women's groups in Asia and witness how they are going through this process of conscientization and what kind of efforts they are making.

One of the signs of the times is that Asian women who have been excluded from the full dignity of the human person by Asian culture and by the patriarchal church have awakened to this harsh reality. Asian church women see the biblical and Vatican II messages cited above as a continuous call on them to experience a sense of being church in a new way. They see how the patriarchal structure obstructs the application of equal personhood and equal discipleship in the church.

Conscientization enhances women's efforts to deepen the study of the Scriptures, their ability to name values and recognize their unique contribution to church and society. As Christians, our lives are closely related to the Scripture and to how the church teaches us to live according to the Scriptures. Many Asian women are trying now to reinterpret the Scriptures and are reworking the text with inclusive language and meaning. The way we interpret things and the way we formulate our language definitely have an impact on the way we live, for this is how our consciousness and conviction are developed.

Most of us Asians have experienced how our colonizers governed us during and even after colonization. Though it was primarily a political and military rule during the period of colonization, it was through the acculturation of the middle-class intellectual to the colonizers' mentality that colonization was prolonged even after the colonizers had physically withdrawn. The medium of preservation of the status quo is often the imposition of the colonizers' language, values, and culture.

Inclusiveness as a Model or Key

Women are called to restore inclusiveness, equality, and harmony in the church. They are called to do away with control and the grabbing of power in all human relationships. They are also called not to abandon the church or surrender to apathy; they are called to be confident in the spirit, deepening their experience of the Christ within the church so that the church can be renewed.

Asian women have long suffered oppression from the patriarchal structure. They do not want to counteract this by replacing it with a matriarchal structure, which can be equally oppressive. Instead they are promoting an inclusive structure. This openness and inclusiveness is not only essential for the Asian women's movement but also a key element for the Asian peoples' movement to liberate themselves from oppression of all kinds. Otherwise women might just replace one dictatorship with another form of dictatorship, if they are also exclusive. Change of structures and change of mindset are consonant with the emphasis of the church on the importance of having both internal and external conversions.

Efforts to be inclusive have brought about a good ecumenical exchange between women of different faiths, first among Catholics and Protestants, then among Christian, Hindu, Buddhist, and Muslim women as well. The inclusive approach that feminist theologians propose leads women to be flexible and open. Since they do not have to defend a particular theory or methodology of their own, they can be more sensitive to the needs of others. They can learn more by listening to ideas and approaches that are different from their own. Thus they will also become more understanding and supportive.

Exclusion of women in teaching theology until recent years was partly due to the patriarchal church. Inclusion of women in teaching theology will help to shape the teaching and preaching of the church for alternative experiences within the accepted patriarchal theology. One of the implications of inclusiveness is an expanding ministry for women or the inclusion of women's priesthood. This movement is stronger within the Protestant churches in Asia. Discussions among, and demands from, the Catholic women are relatively weak. One of the reasons for this is that the Vatican is very strong in its desire to maintain an exclusive and male-dominated hierarchy. Another reason is that women religious cannot make statements on such a serious matter without the approval of their religious congregation, which is subject to Vatican scrutiny. And because many women are as traditional as men, they themselves are not changing so far, sometimes even hindering other women from changing.

The Protestant women who have been ordained as pastors have often had the negative experience of being looked upon as substitutes for men, rather than being regarded as equal and independent. In fact, it is common that the community of Christian leaders will not easily approve a woman candidate who requests to be ordained if she is intending to get married, whereas marriage is greatly favored for male pastors. Protestant women have complained that although more and more women study in schools of theology, by and large these schools adopt a discriminatory approach in education: for men, the training is mostly in preparation for ordination as ministers, but for women the focus is on how to be the pastor's wife or a lay teacher in the parish. To be inclusive is to see ministry as flowing from gifts rather than as based on gender.

Team Ministry

The recent attempts within the Catholic Church in Asia to team up both priests and women for spiritual direction (counseling, retreat work, etc.) have produced new and very positive experiences. Traditionally, spiritual direction is an exclusive right of the male clergy, which, according to some feminist theologians, can be used as a means to control women and the laity in order to maintain the superiority of the celibate male clergy in the church.

So far, this kind of team spiritual direction has been well received in Asia. Priests who are working as co-partners on the team or priests who favor such spiritual direction have remarked with enthusiasm about how they have been enriched by the cooperation of women. Priests have appreciated women's capacity to enhance a warm and loving human relationship, and their ability to relate to a God who is personal and human as opposed to an abstract God. In fact, members of the church—even males—are now beginning seriously to question the patriarchal system and its negative effects on them. They recognize that women can help to restore such values as friendship and intimacy to the church. These values have been largely discouraged by the church culture throughout history, but they are values that modern psychologists confirm as essential to human existence.

In the same way, women can play roles in the parish team and other arenas for action. Women can contribute in curriculum development. They can help write and select the texts for catechetics and schools, pointing out how sex-stereotyping of male-female roles is fostered in the texts and pictures.

Action for Justice

As one who has been involved full-time in justice and peace work for a number of years in Asia, I have the conviction that this is an area where women must open their eyes to discover new ways of being church.

Action for justice has been termed a constitutive dimension of preaching the gospel by the Synod of Bishops' document "Justice in the World." Asian women's experiences allow them to see the effects of working for justice, a concern that the Asian churches have gradually incorporated into their pastoral works.

Through actual exposures to Asia's realities, through training, analysis, and reflection, Asian people begin to see more easily why they are poor and oppressed. They also see why Asia is kept poor and underdeveloped, why militarism has such a strong hold in their countries, and why there is such a violation of human rights. Theological reflections urge Asian people to come up with a Christian response toward this situation.

Asian women are "holding up half of the sky." If they are moved to action arising from this consciousness, Asian societies are bound to change in a positive direction. And women have the power to change societies if they introduce the concept of justice wherever they are present. Women are the frequent churchgoers; they are seen more frequently attending church activities and activities related to their own community of slums, villages, housing estates, and so on; they are the ones taking care of the children at home. Therefore their influence in these areas can be very substantial and penetrating if they have a conviction that things can be changed for the better and if they work toward it.

I would like to emphasize here that women from all walks of life, all levels of intelligence, and differing experience can contribute equally, though in different ways, to the same goal. Some studies on the level of political involvement of women in Hong Kong show that housewives who are living in the crowded, low-cost government-housing estates are frequently and actively involved in matters concerning their community. Their actions are very political on a local level. On the other hand, middle-class intellectual women are not so actively involved in local or community politics, as their common felt needs are not so great. They can live more or less independently in private houses, although sometimes they are geared to politics on the macro level.

Due to the cultural and religious background, and due to Asia's semifeudal system, Asian people and especially women are generally apathetic toward anything political. However, Asian women are now getting involved in political actions that will improve their lives. This is a trend that will grow and will have far-reaching consequences. Asians are beginning to realize that to do nothing is to give their silent consent to the oppressors to continue doing harm to them.

Women can change the Asian church and the society along with it if they work to bring justice and peace education to their families. Asian children are too long under the patriarchal tutelage. They will grow up dominating others as they have learned from their "fathers," the patriarchy, and they will accept domination without challenging it. If Asian women gain social consciousness, they can help to create the same process in the family, in the community, and in the church, where members are invited to express their views freely, to share their problems and find the solutions together. This process demands creative criticism, openness, inclusiveness, acceptance, and democracy—and these are what our church and society need today.

DEMYTHOLOGIZING THE PATRIARCHAL STRUCTURE

The fate of Asian women today reflects the impact of the patriarchal structure, which many Asian female theologians have identified. Within this patriarchal structure, all the positions in the hierarchy (popes, bishops, priests, deacons) are occupied exclusively by a minority of celibate males who either are not aware of women's life and experience or are not open to face the need of change in the patriarchal structure, or both.

Biblical scholars and theologians are questioning whether the patriarchal structure of church and the antiwoman attitude were intended by Jesus when he began to preach and establish the kingdom on earth, or whether these developments are only historically conditioned. In Mark 10:29-30, commenting on Jesus' answer to Peter's question, "Who then can be saved?" Elisabeth Fiorenza says that, in the answer of Jesus, "fathers" are among those to be left behind; "fathers" are not included in the new kinship to which the disciples aspire. For Fiorenza and for many Asian women, this is an implicit rejection of the power and status of the "fathers" and all patriarchal structures in the messianic community. Therefore this rejection gives rise to what Fiorenza terms "the discipleship of equals."[5]

In Mark 3:33-35 Jesus proposes the new structure for the messianic community. In this community, the old way of relationships of "mothers," "brothers," and so forth is to be replaced by a new principle, that of doing the will of God. Christ wants us to be free and to enjoy the freedom of being children of God; we need to take Christ's words seriously.

In principle, as Christians we all believe in the resurrection of Christ, because it is an important proof that Christ is divine. If so, we should also believe that "when the dead rise to life, they will be like the angels in heaven" (Mt. 22:30). In other words, the Christ who rose from the dead is no longer conditioned by sex, race, or nationality. Christ becomes all for all. Everyone in the messianic community becomes a disciple among equals.

Logically therefore, it is no wonder that feminist theologians call it a great scandal to see that, beginning with the early church and continuing to the church of today, the institutional church has not obeyed the command of Jesus to "call no one father." Asian women are just beginning to get involved in reinterpreting the Bible to find its deepest salvific and liberating significance for humanity as a whole. One important step is to demythologize the existing patriarchal structure with all its implications.

NOTES

1. Elisabeth Schüssler Fiorenza, *In Memory of Her* (New York: Crossroad Publishing Co., 1983).

2. Susan T. Foh, *Women and the Word of God, a Response to Biblical Feminism,* (Presbyterian and Reformed Publishing Co., 1979).

3. Kari Elisabeth Borresen, *Subordination and Equivalence: The Nature and Role of Women in St. Augustine and Aquinas* (Lanham, Md.: University Press of America, 1981).

4. Ann Wilson Schaef, *Women's Reality: An Emerging Female System in the White Male Society* (Minneapolis: Winston Press, 1985).

5. Elisabeth Schüssler Fiorenza, *In Memory of Her.*

II. A Protestant Perspective

Yong Ting Jin (Malaysia)

THEOLOGICAL REFLECTIONS ON WOMEN IN THE CHURCH

At the Asian Women's Consultation on Total Liberation from the Perspective of Asian Women, held in Manila (Nov. 21-30, 1985), varied expressions were given to reflect theologically on women in society, and church in particular, as found in the statement below:

> Oppression of women is SINFUL. This systemic sin is rooted in organized and established economic, political, and cultural structures with PATRIARCHY as an overarching and all-pervading reality that oppresses women.
>
> As church people, we have come to realize that the highly patriarchal churches have definitely contributed to the subjugation and marginalization of women. Thus we see an urgent need to reexamine our church structures, traditions, and practices in order to remedy injustices and to correct misinterpretations and distortions that have crippled us.[1]

Such is the existing reality of the church! Apparently the church has become an institution, with all its goods, services, laws, doctrines, liturgies, rites, ministries, structures, and traditions. The entire mechanism developed gradually, resulting in a pyramidal hierarchy. This form of domination is typical of the patriarchal system, pervading all spheres of life. Particularly in the arena of church politics, the power game ranks high, breeding corruption, cultivating and securing superiority, exhibiting abuses of power for political motives and vested interests. Yet this is the leadership model we are given to follow. The image and marks of the church as *ecclesia* are scarred.

Leonardo Boff[2] made a most provocative critique of the Roman Catholic Church and the ways in which power, sacred power, is manipulated and abused. This is in no way any less true of the Protestant church. His contention was that since the fourth century the church has become prey to the forces, the dynamics, of power, which have nothing to do with the power of the gospel. Again, this historical reality is confirmed repeatedly in our experiences of the institutional church today.

These are the old ways of being church—full of distortions, plagued by corruption and high-powered lip service, glaringly unjust practices. Even the so-called renewed community of the supposedly progressive ecumenical movement of men and women is not spared from this critique, as long as we too fall prey to tendencies and practices of the "old"!

The church has lost its real essence, meaning, and effects. Though there have been serious attempts and prolific theological reflections/writings to redefine the meaning of *ecclesia,* it remains an important priority for us to return yet again to an understanding of the church as *ecclesia* and faith community.

While confirming the effects of the present realities of the church and the hurts upon our lives and those of other women, the participants at the Manila Consultation experienced yet again the liberating gospel and spirit of Christ. By Jesus' breakthroughs with a tradition that would diminish one-half of humanity, we felt affirmed and empowered to persevere in our painful struggle for full humanity. Jesus demonstrated this full humanity by his own life; and the teaching of God's kingdom was one with his deeds.

In the light of the gospel truth, Jesus is GOOD NEWS to all women! We have every reason to rejoice, to be hopeful, and to order our lives after the model of the New Creation in Jesus Christ.

WOMEN AND NEW WAYS OF BEING CHURCH

The original Greek meaning of *ekklesia* (a gathering; church) refers to a gathering of people belonging to a community. It has a common history, founded on an event and sharing a common experience. In a theological sense, the *ekklesia* history began when a few women acted together by paying respect to their dead friend Jesus at the tomb on the Sabbath day, during which they were forbidden to do any work. Already they were doing something "new" and profound, though it was treated as an insignificant, small job! And later, as enlightened first witnesses to the (cross-) resurrection-event and a new personal experience of Jesus the risen Christ, their "storytelling" of the Good News was ridiculed and passed over as unsound. Yet this was how the *ecclesia* emerged. It was a new birth with a new identity.

Swept by the unique experience of the Spirit and its charisms at the Pentecost, the faithful believers of men and women were moved to assemble in one place, celebrating and sharing their resources and life in common. Daily they deepened their faith by examining the Scriptures and breaking bread. Care, love, and concern for one another prevailed and increased in the community— a distinctive *koinonia* indeed. The Spirit led and shaped the faith community. It bore a new, distinguishing mark and vision patterned after the life and mission of Jesus. In building up a community, the believers grew in character, individually and corporately—one and all responding to and professing the power of the gospel in the living out of their life together.

We can find, as conceived in the New Testament writings, a host of theological thinking, terms, and expressions used and described to put new meaning and content into this gathering of faithful women and men. Looking at the epistles of Peter and Paul, the *ecclesia* is characterized as the "people of God," the "body of Christ."

In fact, the term "people of God" has its deep historical roots tracing back to Old Testament times. Related to its cultural and sociological terms, the "people of God" also refers to a chosen race, a royal priesthood, a holy nation. In 1 Peter 2:5-10, they are a community called to proclaim God's saving act for all humanity.

Paul described *ecclesia* with reference to the "body of Christ" as a corporate unit. A plurality of gifts is evidenced by the members of the body. Each person has a unique and creative role to play as inspired and sustained by the Spirit. Everyone is charismatic, no one is useless. As such, each member has a decisive place in the community, but all serving one another, all having and enjoying equal dignity. There is no room for any part of the body to despise, oppress, or dominate the other: "The eye cannot say to the hand, 'I do not need you,' nor can the head say to the feet, 'I do not need you' " (1 Cor. 12:21). All charisms that God bestows upon each person, man and woman, young and old, must be used and shared in service and humility to the whole community.

Going back to the gospel accounts, one finds that the nature and character of *ecclesia* was initially enacted in Jesus' ministry. The great following of the "Jesus community" was a dynamic presence in the midst of the sociocultural and political setting of Palestine in the time of Jesus. However, the birth of this "Jesus community" came into being when Jesus announced the Good News of God's kingdom (*baseleia*) as the vision of the new creation. Precisely in this context the *ecclesia,* or the then "Jesus community," was understood to be a visible and dynamic sign of the kingdom vision directed toward a holistic transformation of society. This was the most radical new way of being church in the widest ecumenical sense of the word.

When Jesus sought to communicate a vision of the new era, his core message was leveled against the social, cultural, political, and economic situation of the time. In favor of bringing about a total liberation to each human person and to society as a new way of life as well as a new order of society, Jesus spoke in parables. They depict pictures and scenes of life in a community where old and new values are contrasted. The story of the banquet portrays a scene of the sharing community, where an invitation is extended to people from the streets and lanes—poor, blind, and lame—until the house is full! In Jesus' under-standing, a sharing community does not seek to establish its own exclusive social class, as the Pharisees were doing, separate from those we regard as inferior or subordinate. On the contrary, it seeks for inclusiveness as a definite value and way of life, doing away with social division and all forms of discrimination.

The story of the meal, and how people rush for positions of honor and power, is also far from the way of life in a community. Instead, humility—a lifestyle of servanthood and self-denial, or self-emptying—is needed. Jesus taught that all power and authority must be exercised in deepest humility for the love and service of others. This is something that demands a transcendence of old attitudes and mentality; indeed, a very costly new way to discipleship!

Baseleia is good news for women! Women were the most oppressed and powerless of all, but Jesus associated with them and restored the dignity due them regardless of their social status or stigma. He affirmed the full personhood in women as being created in God's image, a concept that culture and traditions may distort and so cause women to be seen as less than human. Unlike the rabbinic tradition, Jesus taught women openly. Women were among the band of disciples following Jesus because he included women in his teaching and practice of God's kingdom. In historical reality, as the Gospels have it, women were in fact the first in faith, in terms of both their coming to faith and their quality of faith. When Jesus appeared and reached out to them at the tomb, he sent them to carry the Good News of his resurrection to the other disciples. Thus women must today rediscover their original and distinctive role in the Gospel. Precisely because of the primacy of women's faith, women played a decisive role in the disclosing of God's liberation history, as recounted, in Matthew's and Luke's Gospels, in the birth stories of Jesus.

Women were active participants in all areas of the life and mission of the early Christian communities. They were apostles, teachers, prophetesses, providers, workers, preachers, each according to her potential and God-given talents. Indeed, they were full-time partners alongside men in the Gospel of Christ.

Today, women must become fully aware and take confidence in Christ to rediscover their original and distinctive role in the Gospel. In realizing their potential they ought to reclaim their rightful place in the kingdom and God's New Creation through Jesus Christ. They must receive with faith the salvation of God by grace and begin to experience anew the power of the Gospel, which sets free every person from all forms of bondage and oppression. With this faith and hope, women can, with new minds, assume in new ways the role of leaders, decision-makers, pastors, educators, teachers, prophetesses, peacemakers, theologians, and so forth. Women in the New Creation must set aflame their lives and be followed in the order of faith.

The new ways of being church are modeled and implied, based on the values, characteristics, and qualities of the new as embodied in the person, life, and value system of Jesus. Every person, female and male, is summoned to participate in the building processes of the new. When the new era comes, it cannot leave the old structures and lifestyles intact. The new wine will burst the old wineskins, calling for a new creation (Mk. 2:21–22). Likewise, a piece of new cloth does not match the old one. Behold, the old is passing away, and the new has come!

IMPLICATIONS OF THE WOMAN'S ROLE AND CONTRIBUTION IN THE NEW CREATION

In the light of the new-woman consciousness and of women reclaiming power in their significant role, they are empowered to play a creative role and to make positive contributions in new ways of being church. A host of things come to mind calling for a reconstruction of the old and an innovative creation of the new. The challenge is waged at all levels and dimensions of life. It goes further than the verbal, analytical perspective by expanding frontiers of action as well as involving a fuller integration of both personal and corporate lives together in a human community of women and men.

A New Lifestyle

Being a new woman in the new creation, she has to participate in the new, making it relevant by living out a lifestyle that is Christ-like. Right at the start, when Jesus announced and summoned people to the kingdom and its vision, he called for repentance. Living out the life of the kingdom, therefore, requires continuous repentance and faith in the Good News. It calls for a total change of heart, mind, and spirit—at the personal level as well as at the social, in the structures of the heart no less than in the structures of economics, politics, culture, and all other spheres of life and systems of society. Repentance is required of any new person in Christ, without bias or distinction of race, sex, and class. Here the process of repentance causes one to seek first God's *baseleia* and righteousness. Without constant repentance and search on the personal and the corporate levels, a total transformation of society will not be realized. Therefore, women too need to enter into the process of repentance and search in order to remain responsible agents in the building of a new faith community or church. While submitting herself to the spirit of God in this process, the woman must see herself playing the role of educator and preacher promoting new ways of being church as envisioned by Jesus. This is primary, prior to any concrete actions, role, and contribution.

An Ecumenical Role

The woman's role and contribution in new ways of being church must be approached in the widest ecumenical sense, taking into account the realities of social and religious institutions such as the church, home, and society at large. Today, increasingly, women in the church are addressing themselves to the twin tasks of total transformation in the church and in the society.

A New Exercise of Power

In the institutional church, women are faced with confronting and challenging patriarchal structures and traditions. Alternative models are needed to shape and build up a new faith community of women and men. New meanings and definitions of the leadership, power, and authority concepts must be given. In the biblical sense, Jesus speaks of being a leader and handling power in the most unworldly manner. Jesus rejected and opposed strongly the kind of power, position, status quo, and glory offered by Satan in the story of the three temptations. As a leader, Jesus washed the feet of his friends. This power is the blessing for one to live in love, in peace with justice, in community. This power is never violent or destructive, ego-centered or domineering. This power is understood, motivated, and exercised by one's set of values as patterned after the vision of God's new creation. It serves to foster, enhance, and nurture all of life. This power is dynamic and constructive because it has to do with caring, inclusiveness, peace with justice as against racism, sexism, classism, and militarism.

Today, women having past and present experiences of powerlessness may treat this as a special calling to sing of power in a new key. They are capable of exploring ways to move beyond powerlessness into new visions and meanings of power.

The new exercise of power goes with a new approach to leadership. The old model is hierarchical, bureaucratic, and exclusive. It is also based on a one-man heroic show highly motivated by a spirit of competition and a male-macho image. To be followed in the order of faith, women have to show themselves as leaders different from the male style. In Jesus' words, to be a leader, one must be a servant—a suffering servant. Women are presently practicing and sharing collective leadership. This proves a better alternative as they adopt a creative and cooperative process of decision-making, of mutuality and trust based on consensus.

A New Theological Reflection

In the present total life and mission of the church, women have a vital role to play. They are the renewing force. A primary task may be creating an educational program on a rereading of the Bible from the women's perspective. Thus women's contribution to doing theology from their lived experiences in a relevant context is crucial in the order of faith. This too leads to the formulation of worship, its content and form of liturgies; the use of language and new symbols that are inclusive of all people without distinction of gender, race, and class.

While reaching out to women in the church, some kind of creative and regular dialogue is needed between women and men, and among women themselves. This helps to build up and nurture a new community of women and men who are already engaged in struggle for total human liberation, including the women's struggle against oppression.

Among women theologians and women making theological reflections, the need for a partnership of women and men in contributing to the total life and mission of the church is becoming more recognized. This contribution is essential, particularly in terms of maximizing women's participation in all areas and sharing in all forms of ministries, theological dialogue, and education toward partnership.

The New Faith Community

In the broadest ecumenical view, new ways of being church extends to and embraces all of creation and humanity in the whole inhabited world. The church as a faith and human community is located in the midst of the current global realities. Perhaps women find that their role is more than double as they assume the task of analyzing the situation at all levels—global, regional, and local—by translating the Good News of God's kingdom relevant to the social realities. Women become the prophetic voice as they pose challenges to other women and men to repent and live the new order of life.

The woman's role and contribution goes further than merely engaging at the level of social analysis. In the light of the greater human struggle for total liberation and social transformation, more women are moving to the forefront in the people's movement, in the peace movement, and also in consolidating their own movement.

Women in the new faith community can play a part in enabling other women to participate in women's movements around the world. Concrete concerns of the women's situation in the national or local context should be brought to the attention and care of the faith community. This is an important area of contribution by women for and with other women who are among the poorest and most oppressed of all. It can become a new missionary venture, an evangelization on new frontiers. Women in the faith community then can take a leading role in interpreting the church's mission to women who are oppressed in all sectors of the society. Issues, problems, and concerns may vary from country to country in Asia. However, these may be classified under the following broad categories:

militarization and nuclearization, and their effects on women;
prostitution and exploitation of women's bodies;
exploitation of women workers;
customs, traditions, and religious practices oppressive to women;
racism and racial minorities;
women in politics and people's struggles.

Concerted actions will have to be taken in response to the conditions of women listed above. Women in the church can enter into a joint endeavor with women's organizations already existing in their locality that are working with women of various sectors for consciousness-raising and toward mobilization for change.

A New Pattern of Relationship

The home-and-family tends to be a forgotten place even though it is a basic institution of education within the larger society. However, it is a place where patriarchal attitudes, ideas, and values are reinforced daily in all aspects of family life. Children grow up with stereotyped roles defined for their lives as male and female. The pattern of relationship between man and woman, husband and wife is one of a superior and a subordinate, as perpetuated and accepted by social and cultural conditionings. The home, being a most basic social and educational institution, must be transformed. The woman's role and contribution in new ways of being church should also consider educating the young, especially in the formation of minds and hearts, inculcating new values following the vision of the new order where equality, love, justice, and peace will reign.

The need for creating a new form and pattern of relationship between man and woman, husband and wife must be approached on a more personal level. It may be seen as unimportant, but in order to be fully integrated in the new, the old model and pattern of relationship must also go. New ones must be created. Women together with men will have to break through traditions and cultural practices that keep them in their respective gender roles. This involves a long and painful process. Women will have to help themselves, first of all, to break out of the roles defined for them, the image and the position that restrict them from creativity and freedom. By working through this at the personal level, half the job is already done when men and women enter consciously into an equal and mutual partnership in the total life and mission of the church.

CONCLUSION

Women, church, and new ways of being church are viewed in the perspective of God's kingdom and the new creation. It is in the light of this perspective that the woman's role and contribution are discussed. However, it is felt that this is a limited discussion. Nevertheless, the task is very demanding of all of us at all levels of change.

In obedience to our faith, let us in solidarity struggle together as members of the people of God, the body of Christ, new citizens of the kingdom, new creation made in God's image toward the vision of the New Heaven and New Earth where God's spirit, justice, peace, and love will reign and prevail in the order of life.

NOTES

1. Quoted from the statement "Asian Church Women Speak," drafted at the EATWOT Manila Consultation, Nov. 21–30, 1985. See chap. 11, below, page 120.

2. Leonardo Boff, *Church: Charism and Power* (New York: Crossroad Publishing Co., 1985).

10

A Common Methodology for Diverse Christologies?

Virginia Fabella (Philippines)

INTRODUCTION

My original assignment for this Ecumenical Association of Third World Theologians Intercontinental Women's Conference was to offer some reflections on "Women and Christology from an Asian Perspective." As if the topic were not substantial enough, the organizers have asked me to add methodology as well.

Let me explain from the outset why this is not a simple task. First of all, there is the word "Asian." As a continent, Asia is not only immense, it is also extremely diverse and complex. The most extensive among the continents, Asia stretches from Turkey in the west to Japan and Indonesia in the east, encompassing 58 percent of the world's population. Who among the estimated 2,800,000,000 Asians has the proper Asian perspective? In the second place, there is the topic of Christology itself. It was only in 1981 that the Christian Conference of Asia embarked on a long-term project, on a collective basis, to spell out Christologies relevant to the pluralistic societies in Asia. The participants in the project hope to come up with their conclusions by 1989. So there is still no "Asian" Christology in existence,[1] not even from a male perspective. Third, the topic must somehow relate to Asian women, who comprise one-quarter of the world's people. But the majority of Asian women are just beginning to emerge from their culture of invisibility and silence, and most of them have never heard of Christ. So you can see why my assignment is not so simple.

Thanks to the EATWOT Women's Commission, however, I do not have to start from scratch. As part of the commission's four-phased program, thirty women from seven Asian countries gathered in Manila in November 1985 to participate in a continental consultation entitled "Total Liberation from Asian Women's Perspective." One of the topics discussed was "Women and the Christ-Event." Furthermore, the consultation laid the foundation for an informal network among the participants who have subsequently shared pertinent reflections with me. I am thus grateful to all the women doing theology in Asia who form part of our EATWOT sisterhood and have laid the groundwork for my present assignment.

My paper then will be divided into two parts: the first will contain two Christological reflections of Asian women, in summary and composite form, while the second will zero in on the methodological implications of these reflections. To understand the Christological reflections, it is important to recall Asia's twofold characteristic as a continent, that is, the poverty of its masses coupled with the richness of its cultural and religious traditions. As part of the Third World, Asia is marked by poverty and oppression—massive poverty surrounding pockets of affluence, and interrelated oppressions from within and without. What distinguishes Asia from the rest of the Third World is its religious, cultural, and linguistic pluralism. Asia has at least seven major linguistic zones, more than any other continent can claim. It is the birthplace of all the great world religions and, with the exception of Christianity and Judaism, it is the home of most of their adherents. The vast majority of Asians are Buddhists, Hindus, Muslims, Taoists, or Confucianists, with a minuscule three percent Christian. Thus it is actually the "non-Christian" soteriologies that have shaped the myriad cultures that can truly be called Asian."[2]

This brief background is necessary in order to comprehend the two following Christological positions articulated by two Asian women who took part in the Women and the Christ-event workshop at the Manila Consultation in November 1985. The two papers were chosen as representing two different religio-cultural backgrounds. The first, below, is the summary of the revised reflection paper of Lydia Lascano, a delegate from the Philippines. It must be recalled that the Philippines is the only country in Asia that is 92 percent Christian. The second summary represents the reflections of a Korean *minjung* theologian, Chung Hyun Kyung, supplemented with material from other Korean writings.

CHRISTOLOGICAL REFLECTIONS OF ASIAN WOMEN

The Philippine Reflection

The Filipino people are on a continuing pilgrimage toward liberation from all forms of evil—personal, relational, structural—toward a society that is truly free, just, democratic, and sovereign, a foreshadowing of God's reign promised by Jesus. As the people continue to suffer oppression and deprivation and struggle for a more human life, they are living out Jesus' own life, his passion, death, and resurrection.

Despite the February 1986 events, which resulted in Ferdinand Marcos's ouster, life remains unchanged for most people, especially in the rural areas. About 80 percent still live below the poverty line and there are still many victims of harassment and violence. The majority of these are peasants, workers, tribal minorities, fisherfolk, urban poor, and the unemployed. And the majority of this majority are women.

Many women are not aware that they are doubly oppressed, not only because of their class but also because of their gender. Digna is one of these. Together with her husband and children, Digna migrated to Manila from one of the southern islands to escape the severe economic hardships they were undergoing. But life in the overpopulated city turned out worse. After months of meager family diet and a daily long trek to work, Digna's husband contracted a serious illness and lost the temporary job he held. It fell on Digna, then pregnant, to provide for the family and to care for her sick husband as well. She could not get a job because of her condition. In a state of desperation one day, Digna decided to serve fertilizer to her family to end it all. A friend intervened and thwarted Digna's plan. This was a year ago, but Digna remains bitter and sees no real solution to her problem. Digna is among the millions of Filipino women who suffer from the prevailing economic system that offers no assurance of survival for the poor; they are unable to fight or dodge it, much less to have any intention or energy to change it. They are today the Christ disfigured in his passion.

Numerous Filipino women are undergoing this apparently passive moment of Jesus' sufferings. In contrast to the experience of "undergoing" passive suffering, "doing" and "accompanying" are acts of solidarity that constitute the other moment of Jesus' passion. How Jesus was able to stand his ground during his arrest and trial brings us to a consideration of his passion as an act of being in solidarity. This solidarity can be traced back to the instances of his teaching, healing, and acts of compassion and kindness; his deeds were not merely something to be done and forgotten soon after. He identified himself with his suffering people. He welcomed them, spoke to them about God's reign, and cured those who were in need of healing (Lk. 9:11b). Assurance of the promised reign, now inaugurated, accompanied his response to people's concrete needs and their questions on life's contradictions. Because he stood for all he taught and did, he consequently endured suffering at the hands of his captors as a continuation and overflow of his act of identification with his people who saw no clear end to their misery at the hands of the system.

Jesus' passion as an act of solidarity with his people is relived among the militant, protesting Filipino women who have taken up the struggle on behalf of their sisters and of the rest of the suffering poor. Some have become aware that their oppression not only has economic roots, but also stems from a long history of patriarchy. Through centuries of Spanish colonial rule, women have been made to believe, partly through the instrumentality of the Christian religion, that they are inferior to men and hence subject to them. This has made many Filipino women servile, unduly dependent, unquestioning, and fatalistic. This subjugation of women through the patriarchal ideology supported by religion was taught as a kind of "spirituality" for Filipino womanhood. Those with such a "spirituality" (and they are still legion) tend to block the process of genuine emancipation not only for women but for the nation as well. Those who have overcome this "spirituality" have been able, through the power and example of Jesus Christ, to identify with their sisters in their passive suffering and to perform acts of solidarity toward their full personhood and womanhood. Women, once bent over double, are allowing Jesus' miracle to be repeated again and again (Lk. 13:10–17). During the drafting of the new Philippine Constitution, the six women commissioners threatened a walkout unless their forty-one male colleagues included an explicit provision on equal rights for women and men.

Like Jesus' suffering, women's active suffering has salvific value, for from the perspective of faith, every suffering, whether personally or vicariously experienced for the sake of building a more just world, falls within the ambit of salvation history. This historical salvific process culminated in the coming of Jesus Christ to inaugurate God's reign. All suffering, all hoping, all struggle ultimately find meaning from the viewpoint of the reign of God that Jesus proclaimed. The assurance that God's reign will come in its fullness is Jesus Christ, crucified and risen, the anchor of hope (Heb. 6:19). Christ today in the Philippines is simultaneously going through his agony, being crucified, and alive in the struggle of women from their captivity toward full humanity in a just, egalitarian society.

The Korean Reflection

Korea has a long history of invasion, colonization, and domination by powerful foreign countries. Besides the many ills inflicted by the superpowers on Third World nations, Korea bears the additional pain of being a divided country, which is not of its choosing. State repression, along with poverty, disease, and starvation, are not unknown to the Korean people. Those who have borne the greatest burden of their historical tragedy are the *minjung,* that is, the Korean masses, the common people deprived of their basic rights. Although there is no precise definition of the word, it is generally agreed that an accurate description of *minjung* is "those who are oppressed politically, exploited economically, alienated sociologically, and kept uneducated in cultural and intellectual matters."[3]

Under the weight of what is perceived as unjustifiable suffering, both personal and collective, it is no wonder that the *minjung* have a feeling that combines resentment, indignation, and the will to overcome, on the one hand, and defeat, resignation, and nothingness, on the other. This is the *han* of the *minjung,* and *minjung* women especially have an accumulation of *han.* For not only do Korean women suffer the most under the current economic oppression and political repression, they are also the victims of an age-old Confucian system of ethics, which inculcates male domination. Under the Confucian family code, women owe a triple obedience to father, husband, and son. This extends beyond the home to the work place, to the churches, and to political life in general. In many cases, obedience means complete submission, even at the cost of one's dignity.

Lee Ok Soon, a miner's wife, recounts:

> Miners have a superstition that a woman crossing the road in front of them brings bad luck, so women must be careful particularly at the change of shift. Miners have three shifts in rotation so the wife's pattern changes accordingly. However, it's easy to forget after our husband has gone off for his shift, to be careful about crossing the road. If a woman does happen to cross in front of a man, he will shout abuses at her. Usually, the woman will kneel in front of him and beg forgiveness. If she answers back instead, he is apt to beat her. If a woman has crossed the road in front of a man and there is an accident at the mine, the workers will be sure that is the reason. Even if the woman apologizes, the offended man may demand a day's wages from her.[4]

Women in the factories or on the farm share similar stories. The subjugation of women is so evident and extreme in some cases that one male *minjung* theologian observed that "under Confucianism's strict imposition of laws and customs discriminating against women, the existence of women was *han* itself."[5]

Given this situation of *minjung* women, what would be the significance of Jesus Christ to them? In the answer of one Korean woman: "If Jesus Christ is to make sense to us, then Jesus Christ must be an exorcist of our *han*." He must be a "priest of *han*." For the *minjung* women, salvation or redemption means being exorcised from their accumulated *han,* an untangling of their many-layered *han*.

Exorcism is nothing new or strange to Jesus Christ, as is evident to any reader of the Synoptic Gospels. But neither is exorcism new or strange to *minjung* women. Korea has a deep-rooted tradition of shamanism, which features the expulsion of evil spirits, believed to be of those who have died with *han*. As a form of folk religion, shamanism is based on a strong belief in an unseen world of gods, demons, and ancestral spirits that affect daily life. A good third of Korea's population are practitioners of shamanism, but it is only the shamans, or priests, themselves who have access to this spirit world through certain rites. Thus shamans play an important role in casting out evil spirits and comforting people who live under severe life conditions. An interesting phenomenon in Korea is that, despite its predominant patriarchal culture, the majority of shamans have been women. Women shamans have been "big sisters" to many deprived *minjung* women, untangling their *han* and helping them to cope with life's tribulations.

In this context, Jesus Christ must be a priest of *han* for the *minjung* women, as healer and comforter. The objection is made that as a "priest of *han*," Jesus Christ would be contributing to the "status quo," for shamans are not generally known to make the connection between personal *han* and structural evil.[6] This is to misunderstand and underplay the role of spiritual emancipation in the quest for total human liberation. The error in many Asian attempts at social change is precisely that they lack integration between external progress and transformation, on the one hand, and interior liberation, on the other. The two elements must interpenetrate if liberation is to be holistic, authentic, and long-lasting.

Jesus Christ as priest of *han* will not only be healer, exorciser, consoler, friend; he will also be transformer. For he who expelled demons and cured the sick of their infirmities also denounced hypocritical practices and reversed customs and tradition. The feeling of resignation may be misconstrued as defeat, but indignation as such is what underlies the tenacity of will for life, which allows powerless people to survive. The former can be, and has been, sublimated to great artistic expression, while the latter can erupt as energy for revolution. Jesus Christ can transform the *minjung* women's *han* into an energizing force for social change. The *minjung* women have already shown this capacity in their open protests against injustices and in their struggle for human rights.

Commonalities and Differences

Before moving on to the next section, let us draw a few similarities and differences from the two foregoing Christological reflections, which point to an emerging methodology among women doing theology in Asia:

1. The two reflections are grounded in experience.

2. Both bear the mark of a colonized people.

3. The influence of both the socioeconomic and religio-cultural realities is apparent in the development of the two positions.

4. A thorough "Christian" background is evident in the first, while the influence of other Asian religious practices is notable in the second.

5. The focus of both papers is not "who" is Jesus Christ but "where" or "what" is Jesus Christ for Asian women, the Filipino statement emphasizing the "where," the Korean statement, the "what."

6. In both cases, Jesus Christ is seen as a liberating figure for both men and women.

7. Neither position is disturbed by the maleness of Jesus (implying that it is "accidental" to the liberation process).

8. Neither of the two statements dwells on abstract controversies such as "the historical Jesus vs. the Christ of faith," or on Jesus' traditional titles such as "Son of God" or "Son of Man" or "Lord."

9. Though both are aware of patriarchy as a main source of women's oppression, there was no indication in either position of an exclusive fight against it.

10. Women's struggles are placed within the broader struggle toward full humanity for all.

METHODOLOGICAL IMPLICATIONS

The foregoing Christological reflections indicate the possibility of diverse Christologies from the perspective of Asian women. Given the multiplicity of contexts, particularly in the realm of the religio-cultural, what could be the unifying element of these diverse Christologies? It is proposed here that a common methodology may be one of the unifying factors in Asian women's efforts toward a contextual Christology, or to put it in broader terms, a contextual theology. The samples cited, as well as the work the EATWOT Commission has already done on the national and continental levels, point to common methodological elements for doing women's theology in Asia.

First of all, if theology is to have an Asian women's perspective, then it has to be done by Asian women themselves. There can be no substitute or shortcuts for this. However, this does not mean that all Asian women, even those trained theologically, automatically have what we term as "an Asian women's perspective." Rather, this means women who have not only become aware of women's inferior status and discriminatory treatment in our societies, but have also committed themselves to the women's struggle for their rightful place in history. This element can be detected in both Christological samples presented above.

In Asia, the Christian theologian must bear in mind that the vast majority of women are poor and adhere to other religious traditions. Unless this fact remains in the forefront of the theologian's consciousness, her "theology" will be irrelevant to the great multitude of her struggling Asian sisters. Chung Hyun Kyung, whose Christological reflection forms the major portion of the Korean position summarized above, expresses it well in her full paper:

> My theological audience will be the Korean poor women who are searching for full humanity in their struggle for survival. Whether they express their yearning for liberation and wholeness in Christian terminology or not cannot be the main issue for my theologizing, because Christianity is still a minority religion in Korea. The main issue is whether I can recapture the message of liberation and salvation from the Christian Gospels and make it communicable to the women in the struggle for justice. Our purpose for theologizing is to sustain our power and to empower each other to overcome the fear of torture and death and to hope for the future in the midst of our brokenness.

As can be noted in the Philippine and Korean reflections, when Asian women speak of their struggle, they have in mind the broader struggle for full humanity for all. If there is a focus on women in our present involvement and theological efforts, it is because this is a necessary preliminary stage toward a more just and egalitarian existence for all. Women's ultimate goal is not just to gain more rights or a better status for themselves but a life-giving and truly mutual relationship among human beings, which involves the liberation of both women and men in a transformed society. It is that "all may have life and have it in abundance" (Jn. 10:10).

Another element of an emerging common methodology is the importance given to the context, as in all Third World theologies. Asian women have to deal with their two disparate but interacting contexts: their Asianness and their womanness. As already alluded to earlier, Asia's overwhelming poverty and its multifaceted religiosity are the "two inseparable realities which in their interpenetration constitute what might be designated as the Asian context and which is the matrix of any theology that is truly Asian."[7] Both Christological reflections above show the marked influence of both the socioeconomic and the religio-cultural contexts. But the theologian needs to be conscious of those influences, so she can reject those that enforce women's subjugation and exploitation and accept those that contribute to their emancipation. In order that knowledge of the context does not remain on a theoretical, or worse, a mythical level, the theologian must be engaged in a "dialogue of life" not only with the poor, who are mostly women, but also with those of other religious and cultural traditions and different ideological convictions. In this way, one develops an experiential understanding of the Asian context.

But to understand Asianness is not sufficient for women doing theology. Their womanness is the other important and more pressing reality to consider. By "womanness" is not meant a mere conglomerate of biological or psychological factors but an awareness of what it means to be a woman in the Asian context today. It is to have experienced our common lot as women, but it is also to have awakened to the fact that our world of subjugation and subservience is neither our fate nor our due, and that it is possible to change it. Suffering, multiple oppression, growing awareness, struggle for full humanity—this is all part of being a woman in Asia today.

Women's experience is basic to our theology. In the Manila Consultation, the participants summarized Asia's experience in their final statement as follows:

> In all spheres of Asian society, women are dominated, dehumanized and dewomanized; they are discriminated against, exploited, harassed, sexually used, abused and viewed as inferior beings who must always subordinate themselves to the so-called male supremacy. In the home, church, law, education and media, women have been treated with bias and condescension.

The situation of women depicted in the Philippine and Korean examples is but a microcosm of a continentwide reality. Women fare no better in economically advanced Japan. They still suffer from the "good wife and wise mother" ideology, which is deeply ingrained in their society, restricting their initiatives and activities. In a modernizing country like India, women continue to be victims of the ancient dowry system, wife burning, genital mutilation, *sati,* and more recently, forced sterilization and sex-determination tests. Women from all Asian countries have their own personal stories to share.

The process of doing theology demands that we go beyond giving our individual testimonies or describing our collective situation as women. We need to employ a comprehensive analysis of all the systems and structures that affect human lives. Although we bear socioeconomic exploitation and deprivation similar to our Asian brothers, women are the more direct victims of the social system called patriarchy. Both reflections in this paper acknowledge this, but for our theologizing purposes, a more thorough and critical study is needed to show how patriarchy has penetrated our cultural and religious structures and traditions, our laws, practices, attitudes, and psyche—in short, the very woof and warp of the fabric of our daily life. This is the reason why a comprehensive analysis is a must in our doing of theology: not only to uncover the roots of our oppression—economic, political, religious, cultural, and even ecological—but to see how these different forms of oppression are interrelated and reinforce one another.

Because ours is a Christian theology, it is in the light of our Christian faith that we reflect on our life-experience and so our Judeo-Christian Scriptures are an indispensable source. But there is an urgent need to reread Scripture from a woman's standpoint, that is, from a more inclusive perspective, before it can be utilized properly and validly as a basis of theological formulation. A reinterpretation of Scripture from a feminist perspective has already been begun, particularly in the First World. Our use of Christian Scripture as a vital part of our theologizing process does not preclude availing ourselves of the Scriptures of other faiths as well, for they too are a vehicle of God's revelation. However, in using Scriptures, Christian or otherwise, we are warned to discriminate between what is described as a social norm of the day and what is prescribed as essential to the religion. For example, Jesus' maleness was not essential to his salvific mission. In the Asian Women's Consultation in Manila, the fact that Jesus was male was not an issue, for he was never seen as having used his maleness to oppress or dominate women. Nor does the fact of his maleness necessarily lead to the conclusion that God is male.

Tradition is also an important source for doing theology on our continent. This entails delving into Asia's history and literature, its age-old cultures, its folk religions, and its spirituality, to see how God is at work among the Asian people. But again, all these sources that are found in the vast storehouse of Asia's past and present must be reexamined and read anew from women's point of view to distinguish between what contributes to women's emancipation and what leads to women's further enslavement.

As mentioned earlier, the goal of women's theology is the liberation of all men and women from whatever binds them both internally and externally. Internal liberation is integral to the Asian style of being, thinking, and doing— thus freedom from greed and acquisitiveness is as vital as liberation from exploitative, capitalistic structures and imperialistic domination. This is putting it simplistically but, for Asia, liberation must be total. This further means a deeper commitment to Asia's struggle for full humanity in general and to the women's movement for a more just and egalitarian society in particular. It means working for the transformation of persons and structures in our Asian societies so they will be reflective of God's reign in our midst.

Women's theology in Asia is only now being born. Actually what we have presented is an overview, a report if you will, of what the EATWOT's Commission on Women's Theology has done in terms of both Christology and methodology. What will be the shape of Asian women's theology? As we were forewarned in the Christological examples, Asian women's theology will have many shapes; but these will not be known until they are done, and when they are done they will still be tentative and provisionary. However, we know they will all be liberation theologies. For Asian women cannot speak of religions and cultures without speaking of poverty and multiple oppressions. Neither can they speak of liberation from poverty and oppression without speaking of "spiritual" liberation.

Like all liberation theologies, women's approach in doing theology is inductive, drawn from experience and commitment, but it is also ecumenical and collective in its approach and inclusive in its perspective and goal. Without women's perspective and their contribution to theology, God, Jesus Christ, the Holy Spirit, salvation, church, and mission will be only half understood. God's image and God's plan will continue to be distorted in our world. So it is indeed imperative for all of us to take our theological task seriously. As we assume this task, let us invoke the Holy Spirit who will surely help and guide us.

NOTES

1. See below, p. 115, regarding the term "Asian." Barring that, it can be said there are books on Christ written by Asians, one of the most well-known being *The Unknown Christ of Hinduism,* by Raimundo Panikkar, first published in 1964 (rev. and enl. ed. [Maryknoll, N.Y.: Orbis Books, 1981]).

2. Aloysius Pieris, "Towards an Asian Theology of Liberation: Some Religio-Cultural Guidelines," in *Asia's Struggle for Full Humanity,* ed. Virginia Fabella (Maryknoll, N.Y.: Orbis Books, 1980), pp. 75–96.

3. Han Wan-Sang's definition, cited by James H. Cone, "Preface," in *Minjung Theology,* ed. Commission on Theological Concerns of the Christian Conference of Asia (Maryknoll, N.Y.: Orbis Books, 1981), p. xvii.

4. Statement given at the national meeting of Korean Association of Women Theologians (KAWT), held in Seoul, Korea, Oct. 25–27, 1984.

5. Suh Nam-Dong, cited by David Kwang-sun Suh, "A Biographical Sketch of an Asian Theological Consultation," in *Minjung Theology,* p. 25.

6. Chung Hyun Kyung reports in an interview that some of the new breed of shamans (who are in their late twenties and early thirties) have begun to see and articulate this connection.

7. Aloysius Pieris, "Asian Theology," pp. 75–76.

11

Final Statement: Asian Church Women Speak (Manila, Philippines, Nov. 21–30, 1985)

INTRODUCTION

We, church women from Hong Kong, India, Japan, Korea, Malaysia, the Philippines, and Sri Lanka, bound by a common vision of a just and free society, have come together from November 21 to 30, 1985, in Manila, Philippines, to reflect theologically on Total Liberation from Asian Women's Perspective.

We belong to different Christian denominations; we come from diverse and complex cultures and backgrounds, but we experience a common bond and a common bondage—as Asians and as women.

In this light, we came together to reflect on the situations we find ourselves in and to examine the effects of these realities on the lives of our people, particularly the women.

During our first days in the Philippines, we exchanged views with Filipino women from different sectors of society. We also immersed ourselves, even for only a very short while, among the poor and oppressed—the farmers, the workers, the fisherfolk, and the urban poor—and experienced for ourselves the deplorable conditions they are in.

During the consultation, we shared experiences and insights, we discussed and analyzed, at times with much pain and effort, in order to understand one another and the realities that surround us. We later realized, however, that we did not delve deeply enough into other important facets of our Asian roots— the great Asian religions and traditions that have shaped our Asianness.

We examined the contributions we have made and the role we have played in the past, even as we planned for the tasks we have to undertake in the future. In silence and prayer, with dances and songs, we celebrated and offered to God our hopes and joys, our wounds and pains—as Asians and as women.

REALITIES AND ANALYSIS

We are alarmed by the increasing poverty and oppression engulfing Asia today, resulting not only in the dehumanizing of persons but also in the extreme degradation of women. Foreign domination, state repression, militarization, and racial strife have reduced our people to being mere pawns in the deadly games of the powerful. In the interplay of these evil forces, it is the women who suffer most.

In all spheres of Asian society, women are dominated, dehumanized, and dewomanized; they are discriminated against, exploited, harassed, sexually used, abused, and viewed as inferior beings who must always subordinate themselves to the so-called male supremacy. In the home, church, law, education, and media, women have been treated with bias and condescension. In Asia and all over the world, the myth of the subservient, servile Asian woman is blatantly peddled to reinforce the dominant male stereotype image.

Indian women still live under the shadow of a patriarchal tradition that manifests itself in violence against women, namely, the dowry system, bride burning, forced sterilization, and sex-determination tests. Hindu mythology, which depicts woman as the seductress or the evil one incapable of moral self-control, has helped to institutionalize these unjust practices.

Filipinos, like many of their Asian sisters, are subjected to job discrimination and are exposed to health hazards in factories, multinational corporations, and export processing zones. Because of the severe economic crisis, and with the advent of sex tourism and the presence of U.S. bases, many Filipino women and children have been plunged into prostitution. Many leave home to become migrant workers in hostile alien lands. Furthermore, many are raped, tortured, imprisoned, and killed for their political beliefs.

In Malaysia, where there is a resurgence of religious fundamentalist trends, widening economic inequalities, worsening communal relations, and diminishing political freedom, women are the worst hit. In Japan, the male-oriented emperor system is still firmly established. And even as the people continue to bear the stigma of the nuclear havoc wreaked upon them, Japan steadily moves into a highly dangerous technological stage with its concomitant deadly hazards.

In Korea, people suffer from pain of separation and division of their homeland; they live under a government preoccupied with national security and militarism, while remaining in the grip of the Confucian family law that makes men absolute masters in all aspects of life.

Oppression of women cuts across class, caste, creed, race, profession, and age. But even among women there is division and misunderstanding because of differences in perceptions.

Living in the Third World, we see and experience double oppression from the all-pervading patriarchal system deeply ingrained in our societies, aggravated by the unjust structures which have been perpetuated by the rich and the powerful in collusion with the foreign forces that dominate us.

In the midst of all this political, economic, and cultural turmoil, strong people's movements are emerging, with the women contributing great force and militance to these movements. Women's growing awareness indeed heralds new life and liberation from the shackles that have long stifled us. We have reason to rejoice and be hopeful.

THEOLOGICAL REFLECTIONS

In our theologizing, we attempted a creative and collective work style, which we felt mirrored the vision of that community toward which we are striving. Instead of working individually on separate papers, we developed composite papers on six theological themes in relation to women. In the process we uncovered hidden realities and arrived at conclusions:

Oppression of women is SINFUL. This systemic sin is rooted in organized and established economic, political, and cultural structures with PATRIARCHY as an overarching and all-pervading reality that oppresses women.

As church people, we have come to realize that the highly patriarchal churches have definitely contributed to the subjugation and marginalization of women. Thus we see an urgent need to reexamine our church structures, traditions, and practices in order to remedy injustices and to correct misinterpretation and distortions that have crippled us.

We saw how theology itself has added to these distortions. We unearthed theological premises, traditions, and beliefs that have prevented us from becoming fully human and have blurred the image of God that we are. These elements are:

—the patriarchal image we have of God;
—the predominant male interpretation of the Bible;
—the overemphasis on the maleness of Jesus, which has been used to discriminate against women in the church and society;
—the propagation of a "Mary cult," which not only vitiated the person of Mary, but also dislocated her and minimized her active role in salvation history; and
—the bias against woman in Christian tradition buttressed by male-oriented Asian religious beliefs.

On the other hand, we rediscovered Christ's liberating and salvific mission which encompasses all; we encountered the Christ of the poor, we saw his power over sinful structures and situations. Most of all, we felt confirmed by Christ's radical breakthroughs and supportive stance for women during his time.

We saw Mary, the mother of Jesus, no longer as a passive, ethereal being, detached from the suffering millions of Asia. We now see her in a new light, as a strong woman who can identify and be with today's grieving mothers, wives, daughters in the bitter fight for freedom.

Even as we identified repressive elements in other religious traditions, we recognize that there are also life-giving elements in these great Asian traditions.

In the process we recognized the need for new symbols and an inclusive language to formulate a theology that is contextual and liberating, as well as a need for renewal in the churches and in communities of faith so that *koinonia* will be realized.

Through all our reflections, we were aware of the Holy Spirit's bonding presence among us. Thus we prayed to the Holy Spirit—that our varied gifts and insights may be welded into one powerful tide to help overcome the forces of death and evil, and usher in the New Creation in Asia.

TOWARD COMMITMENT AND ACTION

We, Asian church women, declare our strong solidarity with our oppressed people—the workers, the farmers, the fisherfolk, the urban poor, the tribal and ethnic minorities, and most especially the women—in the painful struggle for full humanity.

We denounce foreign domination, state repression, militarism, dehumanizing capitalism, and all forms of evil that subjugate women.

We offer our collective strength and power to our Asian sisters in the fight against poverty and oppression.

We staunchly support women's movements in confronting patriarchal structures and traditions; we are one in struggling for democratization in the home, the church, the schools, and society in general.

We will constantly exercise vigilance in upholding women's right to equality and self-determination; we will work unceasingly to lift our suffering sisters—the battered, the tortured, the hungry, the silenced, and the unfree.

We firmly resolve to promote authentic feminist education and the development of a liberating theology from the perspective of Asian women.

We strongly encourage new forms and ways of communication that will make us aware of issues that affect our lives and our fortunes.

We reach out and join hands with our sisters beyond our shores. Together we will rise from our bondage and heal wounds; together we will continue to hold up half the sky and move mountains.

WE CALL FOR UNITY AND SOLIDARITY, FOR IT IS ONLY BY WORKING TOGETHER TOWARD A NEW COMMUNITY OF WOMEN AND MEN THAT THE WORLD WILL WITNESS THE COMING OF THE NEW KINGDOM, WHICH IS THE EMBODIMENT OF JUSTICE, EQUALITY, PEACE, AND LOVE.

Part Three

LATIN AMERICA

12

Women Doing Theology in Latin America

Ivone Gebara (Brazil)

The expression "women doing theology" is new, as is the explication of what the expression means. Previously, there was never any mention of sexual difference with regard to those who wrote theology, since it was obvious that the task was something proper to men. Today it would seem that the matter is no longer obvious, and the gender of the authors must be specified. Gender is understood not only as a biological difference prior even to birth, but especially as a cultural dimension, that is, as a stance or an aspect that affects the production of other cultural values, of other kinds of human interrelationship and other ways of thinking.

The fact that women have entered the world of economic production and, more broadly, into politics and culture and the consequences for change in society and in the various churches deserves deeper reflection on its own. Such a deepening would go beyond the scope of our contribution, since right now we have another aim.

I am going to devote my attention especially to the question of the task of theology, emphasizing some points of reflection on what has already been said, and I shall continue my reflection beyond issues that are properly theological.

WHAT CHARACTERIZES THE WAY WOMEN DO THEOLOGY?

In order to sketch a response to this question, we must first explain what we understand today by the theological activity of women. I should make it clear that my starting point is the Latin American context and, more specifically, the situation in northeastern Brazil. Placing myself at that starting point is cru-

---

Translated from Portuguese by Phillip Berryman.

cially important, since it conditions my reflection as a woman out of a particular socioeconomic, political, and cultural situation. This situation shapes my being and my acting, my seeing and my feeling, my speech and my silence.

To speak or write from northeast Brazil is to situate myself in a region where misery and exploitation take on extremely dehumanizing forms and where most of the people, and especially women, are its victims. This region is the victim of internal and external contradictions of the capitalist system and is marked by various kinds of contrasts: *(a)* by economic and social contrasts: a few large-scale property-owners, most people landless, very high unemployment; *(b)* by political contrasts: power of the "colonels"—sugar-mill owners, industrialists, and politicians—alongside the lack of decision-making power on the part of millions of people in the northeast; *(c)* by cultural contrasts: utilization of popular culture to serve the dominant culture, machismo, and subjection of women.

As we know well, these contrasts entail enormous social consequences, reducing most of the people to subhuman living conditions. It is out of this situation, which sustains my being and my reflection, that I can speak of women's theology. I recognize that I am a woman who lives in privileged conditions, conditions that give me enough space to reflect, to speak, and even to write. I speak of the woman that I am myself, and of others, the poor women of my region, in an effort to move over into their world on the basis of my option for our liberation, as well as on the basis of our common human condition as women.

As I see it, the theological task is multiple and varied. There is nothing new about such a statement. What may be new is the fact of explicating it from the starting point of the situation of women. Hence, I speak of different theological tasks.

Shared Experiences

There is a way of doing theology that starts with shared experience from oral transmission, from the simple fact of sharing life. I believe this way of doing theology is what is most representative of the popular milieus. Many women are especially gifted with a deep intuition about human life and are able to counsel, to intuit problems, to express them, to give support, to propose solutions, and to confirm the faith of many people. They explain biblical passages on the basis of their experience and respond to doctrinal questions by simplifying them and setting them on the level of existential reality. Some of these women are illiterate. That would pose problems for a more academic doing of theology, but it does not hinder the exercise of this ministry. This activity is sapiential; it springs from life, and life is its reference point. It is received as a gift from God and handed on as a gift.

Discourse dealing with the important issues in life is the heart of every theology. God's life is related to the life of humankind, and the life of humankind is related to God. All subsequent systematizing, all thematizing, all connecting of ideas, is vitally linked to this most basic aspect.

With regard to this primordial religious experience, it is important that we take note of the function of women in Candomblé,* especially in northeast Brazil. I draw attention to this point simply to underscore the fact that even in machistic cultures like our own, in Candomblé the woman has a special place in carrying out religious tasks. The "Mother of the Saint" is "queen" in her own territory. She is the recipient of the wish of the saint, male or female; she transmits or presides over and coordinates religious ceremonies. Generally speaking, this sort of thing does not take place in Christian churches, although one can cite some similar nonofficial functions: counselors, prayer leaders, faith healers, and providers of other services deeply connected to the religious dimension of human life. In some Protestant churches, female priestly ministry is allowed, but it is not exercised at all among the popular sectors in northeast Brazil.

Efforts of Popular Catechists

The theological efforts of the so-called popular catechists, who are responsible for more systematic initiation into Christian doctrine, especially among children and young people, can be one of repeating written materials, things learned in their own childhood, or ideas imposed by priests. One can also find a dimension of impressive creativity, which has a strong influence on the life of children and young people. Today in Latin America one can speak of a "revolutionary role" played by many catechists who open themselves clearly and effectively to the problems of their people and who have shown that they can both take an active role in popular movements and pass on to children and young people a Christianity characterized by the struggle for justice, a high value placed on life, and the sharing of goods. In so doing, they provide alternatives to this consumerist and individualistic society.

Catholic Sisters

The theological effort of Catholic sisters among the popular sectors is a kind of work that became significant in Brazil, especially during the 1970s. The "migration" of sisters to popular milieus, and the fact that young people in those areas have taken on religious life while remaining to serve in those milieu, have strengthened and continue to strengthen a consciousness and militancy in the popular organizations as well as a reading of Christian faith whose starting point is the problems and hopes of our people.

The presence of these sisters has stimulated and motivated a rereading of the

---

*"Candomblé" is an Afro-Brazilian religious ceremony composed of prayers, dances, and offerings led by a priest (Padre Santo) or a priestess (Madre del Santo) with the purpose of invoking the good spirits and expelling the bad ones.

Bible as the history of a people to whom we are linked by religious tradition and from whom we must learn fidelity to life, and in particular fidelity to a book that tells us about Jesus and Mary, figures who set in motion a new way for people to relate to one another.

Something new is happening in the people's theological expression. There seems to be a before and an after, that is, the presence of these sisters often seems to establish the context that enables the poor to experience certain elements of change in the way they formulate and live their religion. The image of a God committed to the liberation of the poor, of a Mary closer to women's problems, of a Jesus who is less remote and whose words are understandable in our own situation—these are just examples of the enormous change that gradually takes place.

Doing Theology from Daily Life

The theological activity of women who teach in theology departments and institutes is a ministry not limited just to courses but involves advising the various groups and movements in the Christian churches. Above and beyond the academic theological formation, which both men and women receive in higher institutions of learning where men are the majority, there is something quite special in the way that women do theology. The elements of everyday life are very intertwined with their speaking about God. When women's experience is expressed in a church whose tradition is machistic, the other side of human experience returns to theological discourse: the side of the person who gives birth, nurses, nourishes, of the person who for centuries has remained silent with regard to anything having to do with theology. Now she begins to express her experience of God, in another manner, a manner that does not demand that reason alone be regarded as the single and universal mediation of theological discourse. This way of doing theology includes what is vital, utilizing mediations that can help to express what has been experienced, without exhausting it, a discourse that leads to the awareness that there is always something more, something that words cannot express.

What is vital cannot be expressed through formal mediations. It can be done only through those mediations that are proper to a sapiential discourse in which relationships with others express the diversity and complexity of human situations and challenges. Theological speech is expressed in the kind of prophecy that denounces the present, in songs of hope, in lament, in the form of counsel. It is as though the aim were to bridge the gap between speech and reality, the distance that the formal and idealist discourse of religion has imposed on us for a long time. It is as though we were discovering, very powerfully and starting from our own situation, the mystery of the incarnation of the divine in the human, not just because "we have been told," but because we experience it in the confines of our lives as women.

The experience of this theological activity is still in its early stages. In Brazil there are not many published works to confirm it and make it known. There is only what I regard as most basic and prior to theological elaboration: faith and its expression based on an encounter with the experience of the oppression of women as an experience of the oppression of the poor. This expression has been more oral and more direct, and has proved to be effective.

At this point, I am limiting myself to taking note of this kind of activity. Further on, I shall seek to explain some characteristics, intuitions, and efforts involved in this activity.

HISTORIC CONTEXTS

The different theological activities spelled out above take place on different levels and in different situations, characterized by various kinds of conditionings. At this point, I propose that we reflect on some "historic contexts" and some characteristics that, I think, are proper to women doing theology in Latin America during these last few years. The basis on which I point to these contexts and their characteristics is my own observation and the way I exercise this ministry, which is confirmed by the practice of a few of my colleagues and by the reception given by the audience I address.

I cannot avoid speaking about my own experience. In a vital way it makes me what I am. My theological experience is the product of my relationship with people, of mutual influences, of my philosophical and ideological stance, situated in time and space. The faith I have received from my childhood onward, the difficult and twisting path of my life, the discoveries I have made, the past and the present, have all left their mark on my experience of theology.

It is hard to draw a line between the subjective and the objective, or a line between what I say about others and what I say about myself. In life, such things are mixed together and interconnected, and we risk killing something vital within them if we try to "divide the waters" too precisely. Every "theory" includes something very personal, something deeply involved with the one who elaborates it, something that is part of the very desire to know and change the world. To speak either as a single person or universally seems to show or reflect something that we experience in the everyday reality of our life within our different social and cultural conditionings: the partial nature of our perception and the partial nature of our interpretations.

Thus it is within the boundaries of my subjectivity/objectivity and within the limits of my experience and observation that I set forth the following three historic contexts and three characteristics.

Irruption of History into Women's Lives

When we speak of the irruption of history into the lives of women—and especially the theological expression of their faith—we do not mean the entrance of women into history; they have always been present. What we have in mind is something qualitatively different and new, that is, the irruption of historic consciousness into the lives of millions and millions of women, leading them to the liberation struggle by means of an active participation in different fronts from which they had previously been absent. It is as though a strong wind had begun to blow, opening eyes and loosening tongues, shifting stances, enabling arms to reach out to new embraces and hands to take up other tools, impelling feet to take other steps, raising the voice so its song and its lament might be heard. Woman begins to take her place as agent of history. The fact is that with her activity and new stance toward what happens in life, a new awareness is clearly coming into being. Participation in labor unions, neighborhood movements, mothers' groups, and pastoral leadership all manifest a change in the consciousness and in the role women play today. Entering into history in fact means becoming aware of history, entering into a broader meaning, in which women are also creators or increasingly want to be forgers of history.

Discovery Causality within Women's Experience

In connection with history, one can speak of the causality of things. The condition of women is the result of an evolution: it has been different, and it can be different. Their present state can be partly explained on the basis of historic causes. The discovery of the causes of the oppression of the poor and, among them, of the oppression of women, has changed women's understanding of themselves as persons individually and corporately. Woman is not marked for an unchangeable fate, nor is she the object of alien wills that shape her existence. Despite the conditions inherent in human existence, she can conquer spaces in which to express her word and her being. This new historic moment of hers is pregnant with future, a moment that announces a Good News that is both present and yet to be lived in its fullness.

It is worth noting that the discovery of causality within women's experience bears the characteristic marks of the particular way in which they perceive and approach the problems of life. No one single cause is absolutized but, rather, the causes are multiple. This way of looking at matters is obedient to their perception, as women, in its complexity, diversity, and mystery.

Entering the Labor Force

The fact that more and more women are entering the world of paid labor, and the world of work and struggle for survival, has awakened them to struggle in other areas where human destiny is also at stake.

Entering the labor force has changed the expression of women's faith. From their previous horizon of home and family, women have opened out to a broader reality. God is no longer one who addresses a world limited to the activities of home and family; God becomes the one who addresses socioeconomic and political challenges in the new militancy of Latin American women. The image of God is no longer that of the father to whom one owes submission; rather, God is basically the image of what is most human in woman and man, seeking expression and liberation. A working woman said, "God is the force that won't allow me to surrender to the will of those who oppress my people." Women's entry into the struggle of the world of paid labor has thus brought about a change in the way they relate. Obviously, this is not the only factor, but it seems important to remind ourselves of it, since it tends to be forgotten or left as a purely accidental aspect within a traditionalist or reactionary theological vision.

CHARACTERISTICS OF FEMINIST THEOLOGICAL ACTIVITY IN LATIN AMERICA

Living Realities and Theological Elaboration

Feminist theological expression always starts from what has been lived, from what is experienced in the present. Consequently it rejects an abstract type of language about life and those matters deeply affecting human relationship. That is why there is a growing effort to clear the field of old theological concepts in order to discover what vital realities they correspond to, and to what extent they really do so. Living realities are the takeoff point for theological elaboration; they are rational symbols that arose in a particular period, the product of a series of conditions, and they were able to bring together rationally certain experiences of reality. It is urgent that we get to know them and discover their meaning for today, and for our history. In their theological work, women seek to retrieve existential realities, to let them speak freely, to allow them to become reorganized on the basis of our context today, and only subsequently to connect them to a prior tradition.

This way of proceeding represents an attempt to restore to theological language its capacity for touching some vital centers of human existence. In other words, to some extent this procedure means returning the poetic dimension of human life to theology, since the deepest meaning in the human being is expressed only through analogy; mystery is voiced only in poetry, and what is gratuitous is expressed only through symbols.

Purely rational concepts do not take into account the meaning, desire, flavor, pleasure, pain, and mystery of existence. Given their own history, women are bolder in questioning concepts, and they have a creative curiosity that opens new paths and allows new understandings. This new mode makes possible a kind of theological creation in community. That is, the new formulation gathers a broader number of experiences and is not narrowed to a formulation or a text with individual "authorship."

This is a "new way" of expressing something after it has been heard, lived, and felt many times and in many ways, so that people recognize themselves when they hear it spelled out, and they feel invited to a deeper reflection on the questions that life poses. It is their own issues that they see reflected on, questioned, or clarified so that the reflection proposed touches most deeply the questions and doubts present in the lives of millions of people.

Recreating Tradition

In women's theological discourse, the theological tradition shared by the different churches does not function as a legitimizing justification that we need only to go on repeating. If we do repeat, it is because that is what today's situation demands, because it does touch the roots of our existence, because to some extent it responds to the problems that ongoing history sets before us. In this sense, what is normative is primarily the present, what calls out today; tradition is viewed in terms of the present. Thus the tradition of Christian communities in the past is continually re-created, and one may even speak of fidelity to that tradition to the extent that both today and yesterday are faithful to the Spirit of God manifest in history and demanding absolute respect for life. The past is not only information, but enlightenment, teaching, and witness for the present to the extent that it relates to the question of being human.

Human Complexities

The theological work of women reflects an ability to view life as the locus of the simultaneous experience of oppression and liberation, of grace and lack of grace. Such perception encompasses what is plural, what is different, what is other. Although this way of looking is not the exclusive property of women, we must say that it is found to an extraordinary extent among women. In popular struggles, in which women have played a very important role, this ability to grasp in a more unified way the oppositions and contradictions, the contrasts and differences as inherent in human life, has been a characteristic feature of the way in which women live and express their faith. Such behavior enables them to avoid taking dogmatic and exclusive stances, and to perceive or intuit the real complexity of what is human.

The Tapestry of Human Life

In addition to these factors or characteristics of the theological work of women, we cannot fail to recall the inestimable contribution of the social sciences—anthropology, psychology, and different theories about language—as elements that have been changing, directly or indirectly, women's understanding of themselves. These same elements have contributed to the emancipation of women's power in the social dimension of human relations and in the way these relations are organized.

All these contributions form part of the tapestry woven by women expressing and reflecting human life as this century ends. The threads, colors, flowers, and other designs—all taken together, interconnected, and linked to each other—are forming the embroidery of life while the artists themselves are beginning to appear, to show their faces in public, to demand respect and appreciation. It is also worth noting that the international women's movement, in its expressions and organizations, has played a role in opening up the oppressed situation of Brazilian women so they could be aware of the situation of women in different areas of the world. For example, the resistance of the *Madres de Plaza de Mayo* in Argentina, and of our sisters in Bolivia, Nicaragua, and El Salvador, has become well known and has led to solidarity and energy, which has confirmed us in the struggle, even though our contexts are different.

The persistence of women in the struggle for life and the restoration of justice have been linked together and lived out as expressions of faith, as the presence of God in the struggles of history. Many women see in these developments the expression of their desire to struggle for a more human world, in which certain values presently dormant may be aroused, where people can accept affection, where life may triumph over the powers of death.

Basic Ecclesial Communities

Finally, I want to take particular note of the work of women in basic ecclesial communities. No doubt this work has been present throughout this reflection, but I can not avoid dealing with it more fully at this point, before concluding my thoughts. I am not going to describe what women do in basic ecclesial communities. That would fill a long essay, and besides it is well known to all of us.

I would simply like to emphasize how their active role is prefiguring within the Christian churches a new way of organizing ministries. Even though these ministries are not sanctioned by church officials, they are recognized by the poorest, those to whom this service is especially directed. The new element in this service is found in the way it responds to a certain number of the community's vital needs and in the fear that it is generating in those who are in charge of the churches and who are gradually losing their former prestige. Women's ministry is shaking up men's ministry, challenging their practice and the exercise of their authority. This is taking place, not because of some decision taken by women to make it happen, but because of the nature and quality of their service and of the new social role that they are winning in the world. To the extent that women actively move onstage in the churches, their organizations, institutions, and expressions must be revised to meet the challenges continually posed by today's world.

IN CONCLUSION: MY HOPE FOR THE FUTURE

Theological formulations that are extremely machistic, privileges of power over what is sacred, and the need for male legitimation for things to "happen" in the churches are beginning to be affected by the clashes that hint of the future. Such a statement in no way intends to replace the "masculine" model with the "feminine" one but to anticipate a new synthesis in which the dialectic present in human existence can take place, without destroying any of its vital elements.

This is my hope: The day will come when all people, lifting their eyes, will see the earth shining with brotherhood and sisterhood, mutual appreciation, true complementarity. . . .

Men and women will dwell in their houses; men and women will eat the same bread, drink the same wine, and dance together in the brightly lit square, celebrating the bonds uniting all humanity.

13

Women's Experience of God in Emerging Spirituality

Luz Beatriz Arellano (Nicaragua)

Speaking about the living experience of God in the new spirituality of Nicaraguan women means speaking of a faith incarnate in the revolutionary process that the people of God are experiencing in Nicaragua. The new spirituality springs very much from these concrete experiences of building the new society. It is our lot to live in a time that is a privileged theological locus in which is incarnate, and from which springs, a new spirituality. This newness arises more from an everyday practice than from any theoretical reflection. Faith here enters into history and becomes incarnate in the process of the daily life of the people's journey. Thus it arises out of their struggles and their hopes.

The commitment of women to the people as a whole is very deep, so much so that we could say that this involvement of women is a characteristic feature of this new process in which the Nicaraguan people are engaged. The ongoing striving for freedom, for sovereignty, the challenge of attaining it fully and holding onto it is also part of an ongoing dynamic. Nevertheless, it should be pointed out that living a new spirituality continues to be a challenge for many women. We can speak only of an ongoing movement of women to live and incarnate their faith in a way that is consistent with what we are experiencing.

Thus my presentation will approach the topic by way of three steps: first, I shall describe how a new experience of God emerged during the liberation struggle in Nicaragua; second, I shall speak about some traits of the spirituality of women in the present Nicaraguan revolutionary process; finally, I shall point to some challenges connected with deepening the experiences and spirituality of women in Nicaragua.

Translated from Spanish by Phillip Berryman.

THE EXPERIENCE OF THE LIBERATION STRUGGLE: GOD PRESENT IN FACES OF THE POOR

Our first experience of God was that of allowing ourselves to feel the impact of the situation of suffering and oppression that our people were undergoing. From that moment on, we began to discover God present in the suffering, oppressed, and outcast countenance of our poorest brothers and sisters. What struck many women, and also many men, in Nicaragua at this point was discovering the situation of children, children in the street who were working from the time they were little; finding out that many women died in childbirth and that many children died because they had no way of getting proper attention; and finally discovering the situation of young people in our country who had no future because they were suffering brutal repression at the hands of Somoza's Guards.

Another aspect that left a deep impression on us was the situation of men and women in the countryside who had to work very hard simply to live, and sometimes in conditions that were worse than those of animals. Personally, I was struck one day to find how a Christian lady with a lot of money was treating peasants, both men and women. When a peasant woman asked if she could buy a pound of pork loin, the woman answered, "How outrageous! You want to buy the best kind of meat and you don't have enough to pay for it. You should be happy if we sell you the bones." It pained me to see that, and I wondered, "How can we say God is love in a situation like this?" And I realized that this situation would remain unchanged unless we struggled to change it.

God Present in Our History: The God of Life

Thus in this new experience of God we were not only discovering the Lord in our poorest, most oppressed, most outcast brother or sister, but also finding that God was asking us to work and to do all in our power so that this situation would not continue. We have gone from an experience of oppression, marginalization, and suffering to a realm of hope that is impelling us toward change, toward transformation. From that time onward, we have begun to discover the Lord present in our own history, inviting us to live and refashion this history of oppression into a history of liberation.

Even in the 1960s many men and women did not see this situation of poverty as something natural, and they began to ask questions such as, "What is our role as Christian men and women in this subjugated, dependent, oppressed society where life is impossible?" In a very natural way, we began to search and we tried to uncover the roots of these problems. We began to confront this situation with the word of the Lord. This helped us to find specific approaches to solutions and changes. We were also discovering that God was different from what we had been taught. We were discovering God as the God of life, closer to us, as one who journeys with us through history.

I recall that it was women who most insisted on discovering God as God of life. I believe that women were better able to make this discovery and translate it into life more easily because of their calling to motherhood, among other reasons, since that is a calling to life and peace. Being essentially bearers and sustainers of life, women find a new meaning in the discovery of God as God of life, and they themselves become stronger and more conscious as defenders and bearers of life, not only in the biological sense but in all its dimensions, the fullness of life to which Jesus calls us as his followers: "I came so they might have life and have it in abundance" (Jn. 10:10). From this angle, Nicaraguan women walk beside their people in creating new life, in giving a meaning to life, taking part in and actively defending a project in history, one that is liberating and is generating new rights to justice.

In this journey, women discover feminine elements in God: care and concern for children, even those who are not their own, defense of life, love, affection, and empathy for suffering. Such characteristics—more feminine, if you will—of a God found to be closer to us and more tender-hearted, led to a rediscovery of God as mother, not just as father, not just as protector, but as one who is immensely concerned for the poor and for the least, for those who have been left unattended, and it gave us a deep hope and a deep sense of having found something new.

At the same time, women encounter the hope of a whole people, where the emphasis is especially focused on what is small and weak, on the poor as protagonists in a history of life. This new, creative, and committed spirituality enables us to overcome all obstacles and even to accept our present life with aggression on all sides, because all those who are guided by the Spirit are children of God (Rom. 8:14).

A New Image of Jesus

Out of their participation in the suffering of our people while also battling through their own struggle, women discover a new image of Jesus—a Jesus who is brother and sister, in solidarity on the journey toward liberation, the people's journey and their own journey; a Jesus who is a *compañero* [colleague, fellow revolutionary] in building the new society.

Jesus' face is present in all the men and women who endure weariness and give their life for others. Jesus is identified as God, man and woman, standing in firm solidarity with the struggle. This is a God who is sensitive to suffering, a God who goes along with the people incarnate in history. The discovery of, and faith in, a God who is in pilgrimage with the people,

> the God of the poor,
> the human and simple God,
> the God who is sweating out in the street,
> the God with the gnarled face
> [from *Misa Campesina* of Carlos Mejia Godoy],

identified with the cause of justice, is a discovery that gives meaning to their struggle and makes everyday life bearable in the midst of oppression—and today in the midst of the aggression, shortages, and unceasing threats caused by the war the United States is financing against the people of Nicaragua.

A New Relation with the Community

As we discovered the God of life and Jesus as *compañero,* we also were discovering that the church must be a community, one that not only questions itself, but also takes on responsibility for the poorest and the least. In this sense, we began to focus more on the kingdom than on the church, that is, we began to see that Jesus' basic message was announcing the kingdom.

We began to ask ourselves: How are we going to announce the kingdom as Good News, to announce the Good News of Jesus with deeds and not simply with words? And the more we reflected on it, the more we began to take on small tasks aimed at transforming society. That is, it was our experience that the love between us women, the love that is the Lord's basic command, had to be not only affective but effective as well. All of this meant that we were experiencing the Lord out of our own painful experience.

From the beginning, women have been outstanding in their involvement in this process. Right away, we women discovered that no one was going to liberate us from outside. We discovered that the Lord was really present within us, and this impelled us to change our own situation.

Hence, when the first basic ecclesial communities were organized in the 1960s, there were more women than men involved. A new dimension of spirituality came to the fore: the "pious" woman, praying a novena, calling on the Lord, became a committed woman, reading the Bible in terms of her own situation and in terms of a new responsibility within history. In this manner we began to experience that there was much more space for women in the life of the church.

This kind of commitment led to a change in the relationship between women and their community. Women gradually overcame the hierarchical relationship of men over women. Galatians 3:28 is becoming something real, since women are finding that they are protagonists in history, history-making subjects liberating themselves and liberating their people. The community takes on solidarity with the pain and suffering of mothers. Thus women find the space in which they can denounce the situation of pain and suffering, and also announce, out of their own practice, the new spirituality, which is arising out of concrete life experiences. Their combative spirit commands the respect of others. Thus their sense of community is deepened. It is in community that women find their true place; it is when the community comes together that people pray for the situation of the country, for the men and women who are defending their homeland, for peace and justice. The community is also the place for celebrating those small victories that represent the hope for something new, that which is becoming new.

Woman's Dignity as Image of God

We have also discovered another important aspect for women, that of human dignity. Reading and practicing the word of God in relation to the real situation, as their involvement in action became more prominent with each passing day, women discovered their own dignity. In the community they now began to speak of women's rights, of woman's dignity as human person, and they began to discover that they were cast aside and mistreated in their own houses; they began to realize that if they wanted a different future for themselves and their children, they had to struggle. In this sense, reading the word of God from woman's perspective played a very important role in developing the consciousness of both men and women. I recall how some of the passages that people in the communities—especially women—most enjoyed reading were in Genesis, the passages about the creation of man and woman. I also recall the joy with which women discovered that they were equal, that they had been created in the image of God just as much as men. That was the starting point for demanding their own rights and their own opportunities. They encouraged other women to form new groups and to encourage their husbands to go to the meetings and to urge their children and everybody else to discover this reality of the dignity of the children of God as a new experience of God in a church that was beginning to be changed under the impulse of the word of the Lord. This made the women of Nicaragua more and more aware that their new role was not that of simply "taking care of their house and going to pray in church"; their role was to be history-making subjects of their own liberation, and hence to take part in the struggles to transform their country. Later on, we were to find that women of all ages played a very active, dynamic role in the people's liberation struggle because they had found this liberating dimension in the word of the Lord.

This new women's spirituality that enables them to bear suffering in struggle and still to maintain strong hope finds expression in this poem by Michele Najlis, a Nicaraguan who has been active in the struggle since she was thirteen, and who is a Christian and a revolutionary:

> They pursued us in the night,
> they surrounded us,
> and left us no defense but our hands
> linked to millions of hands linked together.
> They made us spit up blood,
> they scourged us;
> they filled our bodies with electric shocks
> and they filled our mouths with lime;
> they put us in with beasts all night long,
> they threw us in timeless dungeons,
> they ripped out our nails;

with our blood they covered even their rooftops,
even their own faces,
but our hands
are still linked to millions of hands linked together.

Women in the Liberation Struggle

Understanding that women's liberation would be incomplete unless there
was pressure for the liberation of all the people, the women in the basic ecclesial
communities became involved in the struggle against the dictatorship. They
were particularly involved in the first women's organization in Nicaragua,
the Association of Nicaraguan Women to Deal with National Issues
(AMPRONAC). After that, women participated, for example, in marches to
denounce the murder and crimes being committed. At one point, they took
part in a very important action in the church in Las Palmas, to denounce the
fact that more than a thousand peasants had disappeared from the countryside. Women went to the streets shouting the slogan, "Donde estan nuestros
hermanos campesinos—que contesten los asesinos" ("Where are our peasant
brothers and sisters? Let the murderers answer!"). They were also involved in
occupying the United Nations building in Nicaragua to protest against the large
number of political prisoners then being held. Women were very creative: they
not only took part in marches and protest actions, but also served as couriers
between organizations or persons involved in underground work, and later
they also supported the organizations involved in direct struggle, became
involved in the underground, and so forth. Women were really quite conscious
that their faith impelled them to do this, and that it was impossible to be a good
Christian and not take part in this struggle.

Women arrived at this point of participating in AMPRONAC and other
activities related to the struggle as the fruit of a powerful experience of God. We
reasoned that if God is the God of life, and life was being repressed and
destroyed in every way, we had to struggle to make life possible in Nicaragua.
This arrival point was also the starting point from which women experienced
solidarity: it is precisely by being organized that women discover that a new
force is coming into being. This solidarity among women to defend life
was likewise an experience of solidarity to defend the life of the people as a
whole.

An Ecumenical Spirituality

The new spirituality of Nicaraguan women that I am trying to reflect is a
truly ecumenical spirituality, a spirituality shared not only with Christians who
belong to the various churches but also between Christians and non-Christians.
The struggle for women's rights and dignity—although women in Christian
communities discover it through their Bible discussions—is also a broader
expression of values found in the struggle for women's liberation, values that

are at once Christian and human, with no need to attach any religious term. An excellent example of this spirit, of a church without borders, is found in the letter of Idania Fernandez, a young Nicaraguan woman who became aware of the situation of her country in a group called Metanoia, one of the church youth groups that I served as adviser. She wrote this letter on International Women's Day in 1979, a few weeks before she was killed in the liberation struggle. The letter reads:

My dearest little daughter:

Right now we are living through moments that are extremely important for humankind: today in Nicaragua, soon throughout Latin America, and some day it will take place on every continent around the world.

The revolution demands our all from each one of us, and our own level of consciousness impels us to make demands on ourselves as individuals, and to put every possible effort into being useful to the revolutionary process.

My greatest desire is that the day will soon come when you will be able to live in a free society where you will be able to fulfill yourself as a true human being, where people will be brothers and sisters rather than enemies.

I would like to walk arm in arm with you through the streets, and see happy smiles on all the children, and see the parks and rivers. I would like to smile for joy, see our people growing like happy children, see them become the new person, honest and conscious of their responsibilities to all humankind.

You will have to learn to appreciate this whole paradise of peace and freedom you are going to be able to enjoy. I say that because our most wonderful people have spilt their precious blood for this cause, and they have done so with love, out of love for the people, for freedom, and for peace, for the sake of future generations, for children like you, so you will not have to experience the repression, humiliation, hunger, and misery in which so many men, women, and children have lived in our beautiful Nicaragua.

I am telling you all this in case it happens that they don't tell you, or I don't make it to tell you. That is possible because we are all well aware of where we are going and who the enemy is, and we feel at ease if we know that we die as true revolutionaries in the full sense of the word. For we have known how to take our place in our historic context, and we have known how to take on our responsibility and our duty. That is our greatest satisfaction as revolutionaries, as human beings, and as mothers.

"Mother" does not mean being the woman who gives birth to and cares for a child; to be a mother is to feel in your own flesh the suffering of all the children, all the men, and all the young people who die, as though they had come from your own womb.

My greatest wish is that one day you become a true woman with pure feelings and a great love for humanity. And that you know how to defend justice whenever it is being violated and that you defend it against whomever and whatever.

To do that, to know what it is to be a true human being, get to know, read about, and assimilate the great figures of our revolution and of all revolutions in other countries. Take the best of each one as an example and put it into practice so that you will be better each day. I know you can do it, and are going to do it. This gives me a great sense of peace.

I don't want to leave you words, promises, or moral platitudes. What I give you is an attitude toward life, my own attitude (although I'm aware that it is still not the best) and that of all my Sandinista brothers and sisters. I am sure you will be able to assimilate this attitude.

Okay, kid. If I have the privilege of seeing you again (which is also quite possible), we will have long talks about life and revolution, and we will go hand in hand to carry out the tasks the revolutionary process entrusts to us, and we will sing with a guitar and we will be together to play, to work, and to get to know each other better, and learn from one another.

> When I recall your beautiful face
> Beautiful like flowers and like freedom,
> I work even harder in the struggle,
> Joining your smile to our situation.
> I remember you every day.
> I always picture you as you are.
> Always love our people and humankind.

With all the love that is in your mother, Idania.
Ever on to Victory! Free Country or Death!

WOMEN'S SPIRITUALITY IN THE REVOLUTIONARY PROCESS

Nicaraguan women are outstanding in their tremendous dedication to work and their yearning for study, training, and self-improvement, and that is how they press for recognition of their dignity as women. In this revolutionary process, Nicaraguan women feel spurred by great feelings of gratitude, and also by an awareness of their responsibility in the historic moment that our country is experiencing.

Accepting the presence of the Spirit who creates life, who gives life and makes everything new, along with the challenges posed by the Spirit, is one of the first steps that enables us to speak of the characteristics of a new spirituality in today's Nicaragua. Both personal conversion, which since 1979 is expressed in the establishment of more just structures for the benefit of the poor (which includes the bulk of our people), as well as the formation of a new woman and a new man are ongoing dimensions of this spirituality.

Since victory, women continue to be quite active. We see women present in the reconstruction process. Women were massively present in the literacy campaign, and were very ready to go out to the countryside and teach reading and writing to their brothers and sisters who have been deprived of education for such a long time. We see women present in all aspects of rebuilding the country: in activities relating to health, in guard duty, standing guard to defend life. Women are participating in a very strong and intense way in this deep experience of the Nicaraguan people as they move from slavery to freedom: a deeply paschal experience.

Women's lives are changing. The revolution has disrupted traditional cultural patterns through which the traditional image of women had been created. In our traditionally macho society, woman was idealized as the reverse side of the exploitation she suffered as victim: besides her sexual image, her idealized image was one of motherhood, which gave her back, or tried to give her back, as a mother, what had been taken from her as human person and as woman: her dignity, her participation, and the chance to be not just one who reproduces human life but also one who creates new life and transforms her own society and her own culture. From this traditional perspective, in addition to being doubly exploited, as women and as members of the popular classes, women were reduced to reproducing male cultural patterns and even male interests.

The fact that they are following Jesus, who stands in solidarity with the struggles of the poor masses and with the struggles of women, means that Christian women at this momentous period in Nicaraguan and Central American history have a deep feeling of responsibility. They feel the pull of "the freedom of the children of God" (Rom. 8:21); they feel that they must be linked in solidarity with their sons and daughters, with their husbands, brothers, and all those companions in struggle who are on the warfront, defending their country's peace.

One woman who exemplified this commitment to defending life was Mary Barreda, who together with her husband was murdered by the contras (Nicaraguan rebels) after they were kidnapped during the coffee harvest in 1982. As a woman who played leadership roles in the liberation of the people, she could not stand back, but decided she had to engage in practice alongside the least and the poorest. At that moment, such a practice alongside the people meant going out to harvest coffee, knowing that her contribution would become foreign exchange that would contribute to changing the life of the people. Before going out with the harvest brigade, she wrote the following letter to members of her basic ecclesial community in one of the poorest neighborhoods of Estelí:

To my dear brothers and sisters in Omar Torrijos neighborhood:

You can't imagine how much Don Ramón and I have been waiting for this moment. From the time we began to share our lives with one another, you have been a part of us, and we love your streets, your houses, your children and, indeed, everything about you. As far as I am concerned, the best gift the Lord was going to give me would be sharing this moment with you. I was also thinking that I had to give you a good present, but I couldn't come up with anything. But suddenly I've been given the chance to give you a good gift, although it means I won't be with you physically, and that is a chance to go harvest coffee these next ten days. That is why I am writing this brief note, to tell you that this is my gift for all of you: the little I shall be able to harvest will be translated, or rather, converted, into health care, clothing, shelter, roads, education, food, etc. That is why I am going to harvest coffee with all the love and enthusiasm I am capable of, and you can be assured that in every coffee bean I harvest, each one of your faces, those of your children, and even those of people I don't know, will be present. Because of this love I have toward you, I know that the Lord will multiply what we harvest.

I want to ask you that you also make a gift to the Lord this Christmas, in a smile, in taking better care of your wives, husbands, and children.

Wherever I may be, I am thinking about you at this moment while Don Ramón is reading you these few lines.

Greetings to all and a big hug. I love you very much.

Mary

Martyrdom to Defend Life and for the Sake of Justice

Mary Barreda's example shows that their commitment of themselves leads women in the direction of martyrdom. There is an aspect of martyrdom in the lives of Nicaraguan women, an aspect they share with the population as a whole, and especially with young people who fall in battle. Obviously men are more present in the war, but women are also called to experience and suffer this double dimension of martyrdom. There is the martyrdom of seeing their children fall for the sake of the liberation and defense of their country and in order to bring about a more just society, in which a new life for new men and new women may become possible. They may also give up their own lives. Many women go to the warfronts to defend life. They are there to encourage their children, their own and those of others, the children of the people whom they have adopted spiritually as their own. They fortify the *compañeros* who are there in the name of peace and justice, bearing the weight of the aggression on the front line. They do this out of love for their children and their companions in struggle, for "there is no limit to love's forebearance, to its trust, its hope, its power to endure" (1 Cor. 13:8).

The danger of running into the contras is real, and the risk of losing one's life is real. The Spirit, however, does not remain static but, rather, impels us forward, makes us move along, since "it was for liberty that Christ freed us. So stand firm, and do not take on yourselves the yoke of slavery a second time! (Gal. 5:1).

The constant striving for full freedom and for peace as the fruit of justice energizes women to take on full solidarity with our people's struggle for liberation. Endowed with this readiness to suffer and hope along with their sons and daughters, and along with their male and female companions in struggle, women find in the Spirit, who is love, strength to transcend themselves and surrender their lives to support those who are building the new homeland.

Love is the fruit of the Spirit. "There is no greater love than this: to lay down one's life for one's friends" (Jn. 15:13) This has been what Nicaraguan women have understood. The love of mothers has become so strong that it can lead to their giving their lives for their children, as events have shown: on July 31, 1985, eight Nicaraguan mothers were murdered by the contras, after being raped and later barbarously hacked to pieces, as they were on their way to Molocucu to visit their children.

Women find in Jesus the example of the freedom of giving one's life for others, and the example of a life placed at the service of others with utter gratuity.

In addition to facing the possibility of martyrdom, Nicaraguan women, along with the people as a whole, are impelled prophetically and emphatically to denounce to the whole world the increasing aggression our people are suffering. Another characteristic of Nicaraguan women who have heeded the Spirit at this dawn of our history is sensitivity to the present situation of Nicaragua and responding adequately to this historical moment.

Heeding the Spirit not only leads women to act boldly. Action springs from prayer. Women pray and fast for the peace that they yearn for so that life may grow and flourish as a sign of God's reign.

Impelled by the Spirit along this journey, women experience their limits, and the different dangers from the enemy, all aimed at destroying life. Instead of allowing themselves to be trapped by fear, however, they live this situation in a dialectic of boldness, rashness, and weakness that becomes strength. Their weakness comes not from being women, but from being human beings who know that the life of their people is continually threatened and under attack. Thus women are not arrogant in their boldness. Their boldness leads them to move forward, transcend themselves, take on new things they have never undertaken before, but they are weak in the face of death-dealing attacks. Nevertheless, they do not become paralyzed, but march forward and believe with hope in a world that is new, just, and human: the promise of the Spirit emerging, like wheat in the midst of weeds.

Two Realities: Crucifixion and Resurrection, Death and Life

Because of the war of aggression that our people are undergoing, crucifixion and death, resurrection and life are two realities present in all dimensions of life. In death, the mystery of life is already present: many die consciously surrendering their lives to defend an effort to build something within history, convinced of the new life gestating today in Nicaragua. Nicaraguan women feel the stimulus and strength of the Spirit, and out of their faith they actively accompany all those men and women who are defending life along the different warfronts. "God did not give us a Spirit of cowardice, but one of strength, of love, and good judgment" (2 Tim. 1:7).

The incarnation of this new spirituality transcends what is individual and commits us to struggle for the life of the whole body of the people and for all of life. Resurrection is already present in crucifixion. The road toward the building of the kingdom by way of the rise of the new society entails pain, death, and suffering, but it also means the hope of greater life, justice, peace, and love incarnate in history. Both aspects, crucifixion and resurrection, are part of the process of passing from death to life "through the body of Christ" (Rom. 7:4).

Joy Is Paschal

Out of the daily suffering of poor women and out of the lives surrendered in the struggle against the causes of this situation of death, people are living a renewed paschal experience. The experience of death, war, abduction, rape, and abandonment enables them to experience more profoundly the meaning of the Lord's resurrection. Joy is thus the result of the hope that the historic project of life will overcome the situation of death and war that the people are suffering. Hope in the resurrection in no way means escape from present reality but, rather, it means a deeper involvement in the struggle against death. Joy comes from faith, from the hope that death is not the last word. That is why we can already celebrate the joy of resurrection in the midst of war. The following words from the Message of the National Conference of Religious of Nicaragua, after the revolutionary victory, are apt:

God has passed through Nicaragua acting with a powerful and liberating arm. These are some of the signs of his marvelous presence that have been, and continue to be, found in the midst of our struggling people: the hunger for justice in the poor and oppressed, courage, the presence of women, exemplary unity, hospitality and companionship, the responsibility with which each person has taken on tasks in reconstruction, and finally generosity in victory and a joy pregnant with hope that leads the whole population to dream of a tomorrow when things will be better for all and not just for a few.

Joy accompanies the people's journey; we can always celebrate it when life overcomes death, when justice overcomes injustice, when women find their place in society as men have. The signs are already there, we can already celebrate: joy is paschal; resurrection is already something real that we can talk about and celebrate.

Conflict in Society and Church: Incorporated into the New Spirituality

The twofold experience of crucifixion and resurrection, the presence of suffering along with hope, conflict between the project of death and the project of life—here is no reason for Nicaraguan women to drop back, here is nothing that should discourage them. On the contrary, experiencing conflict energizes both women and men to move ahead in the struggle for a more just society that may be a sign of God's reign which is "a matter of . . . justice, peace, and the joy that is given by the Holy Spirit" (Rom. 14:17).

Similarly, conflict within the church, which reflects social contradictions, does not hold Christians back, even though many Christian women find it painful that their pastors do not accompany the people in their anguish and suffering, their joy and hope, rooted in biblical reflection and aimed at a liberating practice to defend life and peace. Indeed, even though in the short run this conflict is preventing Christian commitment to the revolutionary process from growing in a massive way, in the long run it opens up the hope that the church will truly be born of the people and of the Spirit. Thus it is possible that among the communities may emerge a spirituality that will overcome class-based contradictions and the male clerical ideology that presently prevails in the church.

CHALLENGES FACING THE NEW SPIRITUALITY
OF NICARAGUAN WOMEN

We still have a great deal to discover. The process we are involved in is very dynamic, on the move. We are obviously sharing a new experience of God under the guidance of the Spirit, in a history-making process that is generating life for both men and women. We believe it is significant that this new spirituality reflects the attitude that many men and women have taken toward the historic change that runs right through the new society. There are signs that lead us to see this new spirituality as the ability of men and women to take new and bold steps, despite the risk and the uncertainty caused by the constant threat under which people must live, steps toward transforming our history as a sign of life taking flesh in history.

This new spirituality emerges from the new historic situation that characterizes the lives of women in a society that is both in transformation and under threat. Such a spirituality is marked by the signs of gratuity and hope, as experiences of grace encountered in history. However, we cannot say that this experience is yet finished or complete, and hence we can only speak of new characteristics. The conflictive situation within our churches is one of the very factors that most hinder people from becoming conscious and developing new ways of living their faith.

Rereading the Bible in connection with our own situation has certainly been a key factor leading to a transformed consciousness among Nicaraguan Christians, especially women. However, we continue to be challenged by the possibility of rereading the Bible from the viewpoint of women, with women's eyes, with women's feelings, so as to rediscover or continually rediscover, from our own perspective, a new face of God, a more human and closer image of Jesus.

We also recognize that a challenge we women face is the fact that emphasizing motherhood, being a mother, can be dangerous, since it can limit us to our biological functions. Praising mothers can serve as the best disguise for a male ideology. Sometimes we feel we are trying to strike a balance between the just claims of mothers and the male lauding of motherhood. Thus, avoiding male deception is another great challenge.

One thing is clear: it is impossible to come to a definitive conclusion about the new women's spirituality. Nicaragua is changing. In the future there will be new challenges that we cannot yet envision. With the challenges already put to us, we are struggling on our long journey through the desert toward the promised land of peace, of justice, of equality, of liberation, for both women and men.

We women note another challenge in the fact that in Nicaragua today there is more room for women in the life of the revolutionary society than within the church itself. Institutionally, the church continues to be male and clerical. Hence there arise questions of how to translate the new spirituality of Nicaraguan Christian women within the church, not only within basic ecclesial communities, but within the whole ecclesiastical institution.

Finally, we could bring all these challenges together by asking ourselves how we can move from being a people that is sociologically Christian to being a people that is really believing, that deeply lives out its experience of God, that does not center its faith on a body of doctrines, rituals, rules, and "spiritual exercises" from a Eurocentric, male, and clerical culture, a people whose practice is liberating, whose experience is that of encountering the Lord in the experience of the least, the most humiliated, the most impoverished brothers and sisters, so as to be able, out of that situation, to announce and embody the joyful and exhilarating Good News of Jesus, of the coming of the kingdom of justice, peace, and fullness of life.

In striving toward and seeking to embody this new spirituality that we have tried to uncover in this presentation, and in meeting the challenges that lie in store for us, we lift our gaze toward Mary, the mother of Jesus, and we contemplate her as the new woman, the liberated woman, prophetess of the God of the poor, who in anticipation sang of the liberating exploits of God on behalf of the poor, who surrendered her womb and her whole life to the realization of God's liberating plan in history. In her, Nicaraguan women see the model for their own commitment to history and their new spirituality.

I would like to conclude with the text of a simple, popular Nicaraguan Marian hymn* that expresses all the affection and commitment present in this new image of Mary as embodied in the life of our Nicaraguan people:

*Spanish lyrics and music by Carlos Mejia Godoy, poet and composer.

Mary virgin bird,
Joyful virgin bird,
you with the aching feathers,
you with the thorns and roses.
Little bird in the cotton fields,
bird in the coffee groves,
brown-skinned virgin bird,
black bird in the canefield.

We pray to you through your son,
the beloved one from your womb,
the worker, the peasant,
the humble one, the exploited one.
We pray to you through your people.
Virgin bird, when you fly,
don't let your flight be stained,
little bird of peace.

Virgin bird, seed,
Mary of the corn that has been resown,
Mary, bird and mother
of my tortured brother;
Mary, bird out in the sun,
selling fried food on the corner,
little bird up all night,
little bird on militia duty.

Pajarita huasiruca
Virgin bird of maize,
brash little birdie,
border-guarding bird,
little bird from the Segovias,
little bird from San Juan,
little bird from Subtiava,
little bird from Ayapal.

Mary virgin bird,
little bird from Monimbo,
birdie Nicaragua,
bird of Revolution,
freedom-loving birdie,
little bird without borders,
necessary bird,
little guerrilla bird.

Bird with a mature womb,
bitter and sweet beak;
there won't be cages in the future,
little bird of insurrection.
The hope of your wings,
will penetrate all the pain,
birdie Guatemala,
birdie El Salvador.

14

Women's Participation
in the Church

I. A Protestant Perspective

Nelly Ritchie (Argentina)

INTRODUCTION

It is both a privilege and a responsibility to make my contribution to our joint reflection on the participation of women in the church. It is my desire that the contributions of the women present here—and of women in their everyday work—may be hope-giving signs that will lead us all to grow in our real and specific commitment to the reign of God. From the perspective of a faith that gives witness to God's liberating action on behalf of the people and with the certainty that we are called to co-participate in building this witnessing people, I would like to begin by defining what I understand by "church," this sphere, with all its potential, in which women may—or may not—develop fully. I remain aware of the limitations with which we must contend.

CHURCH

In the course of my ecumenical pastoral experience, I have gradually discovered that one of the most important elements, one that is to some extent decisive in the concrete and real commitment of Christians to the process of history, is our notion of church. What I have in mind is not a theoretical and doctrinal comparison of what the church is or is not. The issue is how, when we start from a narrow and restricting idea of what church means, any commitment outside the church building, any activity "toward the outside" is experi-

Translated from Spanish by Phillip Berryman.

enced as something that derives, as a secondary effect, from being church.

Out of our own concrete experiences the data of reality are telling us that a new ecclesiology is underway. I do not intend to spell out this ecclesiology, nor do I think that this panel should spend a lot of time doing so. However, we must mention that out of praxis not only is the concept church, and ultimately the concept of what it means to take part in church, being broadened, but in some manner new ways of being involved in history are opening up to those who call themselves "church."

People of God

In Old Testament language, this people of God is the assembly of those who are summoned, of those who are called. Called for what? The purpose that emerges from the biblical texts points toward the formation of a particular people, God's own, a holy people who can make known its own acceptance by the true God in its options in history.[1]

This purpose, which in the Old Testament seems to be restricted to one race, is in fact a universal purpose. God reminds Israel over and over that truly belonging to God's people goes beyond race. The universal nature of this calling becomes explicit in the incarnate God. In Jesus of Nazareth is revealed the Messiah who continues to create and recreate his own people from among all peoples.

That is how the early community understood its own purpose and mission: to proclaim this universality and this inclusive purpose of God. Thus we have the well-known text of the apostle Paul to the Galatians: "There does not exist among you Jew or Greek, slave or freeman, male or female. All are one in Christ Jesus. Furthermore, if you belong to Christ you are the descendants of Abraham, which means you inherit all that was promised" (Gal. 3:28–29).

This text sheds light on God's universal purpose. However, it is not about an inclusiveness that makes no demands or an unconditioned opening: *(a)* We are part of the people when we respond to the call. *(b)* We belong to the new sphere of relations—with God and with others—when our life is incorporated into the saving process through a clear option, choice, decision for the way of truth and life revealed in Jesus the Messiah. *(c)* We co-participate in the transformation of reality and in building a people of equals.

Community

Those who gather around the purpose of the God of life constitute, and actively take part in, a community. Those who respond to Jesus' invitation and follow him are the company of his associates. Those who with one mind and heart wait for the fulfillment of the promise that they will not be alone as they face the struggle are those who receive the power and dynamism of the Holy Spirit, and this makes them active participants in this new reality, this new way God has of being present in the world.

The New Testament word that describes this reality is *koinonia:* communion, participation in something in common. It is used with regard to relations in

marriage, trade, friendship, and communion with God. The word also translates an attitude: one does not enter into a relationship of dependence and
passive acceptance, but one enters the sphere of creative communication, of
common interests, purposes, and efforts.

The community that is born and grows around the Risen One, around new
life, is one that discovers the key to sharing, a community where this communion that makes them experience true brotherhood and sisterhood becomes
mutual responsibility and a clear exercise of solidarity and justice. Such a
community is concerned not so much with its own self-preservation but, rather,
wants to take stands that can give witness to its Lord's own self-giving.

Is this people of God a "neutral" people? Is this inclusive and universal
community an "amorphous" community? While we do run the risk and we
may fall into the temptation of neutralizing God's transforming message
throughout the ages (words/deeds), it helps us if we recall that in the New
Testament the apostle Paul used the image of the "body" for various purposes:
to show the interdependence of the members, an interdependence made possible by dependence on the head, Jesus the Christ; and to show an organic
character in being and doing, necessary to the enabling of the mission of the
people of God.

I believe that if we take these two concepts, people of God and community,
we shall be able to avoid sterile discussions about who belongs or does not
belong to the "true" church, and about who should or should not participate in
certain spheres regarded as ecclesiastical.

It may even be helpful for us to see our active role as women with the breadth
of people who discern the liberating action of God, as women who really
believe that God is forming, and continues to form, this faithful people from
among all peoples, with a purpose that is particular, but with a vision that is
universal. Furthermore, we may see that it is in the midst of this people, for the
sake of this liberating project, that God continues to summon us and call us
together today out of our particular situations, starting with our limitations—
social, cultural, political, economic, and so forth—as well as our opportunities.

"Church" is the people called together by God, the community of those men
and women who, in response to that invitation, take their place in the saving
plan and are actively taking part in the liberating deeds that make known God's
purpose for humankind: the decision to make all things new.

If we agree on this starting point, perhaps we can now devote our attention
to considering our participation in this plan, our active role as women in this
project.

WOMAN

Limitation or Opportunity?

Here we must certainly take into account our own individual experiences,
the environment in which we have grown up, the social, cultural, economic,

religious, and political conditioning factors that have meant real limitations, without discounting the possibilities we have had—at least those of us here present—to discover our own potentialities, to transform the "given" into the search for what should be.

How do we experience ourselves as women? I believe no definition can successfully translate the wealth of our own experience, of our ongoing search, of our refusal to adjust to the "roles" that it is assumed we must play, of the stimulating discovery that what has enriched us can also enrich others.

Looking Back

Chapter 29 of Deuteronomy recounts God's initiative to enter into a new covenant with the people (this is especially confirmed in 29:9-17). In this instance woman and man are sharers in the agreement, responsible for this commitment and privileged by this "election." Once more it is clearly the case that sharing in the promise is not conditioned by being of a particular race (foreigners are included) or of one gender but, rather, the condition for being incorporated into God's project is the acceptance of Yahweh as true God, and the commitment to respond in fidelity to this faithful God. Despite all the conditioning factors characteristic of that period, in the Old Testament women are incorporated into the saving plan as active participants.

From Old to New Testament we see a qualitative leap in the idea of woman. Jesus' own attitude is that of one who enhances the dignity of women by enabling them to participate fully in announcing the kingdom and anticipating the new humankind.

In the early church we find that equality in Christ is a basic thesis: man/woman, slave/free, Jew/pagan—all are viewed as persons. There is an attempt to live out the new humanity that has been announced. Thus we find women fully involved in the total ministry of the church, recognized as effective co-workers (Phil. 4:2-3) laboring for the Lord (Rom. 16:1-15).

However, the point here is not to find those biblical citations that back the participatory role of women in the early community but, rather, to see the continuity in God's work, one of whose main aspects is the element of communion and encounter, communion between God and humankind and between man and woman, who acknowledge those features that make them different and yet know that they are one: one in the Father's creative purpose, one in the Son's prayer, one in the task of proclaiming and living the message of complete freedom for all, one in the commitment to create the new humankind.

Present and Future

Today no one denies the woman's right to be present in society. At least it is not denied explicitly, although we often receive "messages"—in actions and reactions—of that sort, and many people continue to consider the home and the children to be the proper and primary sphere for women's activity. To a degree, not "obeying" the traditional canons makes our own "being women" (in other words, being really "feminine") questionable.

All of us are quite aware that the "struggle" is not *against* men—who, like us, are victims of the pressures of a society that desires to make us in its own image and likeness, interchangeable parts in a machinery that is already built—but, rather, that our struggle is *on behalf of* a true humankind: participatory, family-spirited, creative, and united in solidarity.

If that is to happen, however, we must uncover within ourselves all our potentialities and help one another in this task of giving birth to all the fruits of this painful childbirth, which has meant, and for many continues to mean, letting our voices be heard, not being seen as a "threat" but as a force bringing about new realities.

I am not speaking of just being "taken into consideration." How many distinctive statements, how many actions of our own, how many enriching contributions have been left by the wayside because of this concern to be taken into consideration! I am speaking of women together seeking new paths so as not to do the same thing we condemn in others (men or women) but, rather, to do everything that we firmly believe can serve as the basis for a new way of life and for a new reality.

I speak as a Latin American woman who recognizes that besides doing away with everything that causes oppression and dependence in our continent, we must strive to do away with the oppressive elements that make women doubly exploited.

Being women, being part of God's people, being agents in the drive toward liberation are three realities that come to expression in different ways. At this moment, however, we shall focus on the specific sphere in which we want to examine this active role: the church.

PARTICIPATION (FROM A PERSONAL EXPERIENCE)

In a way, from the beginning of this paper, we have been attempting to open up the idea and the reality of the church by taking it out of the strictly institutional sphere. We retrieved the notion of its organic nature, of the church being built around God's liberating plan in the world of interdependence and joint action on behalf of this project. But what is our real situation? How do we live on a daily basis with this tension between the institutional church and the church as people of God? As a community that gives witness to and proclaims this plan, how do we give living expression to our involvement in God's people in the larger community?

Only at this point shall I venture to speak of my own experience, which takes place in a particular church with a particular name, history, and geography. It is not my intention that my experience should be understood as being typical of the participation of women in the Argentine church, nor do I want all these "cries" in the form of questions to be attributed to most women. Out of my own experience, I want to share both the certainties and the questions that arise out of sincere searching and in fidelity to the Good News.

The Evangelical Methodist Church to which I belong is part of the Methodist movement whose origins go back to eighteenth-century England, and which arose as a "movement of spiritual renewal, of evangelization of the lower classes, and of community-transforming witness and social service."[2] I do not want to dwell now on the elements that came into this movement as it passed through the United States experience, but simply to note that the Methodist church came to Argentina through North American missionary activity. After 150 years of Methodist presence in Argentina we may note:

a) It began as *"iglesia de colectividad,"* that is, a church of the converted. Most Argentines (like most Latin Americans) are Catholics by birth, and thus at first only European immigrants felt called to Methodism and represented by it.

b) There followed a period in which an emphasis on community action, especially through education, enabled the Methodist church to become more a part of the reality of the country and to understand it better.

c) Only starting in 1969, the moment when the Methodist Church of Argentina became independent of the North American church, did a new understanding of the church's life and mission open its vision and reinforce its commitment within the reality of Argentina. This process of assuming autonomy and national identity was not easy and some tensions remain unresolved.

d) During the tragic years of the most recent military dictatorship (1976–83), when human life was viewed with contempt and human dignity trampled, there were voices in solidarity arising from within the Methodist Church of Argentina. This commitment by most of the leaders, sometimes in conjunction with the congregations to defend human rights—even risking their own security—enabled a minority church to attain recognition for what it was contributing to the nation. Within the church this commitment to "the least" (the disappeared, their relatives, those who were jailed unjustly, those who came back from exile, and so forth) aggravated some of the tensions mentioned above.

Owing to the urgency of responding to demands as they arose, there was not always a corresponding reflection on the changes and transformations taking place within the church, and there was a certain inability to make the institutional decisions that should go along with this new way of experiencing ourselves as church: people called by God to defend life.

Hence we should not be surprised to see a degree of exhaustion and burn-out affect the presumed unity of action. The church exhibits a dwindling base in the congregations, a bodily weakening, and most disconcerting, a "forgetting" or ignorance of what one has inherited: the inheritance coming from the demand that the Good News be proclaimed to the poor and they be liberated from all slavery, and the inheritance of the Methodist church itself, namely, active involvement by the popular classes in that proclamation.

Women, who have struggled tirelessly in the midst of our people, who cried out for life when it was being treated with contempt on all sides, have become more and more committed to changing the situation, but these same women have not always found in the church a community ready to meet their needs. While we are quite aware of the experience of many people, both women and men, who felt that the church was expressing them, ministering to them, and accompanying them in their needs and in their moments of anguish, it is also true that within the community they did not find all the openness required for posing their basic questions, nor all the solidarity they needed in their pain or searching.

In this church that many recognize because of its participatory style both in its internal governance and in its constant concern for the concrete situations in which it must carry out its ministry, in this church where the so-called "ministry apart" (pastoral ministry) can be exercised by both sexes in response to a calling and with the community's recognition, in this institutional setting we find that questioning voices are being raised and suspicions are being aroused.

After ten years of pastoral work within the Methodist Church of Argentina, certain questions are becoming urgent. I am raising some of them, with no expectation of finding answers to them all. Rather, I want to be honest and present the tensions and contradictions that occur even within a participatory institution.

QUESTIONS AND SUSPICIONS

1. Can an open and participatory community be composed primarily of middle-and upper-middle-class people?

2. Can a community that wants to be a "sign" be contented not to grow? (This is asked not with any proselytizing aim, but simply to recover that ancient yearning of God's people: that the people of hope grow as a sign of life.)

3. Does not exaggerated intellectualism mean a subtle contempt for the people's wisdom?

4. Is not exaggerated formalism a stumbling block to the free expression of the people's spirituality?

5. Should not the energy placed at the service of the institution be directed into discovering the transforming power of the people?

These questions arise when we look at the internal life of a church that is a long way from being a creative center of genuine adoration in which God's liberating deeds are celebrated in the midst of God's own, where the people take nourishment for the daily struggle, where the overall situation is confronted with a faith that must shed light along the way and point the way to liberating options. How many other questions emerge when we take a thorough look at the whole breadth of the activity of God's people!

As women experiencing this situation of tensions and struggles, we try to avoid falling into new dogmatisms. We have the opportunity to be not only participants in, but even the agents of, this transformation that must take place if we are to be faithful to our very reason for being as church. And we have this opportunity alongside many others (both women and men) who, whether inside or outside the present institution, want to build a meaningful community, a sign of God's saving purpose.

We also understand that deep-seated changes will become possible to the extent that we gain new space for activity and are aware of the need for transformation. But there are still many questions. For those of us women who have decided to remain within the institutional church with the hope that our work, talents, and service may not be taken advantage of by a few or lead to a project contrary to the one God proposes, how are we to put this decision into effect? How are we to reclaim for the people what has been until now the privilege of a few?

We live in this continual tension between what should be and what we have in our own hands as *materia prima* for changing the way things are. Our responses (limited and linked to particular sectors) will be closely related to the transformation of the overall reality, the macro-structure to which we must all be committed.

That is undoubtedly where we shall discover a people growing in awareness and participation, this people that is bringing about the new age in hope; this people to which we belong and within which we want to remain in order to struggle against anything that limits fullness of life and to further anything that is a sign of justice, of liberating activity, of transforming commitment.

We look at the present without ignoring its shackles. We look toward the future without ignoring its costs. But if we really want to become a people of equals, our commitment as women will be toward eliminating any kind of discriminatory activity. As church, we shall be for eliminating all sectarianism in order to build together a true community that gives witness to the creative and re-creative dynamism of the Spirit of Truth.

NOTES

1. See, e.g., these biblical texts: Gen. 15:1–7; 35:9–12; Ex. 3:4–10; 19:1–6; Lev. 26:9–13; Ps. 79:13; Jer. 31:31–33; Ezek. 37:27–28.

2. From an unpublished paper on Methodism by Julio Sabanes.

II. A Catholic Perspective

Maria Pilar Aquino (Mexico)

INTRODUCTION

The theme of women and the church in Latin America today must locate itself within the context of a reality marked by oppression, dependence, and the conflict of opposing interests. Within this context a struggle exists to eradicate oppression by changing the conditions that foster dependence and by affirming the right of the poor to *life*. The struggle itself is being translated and expressed in the process of the liberation of Latin America.

The struggle for liberation occurs as a reaction to oppression; thus both liberation and oppression are two aspects of an unjust society. There are those who benefit from injustice and look to maintain it. There are those who seek to escape it and thereby combat it. The church in Latin America is involved in both oppression and liberation.

The church reproduces at its center the situations and relationships of oppression. This is because faith, religious expressions, spiritual experience, the relationships of men and women—all express the same interests of the dominant sector of society. And these are interests of class, race, and gender. Yet we cannot oversimplify. The church also embodies the dreams, defeats, successes, and interests of the oppressed. This has its impact on the church itself, as well as on society.

Therefore, to recognize the role of the church as an agent of oppression should not weaken our recognition of the church as the community of the poor who are loved by God. This church continues to liberate itself in history as it grows in discernment of the path of the community of faith, hope, and love. The followers of Jesus, who are the church, remain the sign and saving instrument of the God of life in the course of history.

It is true that, within the church, processes exist that encourage domination and that consider irrelevant the needs and demands of women. At the same time, processes exist that diminish the action of the powerful and act in favor of the oppressed. The active and dynamic presence of women in the church is proof of this.

Translated from Spanish by Louise Bernstein, C.S.J.

THE OPTION FOR THE POOR IS AN OPTION FOR WOMEN

Historically, the church has served as a vehicle transmitting cultural patterns of patriarchy as well as religious traditions with respect to women, which sought to keep them both domestic and private. Yet in the bold relief of history we see the presence of women who stood in opposition to domination.

Since the late 1960s, the church in Latin America has seen itself in a serious process of renewal. The renewal deals with the invasion of the poor into the heart of the church. The massive number of these poor presents varied questions and solutions in each country and region in terms of conscience, strength, impact, and organization.

The presence of the poor has generated within the church a rediscovery of its own mission and identity. Their presence has led the church to new official positions, such as that of the preferential option for the poor. This option has opened new perspectives in relation to oppressed groups. In the case of women, in particular, it should be noted that the church made explicit recognition of a situation of double oppression in the Puebla Document of 1979. In addition, women have actively participated in the formation and advancement of the basic ecclesial communities. These successes have already been noted in the Buenos Aires Conference.

The church as a whole has not proposed a deliberate, organized, and voluntary action in favor of women. However, to the degree that the Latin American church insists upon meeting the needs, the aspirations, and the interests of the poor, it promotes the participation of women.

The presence of women in the church is necessary in order to deepen and enrich the church's own identity and mission as a community of equals called to serve as sacramental sign of the humanity of Christ. As long as only the masculine presence is seen by the church as the exclusive means of salvation, the church fragments and delegitimizes its unity, holiness, and catholicity.

The question of women, therefore, has to be recognized by the church, because their presence in the church conforms to evangelical thinking and because it contributes to the forging of a more integrated conscience—a bright, new presence of church in the heart of oppressed peoples.

Identification with the oppressed and participation in their struggles of liberation have permitted the reformulation of the vocation and mission of the church in Latin America. This experience finds its best expression in the basic ecclesial communities.

These communities propose a living-out of communitarian values. They assume that evangelization is an integral part of their identity. They are liberating areas of faith. They are also democratic spaces of learning and sharing, spaces where God has something to say. In these communities life and faith find profound articulation, and those who experience this life and faith find that one cannot exist without the other. The basic ecclesial communities generate social and ecclesial practices that recapture a more evangelical meaning of church, precisely because of their commitment to the poor and to the struggle for liberation.

In the genesis of the basic ecclesial communities, the growing participation of women in new and freeing evangelization works has appeared. Women are involved in radiophonic schools, popular catechetics, celebration of the Word, the establishment of new communities, and the creation of para-liturgies.

This incorporation of women into liberating evangelizing tasks has followed diverse rhythms according to country and region. But women's quantitative and qualitative presence is a fact. Their presence is expressed in ecclesial practices that are bound specifically to the new expression of church, which takes its faith as stemming from the practice of liberating the oppressed.

In the case of grassroots catechesis and celebration of the Word, women have received an official church mandate to exercise the ministries. Women now participate in various services that educate in the faith, form conscience and ethical values, and project the symbolic/liturgical Word from a liberating perspective.

However, in the formation of new ministries, there remains a question. Are the cultural traditions of Latin America, in which the woman is assigned the role of protagonist, influencing the direction that creativity in the ministries assumes? The future will answer this question.

As for the debate over priesthood for women, the question is posed in different terms in Latin America than in other latitudes. In many areas of Latin America, priesthood for women is simply not seen in terms of righting a massive wrong. In other areas, where priesthood for women is a goal, it is most concerned with priesthood as a presence, service, and option for the aspirations and struggles of the poor.

The basic ecclesial communities provide a space in which women participate in the basic, primary needs of the community. This participation makes it possible to form a conscience in two dimensions of oppression: as poor and as woman. Involvement brings the realization that the struggle for justice for the poor is a challenge and a task reaching beyond the single community.

The emergence of women as equals in the struggle for justice poses the requirement for a more humanized understanding, rather than a man/woman understanding, of the process of liberation. The new humanity requires a more integrating, more global, more unified face, because it has brought a feminized face into the struggle.

The church is enriched by the quality that women bring to their ministerial, evangelizing, pastoral, and sacramental tasks. But the enrichment reaches beyond that level into theological expression. That expression is altered when the life of faith is celebrated through the eyes of women, because that celebration requires a rethinking of the theological task, freed from the macho culture that has molded both the men and the women of Latin America.

In this dynamic and conflicted state of the new presence of women in the church, many aspects need work in the future. There must be more specific reflection on the themes of gender, on the questions of responsibility in leadership, on the recognition of women's presence, on the recognition of women's theological work, and on the new theological reflection their presence inspires.

OTHER CONTRIBUTIONS TOWARD THE AFFIRMATION OF LIFE

We tend to see in the traditional religious expressions of the poor Latin American woman a sense of resignation and defeat because her church is one that shares with the world a vision of domination. Yet we must see, existing alongside this resignation and defeat, an attitude of resistance to oppression. There exists in Latin American history a long trajectory of practices and a symbolic world that has helped the subjugated woman persist as capable of dreaming and creating.

One example can be seen in devotion to the Virgin. Our Lady of Guadalupe has been expressly linked to the processes of independence and a struggle for the land, a struggle always on the side of the poor.

There has been a deeply consistent devotion to the saints and to the dead as intercessors. There has been a conceptualization of God as a God who saves, and of suffering that will be redeemed in the beyond. All contain elements of criticism and resistance to oppression. All indicate dreams of a new and different society, either before or after death. Yet as an ethical indignation toward the actual situation, it is a timid rebellion, a silent rejection of the status quo.

This divided world, this negation of women as human beings and as agents and subjects in history—these do not correspond to God's plan. Women do not voluntarily identify with the interests and the values of actual society. The opposite is true. There is continually present in the church communities the heartbreaking "why?" of hunger, poverty, lack of work, and repression.

Though the grass-roots woman cannot identify the actual state of society as "good," she remains capable of celebration. Life is affirmed, but not life as the powerful say that it is. The woman as dominated sufferer is not the reality, because that reality has been invaded by a new process in which women take the initiative. They create projects. They enliven celebrations. They multiply communities. Life and hope are affirmed against death. The new society in which men and women drink together of the wine of rights and are the sacrament of Christ in history has already arrived.

The presence of women in the church of Latin America is a presence of tension. The rest of the church and its leaders are pressured by that presence to move toward an option for the poor and to take as their own the question of women.

Like the poor, women are objects of suspicion. In the basic ecclesial communities, women become aware of their dual oppression as poor and as woman. They begin to view themselves as creators of a new alternative. They become dangerous when they question the powerful and masculine model of the internal structures of the church. Once this questioning begins, the process is irreversible. There is posed the urgent matter of power and, what is more, of sacred power.

From the massive presence of women in the church, there can surge a transformation of the church. The transformation will occur in the measure that women affirm the creation of ecclesiality, organize anew, and take the evangelization initiative. It will occur through the building of communities in which power does not flow from an ecclesiastical masculine body, but from the necessities of the community itself.

The institution of marriage, particularly, requires attention in order that it support the dignity of women, in spite of the patriarchal context in which it exists. The medieval church, in fact, recognized the right of women to determine the establishment of the marriage bond. But practice has not upheld this recognition.

Another area of concern is the right of sanctuary. This has to do with the protection and defense of the foreigner or the persecuted. Sanctuary has its roots as much in the Old Testament (Num. 35:10ff.; Dt. 9:1ff.) as in the Middle Ages. Today we continue its tradition.

The church in Latin America is a place of encounter, recognition, expression, communication, celebration, organization, and the strengthening of the oppressed. Conditions such as these have, in all revolutionary times, called forth from the church the protection of sanctuary. In sanctuary, combatants have rebuilt their strength to return to the battle.

In various countries, under conditions of repression and persecution, it is in the church that the persecuted find asylum and protection. Here they are recognized as children of God, they are nourished, they can criticize themselves and grow. In situations of sanctuary, in church, chapel, and convent, women play the dominant role.

The Latin American church has been torn and enriched by martyrdom. This has moved it to a reappropriation of the living God as a God of the poor, the defender of widows, the nurturer of the impoverished. The church has assumed a faith in a greater God, in a Lord of history who, by the fact of the violent and early deaths of its children, has taken sides in favor of the poor against the powerful.

Women, wives, widows, sisters, and mothers raise the cry on every front in defense of human rights. The potential of women is expressed with painful vehemence when parts of the body are wounded. Mothers transcend the limits of fear and take on a warlike struggle to find the son or daughter who has disappeared through the forces of destruction and death.

There emerges, then, as a fruit of the presence of women in the Latin American church, a clearer understanding of love. Or, said in another way, women are now translating with new emphasis what love really means in its strictest theological and social sense. Love means:

—to participate actively in the building of new structures;

—to collaborate for a better quality of life for all;

—to affirm woman's being as woman who complements and broadens the totality of human life;

—to articulate woman's cause as the cause of the innocent, the oppressed of the earth;

—to sustain a persistent battle against an order contrary to the practice of Jesus and the Kingdom of God;

—to verify the original design of God, promoting life from its primary base;

—to reaffirm woman's right to be church, to make church, to build church, creating participation, service, commitment, and celebration.

Women spread love as a dynamism of life and for life.

15

Feminist Theology as the Fruit of Passion and Compassion

Ana Maria Tepedino (Brazil)

In reflecting on my own personal experiences and those of my closest female companions, and through the two national meetings we have held in Brazil,[1] as well as in reading the papers presented in Buenos Aires, I have been able to perceive certain "lines of force" of women's theology in Latin America.

EXPERIENCE OF OPPRESSION AS A STARTING POINT

As a liberation theology from a women's point of view, feminist theology is the result of our concrete experience: of "my being and my acting, my seeing and my feeling, my speaking and my silence."[2]

The starting point of this theology is the existential experience of searching for one's own identity, since our present identity has been imposed upon us by a patriarchal and male-chauvinist culture, and is therefore a product of cultural oppression, exacerbated by economic and social oppression.

Its starting point is also our experience of faith, lived from the underside of power and authority. From these two starting points we reread revelation and reality with a view not only to individual liberation, but to liberation of an entire people.[3]

In Latin America, the cry of women comes from within the massive cry of the poor and oppressed in the midst of the exploitation and misery in which the majority of the population lives. And this is why theological reflection from a woman's point of view wishes to make its voice heard as a service to all of those alienated from society. Therefore, it has to be a "combative and aggressive theology, one that gets at the root causes of marginalization and alienation from a biblical and theological perspective, for the purpose of seeking justice."[4]

We believe that any system of domination dehumanizes both dominator and

---

Translated from Portuguese by Phillip Berryman

dominated, and that is why our struggle is against male-chauvinist ideology, which dehumanizes both men and women. We want to invite our male theological colleagues to join us in this struggle so that together we can give birth to a new theology.[5]

As a result, the starting point for feminist theology goes beyond the experience of oppression, the experience of God, and the struggle for justice; it must also be the "practice of tenderness," that is, seeking to create brotherly and sisterly relationships, which should not exist simply between men and women, but also among the elderly, adolescents, and children—and indeed among all people.[6]

A CONTEXTUAL AND CONCRETE METHOD

Feminist theology in the Latin American context arises out of the realities of daily life. This theology *(a)* seeks to know life through personal experience as well as through human and social science; *(b)* seeks to interpret it in light of the Bible (with the understanding that God's revelation was given to human beings and articulated in human language, thus depending on a culture in time and in space—and accordingly, it can both oppress and liberate); we have to discover the sense that the Spirit reveals to us today through the ancient text of the Bible;[7] and *(c)* tries to retrieve and give a name to the experience of women in a patriarchal society in order to redeem the past, transform the present, and prepare for tomorrow.

Therefore, feminist theology has to be based on certain methodological steps.[8] First, do not accept a biblical text passively, but apply a certain hermeneutical suspicion to the biblical passage and contemporary interpretations of it. Second, discover and proclaim the liberating values in the text that lie hidden behind the historical hermeneutics. Third, rediscover within the text whatever it may reveal about what women have accomplished throughout history, and keep that memory alive. Fourth, creatively give the text a present-day meaning. On the basis of the historical context in which the text was produced, rework it creatively, so that the memory does not get lost.

LIFE AS THE KEY TO THE WOMEN'S INTERPRETATION

Throughout the Bible and throughout personal experience, we perceive that for women the key to understanding is *life,* the valuing of life in all its aspects. This is why women are so involved in the various movements for health, day-care centers, and schools; in the community movements for land reform; in volunteer crews to construct housing; in ecology projects—in short, in activities for better living conditions for all.

This can readily be seen in the role of women in the basic ecclesial communities, an area where they have been very active and where, in fact, they have been important leaders in the movement to create an alternative to this wasteful, consumerist, individualistic, and hedonistic society.

Women constitute the other side of the human experience of oppression, the one most diametrically opposed to power and domination. That is why they experience God in their own manner, as the One who really protects the weak and is the defender of those who have less life. That is why God raises up leaders to liberate God's children from oppression (see Ex. 3:7-8), sometimes to denounce prophetically the present, and sometimes to announce the divine design of love, so that men and women can discover and know one another on an equal basis. In all their marvelous differences, they can experience reciprocity and the responsibility of sharing in generating and nourishing—in justice, love, peace, and joy—the life of the new man and the new woman, making history fruitful with new possibilities.[9]

Since she carries in her womb for nine months a new life that is coming into being, woman feels and expresses her experience of God in a different manner. "It involves a 'relational' manner of knowing which goes beyond conceptual coldness, encompassing all the dimensions of life in this relation."[10] For this reason a woman tends to experience life as a unified whole, "integrating strength and tenderness, happiness and tears, intuition and reason."[11] She encounters life as a place "for simultaneously experiencing oppression and liberation both from force and from misfortune"[12] because she is more closely in touch with nature and because her existential experience teaches her to value small things that occur in daily life, without overemphasizing isolated moments. Certain powerful moments serve to crystallize, transcend, and radiate outward (moments of *kairos,* the time outside of time, which illuminates the *chronos,* the time of the clock, dates, and routine).

FEMINIST THEOLOGY AS THE FRUIT OF PASSION

A woman, by her very constitution, seems always to be extending herself, carrying people—through her experience of faith, of prayer, of life, feeling the impetus to overcome individualism and hearing the call to community experience. She meditates on the things of the heart and opens herself fully to communion; hence her sensitivity to the needs of others.[13]

This sensitivity to the pain of others, this capacity for *syn pathein* (the Greek origin of compassion) calls women to suffer with, to feel with, to be in solidarity with, to be more open to the problems of others, to understand the values of sharing in the struggle for better living conditions—and also to transmit the faith characterized by the struggle for justice.[14] This is, as Paul Ricoeur would put it, a faith marked by love: love close by (the immediate: giving bread to those who are hungry) and love at a distance (the longer term: changing unjust structures).

Woman, who together with man constitutes the image of God (see Gen. 1:26), expresses the tender (*hesed*) side of God, the maternal womb (*rahamim*), concern for those children who suffer the most.[15] "In His mysterious divinity He is a Father, yet the tenderness He has for us makes Him a Mother. The father becomes feminine through loving. We see the greatest proof of this in the Son who proceeds from God's very bosom."[16]

Women do theology with passion: they passionately and wholeheartedly give of themselves, striving to fill their ideas with lived experience. Like the female disciples who followed Jesus, totally surrendering their lives, they dedicate themselves to him and to the mission of spreading the Good News throughout the world.

Passion, allowing oneself to be possessed, is the essence of the mystical experience and of the erotic experience as well, involving every fiber of one's being at one peak moment, which explodes with energy and vitality for carrying on the struggle.

Women discover the importance of what their sisters have accomplished in the history of the people, showing through *passion* and through *compassion* that they really have had an impact even though their presence has often been erased. These accomplishments become visible in household chores, in the multiple forms of struggling for life, in the responsibilities of those who devote themselves to transforming society.

At the Latin American Conference on Theology (Buenos Aires), we recognize that women have sought to unite their domestic experience with pastoral activity and, specifically, with theological reflection. To illustrate this integrating experience, I would like to reflect on the figure of Martha of Bethany, the first theologian, who is presented to us as a servant, as "deaconess" in the community, as well as in her well-known role of preparer of food for a beloved guest. She subsequently receives Jesus' greatest revelation and makes a truly authentic profession of Christological faith.

SEEKING INSPIRATION FROM MARTHA OF BETHANY

Many women identify with Martha in the Gospel according to Luke (see Lk. 10:38–42), the housewife who received Jesus in her home and worked in the kitchen. In the meanwhile her sister, Mary, listened to Jesus' words while sitting at his feet, which was the appropriate attitude of a disciple before a rabbi (Paul is often cited as sitting at the feet of Gamaliel; see Acts 22:3). The text contrasts the two sisters, and tradition interprets the text in the sense of opposing the contemplative life, represented by Mary, to the active life, in the person of Martha.

But can this be the only biblical image of Martha? No! In truth, the picture given to us by the Fourth Gospel (Jn. 11:10–44) is quite different. Martha is presented to us as a disciple with very strong faith.[17]

In the Fourth Gospel the fundamental category is precisely discipleship. The disciple is the person who follows the Master, who believes in Jesus and lives in free service and love, who bears witness to Jesus who loved his disciples to the end (Jn. 13:1).

Through the practice of love (*agapan*), everyone will know who the disciples of Jesus are. For the community of the Fourth Gospel, the highest authority was the "beloved disciple," who knew how to love, and therefore knew how to live faith in an appropriate manner.[18]

It is interesting to observe how the Fourth Gospel presents the Bethany family to us: Jesus loved (*agapan*) Martha, her sister Mary, and her brother Lazarus (Jn. 11:5). This Bethany family was a friend (*filein*) of Jesus.[19] It would seem that when Jesus went to Jerusalem he lodged at their house (see Mk. 11:11; 14:3). There he felt at home amidst his "new family"—those who did the will of the Father (see Mk. 3:35). They were his disciples and Jesus was their master.

The Gospel tells us that when Jesus found out about Lazarus' death (here the Gospel uses the word *agapan*), he became so sad that he wept (see Jn. 11:35),[20] which shows the depth of friendship and sensitivity of Jesus.

In this experience of friendship, of love, is an encounter in which a revelation and acceptance of these persons takes place, and they come to know one another and understand what lies in the depths of each one of them. In this manner, the mystery of each one is revealed. In this environment of the Bethany family, in the company of these persons whom he loved and who loved him, Jesus spoke: he talked of God the Father; he taught; he probably talked of his mission, of the kingdom, of his joys, and of the tribulations through which he was going. He also listened to his friends when they spoke.

Perhaps it is this story of human fellowship, this family story, this experience of dialogue that deepens the communion, which sets the stage for the revelation of Jesus to Martha as well as preparing for the profound experience of faith that Martha reveals.

The text tells us that when Martha learns that Jesus is coming, she runs out to meet him, against the rules of hospitality, which called for waiting until the guest arrived in the home. Although Lazarus has already been dead for three days, Martha is both anxious and confident, for she expects Jesus to do something. (Martha reveals that, at this point, she shares the faith of her people in the resurrection of the dead on the final day.) In the dialogue with Jesus, her faith becomes strengthened.

Contradicting the style of the Fourth Gospel, in which Jesus always takes the initiative in beginning a dialogue, this time it is Martha who begins it. She is presented to us as a person full of life and faith, with initiative and determination abounding in hope.

Although in the original source the miracle of the raising of Lazarus from the dead is at the center of the account, the Gospel places the dialogue and Martha's confession of faith at the center of the text.[21] Indeed, the most important fact in the narrative is not the resurrection of Lazarus but, rather, the affirmation that he who is about to die (Jesus) is the resurrection and the life, and that whoever believes in him (therefore loving his brothers and sisters) has already passed from death to life. It is thus understood that the resurrection of Lazarus is a sign of the resurrection of Jesus himself.

Jesus reveals to Martha precisely what kind of Messiah he is: the one who gives life and new life: "I am the Resurrection and the Life; whoever believes in me, even if dead, shall live forever" (Jn. 11:25).

The revelation that Jesus makes to this woman is the culminating point of his public ministry. Martha confesses her messianic faith, not as a reaction to a miracle (see Bartimeus in Mark 10), nor as a reaction to any statement about her (see the Samaritan woman in John, chap. 4), but as an answer to the revelation and the challenge that Jesus makes of her faith: "Do you believe this?" (Jn. 11:25).

Insofar as theology is rational discourse on faith, coherent reflection on Martha's reply to Jesus' revelation summarizes all the Christology of the Gospels: election, sonship, the incarnation, the whole dense core of faith:[22] Jesus is the revelation that has descended from the heavens, the messenger of God so all humanity may have life (see Jn. 10:10).

In her manner of proclaiming her faith, Martha reveals the process of recognizing Jesus: Yes, my Lord (*kyrios*), you are the Christ (*cristos*, Messiah), titles that the Synoptic Gospels attribute to Jesus on the way toward recognizing him as the Son of God. To this acknowledgment, the Fourth Gospel adds its high Christology of the one sent: the Son of God who came into the world. Martha crystallizes the messianic faith of the community, being its spokesperson in her capacity as the "beloved disciple" of Jesus.

The profession of faith that the Synoptics place in the mouth of Peter (see Mt. 16:15–19: "Thou art the Christ, the living Son of God") is placed in the mouth of a woman by the Fourth Gospel. This is the high point of revelation and of the proclamation of faith. Martha is presented as a person with sufficient faith. She represents the apostolic faith of the community of John, just as Peter represented the full apostolic faith of the Matthean community.[23]

In addition to her powerful theological synthesis, Martha, upon proclaiming her profession of faith, makes a Trinitarian prophecy, since it is the breath of the Holy Spirit that enables one to recognize Jesus (see 1 Cor. 12:3) and proclaim him as the Lord. She refers to the Son, to the Father, and to the Holy Spirit. This enables one to understand and express the significance of Jesus.

The most important thing is that Martha's confession of faith is repeated at the end of the Gospel according to John (20:31), when the evangelist expresses the purpose for which he wrote the Gospel: "These signs have been written so that you may know that Jesus is Christ, the Son of God, and by believing, you will have life in his name."

This summary declaration is perhaps the conclusion of the source material of the signs. Hence it is possible to imagine that the Gospel deliberately put these words, coming from their source, in the mouth of Martha as the climax of the profession of faith of the one who is the "beloved disciple," perhaps "to identify her with the writer of the book."[24]

To conclude, we can emphasize that the Fourth Gospel does not set up oppositions. In the story of the fellowship of the Bethany family, Martha and Mary are not in opposition, as they are in Luke (see Lk. 10:38–42). Rather, both reveal attitudes of disciples.

After receiving the revelation and after expressing her faith in Jesus, Martha goes off to share this joy with her sister Mary (see Jn. 11:28), just as Andrew and Philip call Peter and Nathanael.

The Fourth Gospel presents Martha as "deacon" (John 12:2). Certain experts believe that the only function established in the community of John was that of "deaconship," and thus Martha is presented as exercising this ministry.[25]

Martha, the first theologian, hears the revelation, responds with her faith in a powerful profession, and goes off to serve the community. This combination of listening and doing is precisely what ought to characterize the follower of Jesus.

Martha is presented as a deaconess, concerned with the needs of the community and the guests, a person who is dedicated and keeps the faith, who always acts when necessary, who always radiates confidence and hopefulness. At the same time that she receives the supreme revelation of Jesus, she professes her faith and the faith of the believing community. Afterward, being unable to keep such a tremendous thing to herself, she goes off to call her sister, to share the Good News with her so that her joy may be complete (see 1 Jn. 1: 1–4).

CONCLUSION

Like Martha, who combines domestic service with pastoral work and theological reflection, the Latin American women are trying to do the same, always placing the fruit of this work in service to the one who is Life and life in abundance. Life is the key to feminine interpretation, for a woman knows that life is fragile and needs to be cherished and cared for.

Women do theology with passion, passionately giving themselves to this ministry, trying to put together rationality, scientific precision, and relationality. They accomplish this ministry with compassion, with sensibility for others' pain. For it is in suffering together with the oppressed and marginalized people that they are grounded in reality, searching to collaborate in building God's kingdom. A tree deeply rooted in the earth, with its branches like arms wide open to the sky, giving shadow and a resting place—this seems a good image for women's theological ministry.

NOTES

1. See A. M. Tepedino, "That Woman Who Doesn't Know Her Place," *Perspectiva Teológica,* 17 (1985): 375–79; M. C. Bingemen, "And Woman Broke the Silence," *Perspectiva Teólogica,* 18 (1986): 371–81.

2. I. Gebara, "Women Doing Theology: An Essay for Reflection," *Revista Eclesiastica Brasileira (REB)* 46 (March 1986), fasc. 181:5.

3. N. Ritchie, "Woman and Christology," *REB* 46 (March 1986): 61.

4. E. Tamez, "The Power of Silence," *REB* 46 (March 1986): 157.

5. Ibid., p. 160.

6. Ibid., p. 157.

7. T. Cavalcanti and L. Weiler, "Prophetism of Women in the Old Testament: Perspectives for Today," *REB* 46 (March 1986): 40.

8. See E. Schüssler Fiorenza, *Bread Not Stone* (Boston: Beacon Press, 1983), p. 15.

9. Tamez, "The Power of Silence," p. 164.

10. C. de Prado, "I Feel God in Another Way," *REB* 46 (March 1986): 15.

11. "Final Document: Latin American Conference of Theology from Women's Perspective," *REB* 46 (March 1986): 167.

12. I. Gebara, "Women Doing Theology," p. 11.

13. See M. Brandao, "Mary and Feminine Spirituality," *Grande Sinal* 4 (1986): 257–66.

14. T. Cavalcanti, "On Women's Participation in the VI Interecclesiastical Basic Communities Meeting," *REB* 47 (Dec. 1987): 803–19.

15. M. C. Bingemer, "The Trinity from the Perspective of Women," *REB* 46 (March 1986): 79.

16. Clement of Alexandria, *Riches et pauvres dans l'Eglise ancienne* (Paris: Desclee de Brouwer, 1982), p. 49. This is an insert in the text, a parenthesis on the "sexual" nature of the Father in the middle of a discourse on His charitable nature, as if in some way charity and femininity were equivalent.

17. See R. Bultmann, cited by E. J. Moltmann, *Dieu Homme et Femme* (Paris: Editions du Cerf, 1985), p. 36: "Martha's reply expresses the true stature of her faith."

18. See R. E. Brown, *The Community of the Beloved Disciple* (São Paulo: Paulinas, 1984), pp. 205–18; for the problems involved in inadequate and adequate faith, see J. Tuni Vancells, *The Testimony of the Gospel According to John* (Salamanca, Spain: Sigueme, 1983), p. 172.

19. A. Jaubert, *Reading the Fourth Gospel* (São Paulo: Paulinas, 1984), p. 24, says that Jesus' attitude was unheard of, since a Jew would never enter into the house of women alone, as reported in Lk. 10:38–42.

20. It is interesting to note the emphasis given by the words *agapan* (love) and *filein* (friendship), thus conveying the meaning of a very close relationship. This was the basis for the hypothesis that Lazarus was the "beloved disciple," a theory that has since been discarded.

21. E. Schüssler Fiorenza, *In Memory of Her* (New York: Crossroad, 1984), p. 329.

22. F. Queré, *The Gospel's Women* (Paris: Seuil, 1982), p. 105.

23. E. Schüssler Fiorenza, *In Memory of Her,* p. 329.

24. R. Fortna, *The Gospel of Signs* SNTSM II (Cambridge: Cambridge University Press, 1970), pp. 197ff, cited in Schüssler Fiorenza, *In Memory of Her,* p. 330. Since today we still do not know who is the real author of the Fourth Gospel, it is one more conjecture that can "neither be proven nor disproven, historically speaking" (p. 330).

25. See A. Corell, *Consumatum Est: Eschatology and Church in the Gospel of John* (London: SPCK, 1958), pp. 40 ff., cited in Schüssler Fiorenza, *In Memory of Her,* p. 330.

16

Women's Rereading of the Bible

Elsa Tamez (Mexico)

THE REDISCOVERY OF THE BIBLE

Not long ago, when the Latin American poor burst on the scene of church life in Latin America, the consciousness of a large number of people was stirred. The Bible took on new meaning. That book—read by many but until now assimilated through a safe, unidimensional interpretation controlled by a predominantly unchallenged way of thinking—became the simple text that speaks of a loving, just, liberating God who accompanies the poor in their suffering and their struggle through human history. This is not the only new development on our continent. On the contrary, it appears as one more breakthrough in a fast-growing movement in Latin America, a movement propelled mainly by the strong yearning of the poor for life. For multiple reasons and in many ways, the poor are today stronger than ever in their commitment. This is why we, in Latin America, speak of a new way of being church, of doing theology, of reading the Bible.

A reading of the Scripture that truly liberates responds to the situation that has motivated the reading. It seems that, in a context of hunger, unemployment, repression, and war, creativity more than abounds in theology, hermeneutics, liturgy, and the pastoral field. At least this has been our experience. Both Catholic and Protestant grass-roots communities provide clear examples of the ways in which the Bible has been and still is being rediscovered. The study, discussion, and meditation based on the Word has become an integral part of the meetings of the Catholic grass-roots Christian communities. Every-

Translated from Spanish by Alicia Partnoy.

body studies and discusses the Bible from the point of view of liberation. In the progressive Protestant communities, where the Bible has always been fundamental to the liturgy, hermeneutic keys have changed and the Bible has come to be read from the perspective of the poor. In both communities the Bible has been rediscovered.

Characteristically, their readings are strongly linked to the daily life of the members of these Christian communities. There is an unquestionable bridge between the life of the people of God in the Old Testament and that of Jesus' followers in the New Testament.

This reading of the Word from the point of view of the poor has been consolidated and has become so evident that Holy Scripture is regarded as a threatening or dangerous book by some sectors of society that do not share a preferential option for the poor. The sectors I mention might be either religious or secular, such as the government (particularly in countries where the National Security Doctrine is actively enforced). Some religious circles have even decided to avoid biblical discussions. Do they fear the Bible? The ancient book of Christianity has indeed become new and defiant when it is read from the perspective of the poor.

"HOWEVER . . .," SAY THE WOMEN

Despite this situation, women with a certain degree of female consciousness have started to raise some questions about the Bible. It is not that they don't feel included in the main liberation experiences of the Bible: the exodus and the historical role of Jesus. It is that women find clear, explicit cases of the marginalization or segregation of women in several passages of both the Old and the New Testaments. There are, then, differences between reading the Bible from the point of view of the poor and reading it from a woman's perspective. The poor find that the Word reaffirms in a clear and direct way that God is with them in their fight for life. Women who live in poverty, however, even when they are aware that the strength of the Holy Spirit is on their side, do not know how to confront the texts that openly segregate them. These texts sound strange and surprising to someone who is not familiar with the culture of the biblical world and believes in a just and liberating God.

This concrete problem has not been regarded as such until recently. First, the discovery of the Bible as "historical memory of the poor" was greeted with great enthusiasm by both men and women. This discovery implied that it was necessary to discuss a significant number of biblical texts essential to the history of salvation from a new perspective, starting with those texts where the liberation of the oppressed is most apparent (Exodus, the Prophets, the Gospels). Up until now texts that segregate women have been disregarded and subordinated because the main criterion has been to experience God as a God of life who has a preferential option for the oppressed, including women. Second, only in recent years has a feminine consciousness gained some strength in the theological and ecclesiastical worlds. There have, of course, always been women who have openly questioned the church and theology. This is happening to an increasing degree in our days, especially with the upsurge of liberation theology and the proliferation of grass-roots Christian communities where women are the majority and their participation is key.

For several reasons this problem of the marginalization, or segregation, of women is harder to solve than it appears to be. One of the reasons is that our society is extremely sexist—a phenomenon that can be detected at both a tacit and an explicit level. Nor are grass-roots Christian communities free from this sexist ideology, which has deep historico-cultural roots that are hard to pull out in a single tug. To the extent that there is an easy correspondence between two cultures that marginalize women, it becomes even harder to discuss the biblical texts that reaffirm women's marginality.

Furthermore, it is a well-known fact that throughout history this correspondence of two patriarchal sexist societies has resulted in their mutual consolidation. On one hand, old-time antiwomen customs of Hebrew culture have been declared sacred; on the other hand, certain texts have consequently been held up as biblical principles to prove that women's marginalization is natural in daily life. It is in this sense that the Hebrew-Jewish lifestyle presented by the Bible is perpetuated precisely because "thus is written the word of God." This explains why the Bible has been used to reinforce the position of inferiority in which society and culture have placed women for centuries. Today this attitude is not so apparent as in the past, but in some churches it still manifests itself, albeit in disguise.

Something different takes place in grass-roots Christian communities. They react in different ways to difficult biblical texts. Sometimes they disregard antiwomen texts, at other times they juggle them to come out with a positive side or they soften the oppressive nature of the content. On other occasions they wisely simplify the problem by stating that those were other times, that reality should be different today, that God is a God of life and therefore he cannot favor discrimination against women.

Having experienced all of these attitudes in the context of different religious communities I have never taken this problem seriously. In truth, the problem would not be serious if everybody considered the Bible for what it really is: a testimony of a Judeo-Christian people with a particular culture, for whom holy revelation works always in favor of those who have least. Women would then feel included among the oppressed and they would contextualize those texts that segregate them. I believe this is what happens in many communities.

However, I have come to think that the problem is serious. Its seriousness comes, first, from the effects that these antiwomen biblical readings have produced on so many women and men who have internalized, as sacred natural law, the inferiority of women. Second, there is an inherent difficulty in interpreting texts that not only legitimate but also legislate the marginalization of women. Third, and this is mainly for Protestants, the problem is the principle of biblical authority as it is traditionally perceived. These are three difficulties that women are consciously confronting. Let us look at them in detail.

MYTHS, TEXTS, AND BIBLICAL AUTHORITY

After working with some biblical texts, like the famous narration in Genesis 3, it is easy to perceive that between the text and its current interpretation is a long series of ideologizing (or mythologizing) readings of this narration that are more harmful to women than the actual texts are.

Genesis 3 and the second account about creation have been the basis for creating a mythical framework that legitimizes women's inferiority and their submission to men. Myths—ideologies that distort reality—have been created based on these texts, not so much because of information contained in the story per se, but because of the conditions imposed by a society structured around men as its center; and by a particular way of reading the story, which places emphasis on its peripheral aspects; and by a story-telling technique that employs literal description and repetition as literary devices.

There are also other texts in which the example of a patriarchal culture has been brought in for a specific purpose. However, on many occasions, the readers of these texts have elevated the example to the category of divine law. The result is thus a legitimation and legislation, as if it were holy, of an order unfavorable to women.

Women are called, therefore, to deny the authority of those readings that harm them. It is here, then, that the collaboration of women experts in the Bible or of male exegetes with feminist perspectives is needed to reinterpret the texts, using a new hermeneutic approach.

Thus it would finally be possible for women to do a liberation-oriented reading of a text that for centuries had been used against them. However, on occasion there will be no other way to interpret the text except as a putdown of women. Its exegesis will show only the patriarchal ideology of the author, the commentator, the culture, and the historic moment in which the text was elaborated. This is the other Bible-related problem that women confront.

The tendency of some First World radical feminists to reject the Bible is, it seems to me, an exaggerated reaction. I think that by assigning too much importance to these peripheral texts, many leave aside the central message, which is profoundly liberating. From my point of view, it is precisely the Gospel's spirit of justice and freedom that neutralizes antifemale texts. A reading of the Bible that attempts to be faithful to the word of the Lord will achieve that goal best when it is done in a way that reflects the liberating meaning of the Gospel, even when sometimes fidelity to the gospel forces the reader to distance herself or himself from the text. Therefore, a time has come to acknowledge that those biblical texts that reflect patriarchal culture and proclaim women's inferiority and their submission to men are not normative; neither are those texts that legitimize slavery normative. The rationale behind this statement is essentially the same as that offered by the Scriptures: the proclamation of the gospel of Jesus calls us to life and announces the coming of the kingdom of justice.

German theologian Elisabeth Schüssler Fiorenza, who lives in the United States, proposes a new hermeneutic approach. She tries to reconstruct the beginnings of Christianity from a feminist perspective. Using this method she finds very interesting situations that explain women's active participation in the beginnings of the church. She also discovers contradictions in some of St. Paul's writings, which eventually were used to promote the submission of women. From an exegetical point of view, this is one of the best and newest approaches to the Bible. We must admit that, for Third World women, this is an important contribution regarding the analysis of the text from a woman's point of view. However, it is likely that in some communities, mainly Protestant, it will be hard to accept the idea of questioning a biblical author, not to mention an apostle, as is the case with Paul.

This presents us with the third problem: the classic formulation of the doctrine of biblical authority. I shall refer here to Protestant churches because I know them a bit better.

Women with a certain degree of female consciousness, who move in conservative sectors, at times confront the difficulties of the principle implied in the idea of inspiration, namely, being without error, or God's word in a literal sense. I stress that they confront it *at times,* because, according to my experience, a curious phenomenon takes place in real life: there is a mismatch between belief in the traditionally formulated principle of biblical authority and daily-life practice. Women in both traditional and grass-roots Protestant churches have achieved an important degree of participation in the liturgy and other areas and—except in the case of extremely conservative churches—this has not been a problem even though it is clear to these institutions that St. Paul called for "women to keep silent" in church. The issue is not even under discussion; in practice there is a tacit acceptance of women's participation and an increasing recurrence of texts that suggest the active participation of women. However, in some more traditional churches, when a woman becomes dangerously active or threatening to those in powerful positions, aid is found in the classic Pauline texts to demand women's submission to men. It is in moments like these that some women do not know how to respond. This is because they either lack the proper hermeneutic tools or have a mistaken interpretation of the principle of biblical authority.

On the other hand, when at meetings of Christian women there is an attempt to study texts such as Ephesians 5:22–24 or 1 Corinthians 14:34, the discussion frequently winds up on a dead-end street. The conflict arises because women, although not in accord with the texts nor practicing such behavior in everyday life, yet do concede at the same time that the Bible has all the authority of the word of God. Thus they find themselves trapped within a framework of literal translations, forgetting that the word of God is much more than that.

This situation tells us that it is about time to reformulate the principle of biblical authority, from the point of departure of our Latin American reality.

From a woman's perspective it is time to look for new hermeneutic criteria, patterns that not only will help us to handle patriarchal texts but also will illuminate our re-reading of the whole Bible from a feminine perspective, even texts that do not explicitly refer to women. I shall discuss now some matters that come from my own experience.

GUIDES TOWARD READING THE BIBLE FROM A LATIN AMERICAN WOMAN'S PERSPECTIVE

Gaining Distance and Coming Closer

To counteract myth-laden readings of biblical texts and to avoid the risk of repeating the interpretations of other readers, I believe in the importance of gaining distance from the text, mainly from those parts that have been frequently read and therefore have become overly familiar to our ears. When I say "gaining distance" I mean picking up the book and ignoring the interpretations that almost automatically come to mind even before reading the actual text. To distance oneself means to be new to the text (to be a stranger, a first-time visitor to the text), to be amazed by everything, especially by those details that repeated readings have made seem so logical and natural. It is necessary to take up the Bible as a new book, a book that has never been heard or read before. This demands a conscious effort that implies reading the texts a thousand times and very carefully.

This way of reading is going to be conditioned by or embedded in the life experience of the Latin American reader. Her or his experiences must be very consciously taken into account at the time of the reading. It is this experience, in the end, that will facilitate the distancing of oneself from the all-too-familiar interpretation of the common suppositions in the text, and will help to uncover keys to a liberation-oriented reading. This is the process of coming closer to daily life, which implies the experiences of pain, joy, hope, hunger, celebration, and struggle. It is clear from this process of gaining distance and coming closer that in Latin America the Bible is not read as an intellectual or academic exercise; it is read with the goal of giving meaning to our lives today. In the confusing situation we find ourselves, we want to discern God's will and how it is present in our history. We think that the written word offers us criteria for discerning. Already this is a way of reformulating the principle of biblical authority.

The process I call "gaining distance" and "coming closer" is not only geared to finding a woman's perspective. Every Latin American reading of the Bible needs to shake off rote readings that cloud the text. We must approach it with questions coming from life. However, considering that a reading of the Scriptures from a woman's angle is very new for us, considering that it is mandatory to discern between "macho" cultures and the gospel of life, the process of gaining distance from "macho" readings and texts and coming closer to the experience of Latin American women gains relevance for all women.

The Reading of the Bible with the Poor as a Point of Departure

Every liberation reading from the perspective of Latin American women must be understood within the framework that arises from the situation of the poor. In a context of misery, malnutrition, repression, torture, Indian genocide, and war—in other words, in a context of death—there is no greater priority than framing and articulating the readings according to these situations. The poor (men, women, blacks, Indians) comprise the large majority, and it is because of their discontent that repression and mass killings generally take place. They are in a privileged place, hermeneutically speaking, because we conceive of the God of life as One who has a preferential option for the poor. Besides, the mystery of God's reign is with them because it has been revealed to them (Mt. 11:25). Therefore, a reading from a woman's perspective has to go through this world of the poor. This will be a guarantee that it has a core theme of liberation, and it will shed light on other faces of the poor, such as blacks and native peoples. This kind of reading will also give us methods to develop specific approaches to salvation in each of their situations.

Besides, this reading key, which has as a synonymous parallel "God is on the side of the oppressed," is the key to cancel and disallow those—really very few in number—antiwomen texts that promote the submission of women to men and affirm the inferiority of certain human beings because of their gender.

It should be remembered that a reading of the Bible from the perspective of the poor is a hermeneutic key offered by the Scriptures themselves, mainly through "events that create meaning" such as the exodus and the historical praxis of Jesus. Much has been said about this, and it is not my aim to discuss it more extensively here.

A Clear Feminist Consciousness

To read the Bible from a woman's perspective, we must read it with women's eyes, that is to say, conscious of the existence of individuals who are cast aside because of their sex. This procedure includes not only women. Men who feel identified with this specific struggle might also be able to read the Bible from this approach. This simple step is fundamental to achieve a reading that attempts to include other oppressed sectors besides the poor. It is a stamp that will distinguish this reading from others that consider the oppressed in general.

This approach, as noted above, is recent in Latin America. Therefore, even we women are not entirely conscious of it yet. For this reason, our reading does not come out spontaneously, and a conscious effort is needed to discover new women-liberating aspects, or even elements in the text that other perspectives would not bring to light.

Women, as victims of sexist oppression, will obviously perceive with less difficulty those aspects that directly affect them. Their experiences, their bodies, their social upbringing, their suffering and specific struggles give them keys (insights) to this reading.

Some liberation theologians agree that to the degree women actively engage themselves as readers of Scriptures and participants in other theological activities they offer important contributions to exegesis, hermeneutics, and theology.

It must remain clear that when I speak of reading the Bible from a woman's perspective, I am not referring specifically to texts that mention female subjects, but to the whole Bible. It is here where an enriching contribution from a perspective long absent until now can be made.

The novelty of such readings comes from reflection on the experiences of women. Women, for example, due to their experiences of oppression, can pose new "ideological suspicions" not only to the culture that reads the text but also to the heart of the text itself by reason of its being a product of a patriarchal culture. Furthermore, their "ideological suspicions" are also applied to biblical tools, such as dictionaries, commentaries, and concordances, tools that are regarded as objective because they are scientific, but that are undoubtedly susceptible to being biased by sexism. This fact has been proved true by female exegetic scholars.

If to the oppression women endure we add the fact that they live a particular experience as women—in the sense that they are closer to vital processes, and have a unique stance in their view of the world—we shall see new contributions reflected in their readings (in recent years much has been discussed about women's identity).

In conclusion, the "gaining distance" from and "coming closer" to the Bible, the retrieval of liberation keys from the perspective of the poor, and a feminist consciousness are three basic skills indispensable to reading the Bible from a Latin American woman's perspective.

We are just taking the first steps. We are rediscovering new duties that will benefit Latin American women, and we are yearning to learn more. Consequently, this meeting in Mexico attended by Third World women from Asia and Africa, women who share concerns and hopes similar to ours, is for us an event of immeasurable value.

17

Final Statement: Latin American Conference on Theology from the Perspective of Women

*(Buenos Aires, Argentina,
Oct. 30–Nov. 3, 1985)*

God's happiness is like a woman, who, having lost a drachma, lights her lamp and goes about sweeping the whole house, carefully searching until she finds it, and then calls all her friends and neighbors to share her joy at having found it (see Lk. 15:8–10).

The drachma symbolizes our self-encounter and self-discovery through our experience of God and through our theological work that we experience in our daily lives. This experience continues to expand until it becomes a celebration in the public square in which every woman is invited to dance and to express herself joyfully in a language all can understand.

Buenos Aires, the capital of Argentina, has been the site of this celebration in which we have shared different ways of searching for our drachma, our different ways of doing theology. Twenty-eight of us women, from different churches and from nine countries of Latin America and the Caribbean, sought to share, from the woman's viewpoint, different aspects of the riches present in theology, reflecting the different ways this activity is carried out.

There has been an enormous diversity of experiences, colors, and shadings. Within this diversity we have found common characteristics, some of which we had not foreseen.

Translated from Spanish by Phillip Berryman.

We see that women's theological activity strives to be:

—Unifying, bringing together different human dimensions: strength and tenderness, happiness and tears, intuition and reason.

—Communitarian and relational, bringing together a vast number of experiences that express something lived and felt, in such a way that people recognize themselves in this reflection and feel challenged by it.

—Contextual and concrete, its starting point being the geographical, social, cultural, and ecclesial reality of Latin America, which detects the community's vital issues. This theological activity bears the mark of the everydayness of life as a site where God is made manifest.

—Militant, in the sense of taking part in the totality of our peoples' struggles for liberation at local and global levels.

—Marked by a sense of humor, joy, and celebration, virtues that safeguard the certainty of faith in the God who is with us.

—Filled with a spirituality of hope whose starting point is our situation as women, and which expresses strength, suffering, and thanksgiving.

—Free, with the freedom of those who have nothing to lose; and open, capable of accepting different challenges and contributions.

—Oriented toward refashioning women's history, both in the biblical texts and in those figures of women, who, acting out of their own situation, are symbols of struggle and resistance, wisdom and leadership, solidarity and fidelity, justice and peace.

We have discovered these characteristics, fully aware that it is the Holy Spirit who arouses us and moves us. The same Spirit draws us women out of our own lack of self-esteem and out of the oppression we experience because of our gender, toward an effort to break out of old frameworks, and to build a new person (woman/man) and a new society. All of this we experience out of our commitment to the poor, struggling for our common liberation.

In our celebration in Buenos Aires, we inquired into what methods and what mediations we utilized in our theological activity. We were surprised to note that the characteristics that we discovered amount to our own method, and the mediations embrace a whole range of possibilities that can take expression in many languages. Social sciences, psychology, linguistics, philosophy, sociology of religion, ecology, and other sciences are present there and are woven together with the Bible, Tradition, and Life in a single tapestry, vibrant with color and hope. What is expressed is our unifying and inclusive way of perceiving life.

We work in a constant process of breaking away, as though in an ongoing childbirth, in which we seek to release ourselves from old frameworks and from categories imposed by the patriarchal system, in order to give birth to something closer to life, something more densely packed with meaning for us.

We have discovered that we can widen the horizon of our theological reflection in different directions, taking on different religious expressions, and taking into account the problem of racial discrimination as well as social justice.

We have realized that certain themes must be deepened from the woman's viewpoint, themes such as the image of God, the incarnation, the experience of God, the Trinity, community, the body, suffering and joy, conflict and silence, play and politics, tenderness and beauty.

As a sign of this work as a group, we have accepted responsibility for certain tasks:

—To seek a synthesis in our ongoing formation between cultural values— those practices aimed at changing the situation—and "theories" that operate on different levels of human life.

—To pay attention to the theological experience and reflection that is taking place in base-level groups, especially by women, to take on this experience and to allow ourselves to be challenged by it in the process of a mutual enrichment, while also making our contribution.

—To systematize and transmit our experience and reflection.

—To seek, from this theological perspective, common paths with men, helping them to see the strength and tenderness that are part of the common task of bringing forth and nourishing the life of the new person—woman/ man—and the new society.

When we conclude this conference, we shall be taking many questions away with us, to nourish our lives and to help enlighten our search.

The joy of the woman who found her drachma was full only when she was able to share it. In this sense, we want to share our discoveries and hopes with all our colleagues, women and men, and particularly with the women and men theologians of the Ecumenical Association of Third World Theologians (EATWOT) who sponsored our conference.

18

Final Document: Intercontinental Women's Conference

(Oaxtepec, Mexico, Dec. 1–6, 1986)

An intercontinental conference of women theologians from the Third World was held in Oaxtepec, Mexico, December 1–6, 1986. The theme of the conference was "Doing Theology from Third World Women's Perspective." The conference was sponsored by the Ecumenical Association of Third World Theologians (EATWOT) as part of its commitment to total liberation and the achievement of full humanity for all, women and men alike.

Planned to operate in three stages, the women's project sought:

1. To broaden our understanding of women's situation in our respective socioeconomic, political, and religio-cultural realities.

2. To discover the vital aspects of women's experience of God in emerging spiritualities.

3. To reread the Bible from Third World women's perspective in the light of total liberation.

4. To articulate faith reflections on women's realities, struggles, and spirituality.

5. To deepen our commitment and solidarity work toward full humanity for all.

The first two phases of the study took place on the national and continental levels. The present meeting provided a forum of exchange among the women on their findings of the study in their respective continents. Twenty-six delegates from seventeen countries of Africa, Asia, and Latin America took part in the conference.

Mexico—where an affluent minority and a poor majority exist side by side, where signs of its colonial past and neocolonial present were everywhere evident, where "machismo" is still a given—offered a suitable venue for our theological reflections from the perspective of Third World women.

In their address of welcome, the Latin American women pointed out that even though the nameless concubine of the Levite in Judges 19 did not speak out against the oppression meted out to her, her cut-up body did. Everyone who saw the outcome of this atrocity was enjoined "to reflect, take counsel and speak." So Israel stood together united to act for justice. This story moves us to ponder the oppression of women, to discuss it and then give our verdict, acting as Deborah, the judge, would have done, confident that today is the Day of Yahweh (Judges 4).

PROCESS

One of the notable features of this meeting was the atmosphere of serious study, sisterhood, and friendliness that prevailed throughout. Worship times saw all the delegates praying together, in the typical styles of each continent, to the God of all nations. The themes (reality of oppression and struggle of women; vital aspects of women's experience of God in emerging spiritualities; women and the church; women and the Bible; women and Christology) were presented by skilled panelists from each of the three continents. The open forum that followed each panel presentation gave the participants a chance to question, clarify, or comment on the issues raised.

Variations in the dynamics of the meeting included role-playing, audio-visual presentations, a fishbowl session, small-group discussions, and mural painting by all. Informal exchanges outside the formal sessions strengthened the spirit of friendship and solidarity.

CONTENTS

The panel on each theme brought out some rich commonalities and differences:

1. In all three continents, the oppression of women is affirmed as a hard and abiding reality of life, though this varies in form and degree from place to place. Women have an irreplaceable role in society, yet our contribution is not acknowledged, nor are we accorded equal rights with our male counterparts. This oppression is felt in all sectors of life: economic, social, political, cultural, racial, sexual, religious, and even within the family itself. Having become conscious of our human rights and of the injustices perpetrated against us in all these sectors, as women we are teaming up and organizing various liberating movements and projects to help ourselves.

Some of these movements are motivated by Christian faith; we are aware that our liberation is part and parcel of the liberation of all the poor and oppressed promised by the gospel. Our efforts are rooted in Scriptures. Being created in God's image demands a total rupture with the prevailing patriarchal system in order to build an egalitarian society.

This liberating process happens differently in the three continents. In Latin America, women organize themselves around survival strategies. In Africa, the rebirth of women takes place in their struggle to overthrow the oppressive elements in traditional African cultures and religions and the evils of colonialism. In Asia, the struggle is centered in rediscovering the pride of being woman, in building womanhood and humane communities, and in fighting against political, economic, and sexual injustices.

Nevertheless, we have perceived a common perspective in the three continents. The women's struggle is deeply connected with the efforts of all the poor and the oppressed who are struggling for their liberation in all aspects of life.

2. Among the efforts being made toward liberation from oppression, theologizing emerges as a specific manner in which women struggle for their right to life. Our theologizing arises from our experience of being discriminated against as women and people of the Third World. The emerging spiritualities we perceive in the three continents show that spiritual experience rooted in action for justice constitutes an integral part of our theology. As women we articulate our theology in prayer and worship, in our relationship with our neighbor in whom God lives, and in our ongoing struggle as one with the poor and the oppressed.

Spiritual experience for women of the Third World thus means being in communion with all those who fight for life. This is our motivation for doing theology, which is done with the body, the heart, the mind, the total self—all penetrated by the Holy Spirit. Compassion and solidarity are main elements of this spirituality and this theology, and this is expressed in action: organized, patient, and loving action. The divergences in action are due to religious and cultural differences among the continents, to the diversities within the various regions in each continent, and to the varied ways the different churches assimilate these new experiences.

3. The Bible plays a vital role in the lives of women and in our struggle for liberation, because the Bible itself is a book about life and liberation. This liberation is rooted in God's action in history, particularly in the Christ-event. The Gospels restore to women our human dignity as persons loved and cherished by God. New methods of reading the Bible are emerging in the three continents. In Latin America, the poor have rediscovered the Bible and, in it, the liberating God, and this has allowed women, who are part of the poor and oppressed, to capture the spirit of the text while distancing themselves from the letter. In Asia, where Christians are a minority, the Bible is read in the context of interfaith dialogue as well as in the context of concrete life struggles. In Africa, there is some evidence of openness to new ways of reading the Bible. The fact that there are now some women biblically trained gives us hope that

the Bible will be read and interpreted from the perspective of women, especially since the situation of African women has elements similar to that of women in the Old Testament.

In reading the Bible, we women face the constant challenge of interpreting texts that are against us. There is great commonality in considering these texts in their cultural contexts and epochs, not as normative, but as peripheral and not touching the heart of the gospel. The essentially patriarchal nature of the Bible and the interpretations that reinforce the oppressive elements should be acknowledged and exposed.

We participants felt that instead of rejecting the Bible wholesale, as some women do, we should "mine" deeper into it, rejecting all the patriarchal crusts that have obstructed its true meaning over the centuries, and highlighting those neglected elements that portray women as individuals in their own right as well as God's co-workers and agents of life. It was considered imperative to highlight Jesus' relationship with women and his countercultural stand with respect to them. Emphasis should also be laid on God as lover and giver of life, as well as liberator of all the oppressed. The Bible is normative and authoritative insofar as it promotes fullness of life for each person (Jn. 10:10).

4. In all three continents, women constitute a vital and dynamic force within the church. Our strong faith and numerous services of love keep the church alive, especially among the poor and the marginalized. Yet though we constitute a strong labor force within the heavily institutionalized church, we are powerless and voiceless, and in most churches are excluded from leadership roles and ordained ministries. This deplorable condition urgently calls for sustained efforts to discover new ways of being church, of being in the world as the visible presence of God's reign, and of the new creation.

As the New Testament *ecclesia* started with women who were active participants in all areas of its life and mission, we, as women of the Third World, are rediscovering our distinctive role and place in the renewed church today. Our faith in the power of the cross and the resurrection empowers us to live out the vision of God's new creation, where no one is subordinated or enslaved, but where free people take part in God's liberating project to build a true community and a new society. In Latin America and in parts of Africa, a hopeful sign is the increasing leadership roles played by women in basic ecclesial communities. In all Third World continents, the presence of women who stand for justice in all its forms is both challenging and conflictive. But this is the way in which the church will be able to rediscover its true identity.

5. Christology has appeared to be central to women's theology. In the person and praxis of Jesus Christ, women of the three continents find the grounds of our liberation from all discrimination: sexual, racial, social, economic, political, and religious. By reflecting on the incarnation, that is, the life, death, and resurrection of Jesus, we have come to realize the need to contextualize our Christology in the oppressed and painful realities of our continents. This

means that Christology is integrally linked with action on behalf of social justice and the defense of each person's right to life and to a more humane life. Hence in Africa, Christology has to do with apartheid, racial discrimination, militarism, deficiency syndromes that come in foreign-aid packages, and genocide perpetrated through family-planning programs. In Asia, with the massive poverty, sexual exploitation, and racial, ethnic, caste, and religious discrimination, Christology incorporates the efforts to draw out the humanizing elements in the other religions. In Latin America, where poverty and oppression often give rise to a tendency to use religion to reinforce a passive and fatalistic attitude to life, Christology is necessarily connected with the preferential option for the poor. In short, to Christologize means to be committed to the struggle for a new society.

We remark also that many Christians in our continents are seeking to see in Jesus' suffering, passion, death, and resurrection a meaning for their own suffering. This explains the great devotion our people have to the mysteries of the passion and the cross. Nevertheless, we have a mission to announce that Christ brought a new life for humanity and that this was the whole point of his suffering. Suffering that is inflicted by the oppressor and is passively accepted does not lead to life; it is destructive and demonic. But suffering that is part of the struggle for the sake of God's reign or that results from the uncontrollable and mysterious conditions of humankind is redeeming and is rooted in the Paschal Mystery, evocative of the rhythm of pregnancy, delivery, and birth. This kind of suffering is familiar to women of all times, who participate in the pains of birth and the joys of the new creation.

6. The passionate and compassionate way in which women do theology is a rich contribution to theological science. The key to this theological process is the word LIFE. We perceive that in the three continents women are deeply covenanted with life, giving life and protecting life. The woman in our streets always appears surrounded and weighed down with children: children in her body, in her arms, on her back. Thus, even physically, she extends and reaches out to other lives, other human beings born from her body, sustaining their lives. In doing theology, we in the Third World thus find ourselves committed and faithful to all the vital elements that compose human life. Thus without losing its scientific seriousness, which includes analyzing the basic causes of women's multiple oppression, our theologizing is deeply rooted in experience, in affection, in life. We as women feel called to do scientific theology passionately, a theology based on feeling as well as on knowledge, on wisdom as well as on science, a theology made not only with the mind but also with the heart, the body, the womb. We consider this as a challenge and an imperative not only for doing theology from women's perspective, but also for all theology. The Latin American theology of liberation has already discovered that the rigid, cold, and purely rationalistic theology of the West thirsts to be combined with spiritual flexibility and creativeness. "Minjung theology" and other efforts of contextual theology in Asia, as well as Black theology and other emerging

theologies in Africa, are also finding their way to a theological reformulation that is firmly and deeply rooted in human life, where the Holy Spirit lives and acts. Thus our theology is people-oriented, not something done in an ivory tower, apart from people.

As women, we have a contribution to make in the effort of Christian communities to rethink and rediscover new expressions of their Christian faith. Moreover, since religious pluralism is a reality in our different situations, we, as Christians and as theologians, need to dialogue and work with women of other faiths, convinced that in other religious traditions, there too we meet Christ.

In the task of doing theology, our common goal is to bring a new dimension to the struggle for justice and for promoting God's reign, a dimension that is not ours, but is given to us both by the voices of our people clamoring for justice and by God, who inspired and convoked us here. Humanity as a whole, not only women, stands to benefit from the whole endeavor.

RECOMMENDATIONS

Our rich and intensive reflections and exchanges during these past days inspired many possible lines of action, both personal and communal. However, we have made the following specific recommendations:

1. That the Women's Commission continue its program of consultations on the national and continental levels.

2. That the Women's Commission establish a network among the women of the three continents for information-sharing and solidarity work.

3. That EATWOT initiate a dialogue between the Women's Commission and the male members of the Association for greater understanding and more effective collaboration toward the attainment of our common goal of achieving full humanity for all.

4. That EATWOT create a joint commission on the Bible, which will:
   a. encourage and organize conferences on the Bible,
   b. provide materials for biblical formation,
   c. facilitate the exchange of personnel and materials.

5. That EATWOT publish in three languages (English, French, and Spanish) an official bulletin containing works of its members, with adequate contribution from women.

6. That each region of the Women's Commission express its continuing support of and solidarity with the struggles of Southern Africa and Central America and direct part of its theological effort to their situations.

CONCLUSION

At the end of our days together, we feel identified with the woman in John 12 and Mark 14, who makes a passionate prophetic action in proclaiming Jesus as Messiah, anointing him with the royal ointment. John portrays the woman anointing Jesus' feet, perhaps to show that she is a real disciple, washing Jesus' feet as Jesus himself washed the disciples' feet.

This woman's action is a passionate and compassionate action—passionate, because by anointing Jesus with so expensive a perfume, she shows her extreme love for him; compassionate, because her action gives Jesus the opportunity to direct the community's attention to the poor and to exhort its solidarity with them.

Jesus approves the woman's action and says that it would be proclaimed wherever the Good News is preached. The Gospel states that the fragrance spread by her gesture filled the house. As women theologians of the Third World, we are called to do the same. As we commit our lives to the ministry of a passionate and compassionate theology, we shall spread the fragrance of the Good News to all four corners of the world.

Contributors

From Africa:

Elizabeth Amoah, a Ghanaian Methodist with a doctorate in religion, is lecturer in the Department for the Study of Religion at the University of Ghana, Legon.

Rosemary Edet, from Nigeria, is a Roman Catholic Sister who holds a Ph.D. in religion and culture from Catholic University, Washington, D.C., and teaches at the University of Calabar.

Bette Ekeya, a lay Catholic involved in women's development programs, has a doctorate in African traditional religions and teaches at the University of Nairobi, Kenya.

Mercy Amba Oduyoye, Ghanaian, was educated at the University of Ghana and Cambridge University. Author of *Hearing and Knowing: A Theological Reflection on Christianity in Africa,* she is Deputy General Secretary of the World Council of Churches in Geneva.

Teresa Okure, a Roman Catholic Sister from Nigeria with a Ph.D. in Scripture from Fordham University, is professor at the Catholic Institute of West Africa in Port Harcourt. She is executive secretary of the Ecumenical Association of Third World Theologians (EATWOT).

Dorothy Ramodibe, a Roman Catholic laywoman from South Africa, is the present Administrative Secretary of the Institute of Contextual Theology in Braamfontein.

Thérèse Souga is a teaching religious in charge of religious formation with the Sisters of the Retreat in Yaoundé, Cameroun.

Louise Tappa, from Cameroun, is a Baptist minister. She has a degree in systematic theology and is Director of Christian Education and Theology for the All Africa Conference of Churches (AACC).

From Asia:

Virginia Fabella, a Maryknoll Sister from the Philippines, is academic dean of the Sister Formation Institute in Quezon City and is the EATWOT Asia Coordinator.

Aruna Gnanadason, a member of the Church of South India, is executive secretary of the All India Council of Christian Women and Vice-Moderator of the World Council of Churches subunit on Women in Church and Society.

191

Mary John Mananzan, a Missionary Benedictine Sister from the Philippines, has a Ph.D. in philosophy and is Dean of St. Scholastica's College, Manila.

Sun Ai Park, originally from Korea, is an ordained minister of the Disciples of Christ and editor of *In God's Image,* an Asian women's theological journal.

Christine Tse, from Hong Kong, obtained a diploma in social work in Italy, and is Peace and Justice Coordinator for the Centre for the Progress of Peoples, Hong Kong.

Yong Ting Jin, a member of the Basel Christian Church of Malaysia, is the Asia-Pacific Regional Secretary of the World Student Christian Federation, based in Hong Kong.

From Latin America

Maria Pilar Aquino, originally from Mexico, has a licentiate in sacred theology and is director of the Hispanic Ministry Program at the Religious Studies Graduate Division of Mount St. Mary's College, Los Angeles.

Luz Beatriz Arellano, a Roman Catholic Sister from Nicaragua, is a staff member of Centro Valdivieso, located in Managua.

Ivone Gebara, a Roman Catholic Sister from Brazil, is professor of philosophy and theology at the Theological Institute of Recife.

Nelly Ritchie, an ordained minister with a licentiate in theology, is superintendent of the Evangelical Methodist Church in Argentina.

Elsa Tamez, a Methodist from Mexico, is at present a doctoral candidate at the University of Lausanne, Switzerland. She is author of *The Bible of the Oppressed.*

Ana Maria Tepedino, a Roman Catholic laywoman, has a licentiate in philosophy. A mother of four, she teaches theology at the Catholic University and at St. Ursula's University, both located in Rio de Janeiro, Brazil.